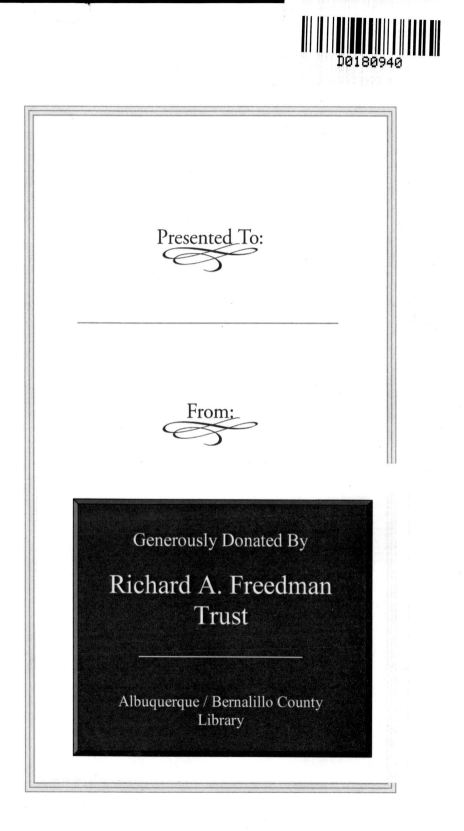

GOD

UNDERSTANDS

DIVORCE

GOD
UNDERSTANDS
DIVORCE

a biblical message of grace

Barry D. Ham, Ph.D.

DESTINY IMAGE® PUBLISHERS, INC.

P.O. Box 310, Shippensburg, PA 17257-0310

"Promoting Inspired Lives."

This book and all other Destiny Image, Revival Press, MercyPlace, Fresh Bread, Destiny Image Fiction, and Treasure House books are available at Christian bookstores and distributors worldwide.

For a U.S. bookstore nearest you, call 1-800-722-6774.

For more information on foreign distributors, call 717-532-3040.

Reach us on the Internet: www.destinyimage.com.

ISBN 13 TP: 978-0-7684-4080-5

ISBN 13 Ebook: 978-0-7684-8912-5

For Worldwide Distribution, Printed in the U.S.A.

1 2 3 4 5 6 7 8 / 16 15 14 13 12

DEDICATION

This book is dedicated to four groups of people

First, to my two sons Jeremy and Jason who have lived so much of this journey.

Second, to my clients; those couples who have sat in my office, hurting, telling their stories, and doing the hard work to make sense of it all, hoping to make it better

Third, to the students in my Marriage and Family classes, who have generously shared their lives, and have endeavored to apply this material and grow in their own relationships

Fourth, to all of those individuals who have struggled in challenging marriages, who have been faced with the threats or devastation of divorce, and yet who strive to honor God above all else in their difficult decisions.

This book is for you!

ACKNOWLEDGEMENTS

A project like this never happens in isolation, and it is imperative that I acknowledge the contribution of at least a few significant individuals, even though there have been many.

Walking through those dark, lonely, and uncertain times following a divorce is awful at best, but is made much more travelable when God provides you with key friends, confidants, and accountability partners. And God was gracious enough to give me many supportive friends, but three were specifically priceless. Mark Berrier, who has been like a brother to me for the past 40 years, has never wavered in his support, his willingness to speak the truth, and his faithfulness, even when I was seemingly out to lunch. Thank you. It was actually out of our discussions that this book began to germinate. I am grateful to Al De la Roche who was always available and never hesitated to ask the tough questions over a #3 combo at Carl's Jr. The trilogy wouldn't be complete without an individual who was willing to endure daily phone calls when I was clinging to an emotional rollercoaster. I am indebted to Bryan Bytwerk, who was that essential person.

One particular couple that was willing to get in the trenches with me and just love on me was Ralph and Kathy Crume. Thank you for adopting me into those Sunday evening dinners and allowing me to process.

Once the writing was complete, then the real work of getting this project published began, and I want to thank my friend and author Paul Batura for his invaluable advice and support along the way. Several individuals reviewed the manuscript for me, but I particularly appreciate the thoughtful suggestions of Georgia Clifton and Al De la Roche. You have both been friends through the storm and therefore knew my heart, understood my words, and knew how to speak into this project.

Finally, I want to acknowledge my website producers, marketing idea gurus, and dear personal friends Steve and Shawna Bryant for all of their contributions both personally and professionally.

Thank you all!

ENDORSEMENTS

As Christian couples experience divorce at an alarming rate, individuals cry out, wondering if there are any real answers or solutions. Does anybody really care? In these pages, Barry reveals that God has been where you are, He knows your pain, He desires wholeness for you, and He offers clear guidance to enable you to get there. He really cares!

GARY CHAPMAN, PH.D.
Author of *The Five Love Languages*

Dr. Barry Ham writes with a marvelous mixture of compassion and conviction. His life's calling is to help others not just find answers to challenges, but to also discover the root cause of their problems.

PAUL BATURA
Author of *Good Day! The Paul Harvey Story*

This book demonstrates that God truly understands divorce—our pain and brokenness, our challenges and struggles, and the oftentimes resulting carnage. As Barry points out, it is because God really "gets it" that He gives us clear insight and direction to help us avoid the "train wrecks" and actually restore marriages that, at first glance, appear to be dead. For those walking this dark and lonely journey, Barry offers, in these pages, real, practical solutions and a genuine hope.

BILL BUTTERWORTH

Author of *The Promise of the Second Wind*

In a world where divorce has become the new "normal," Barry shares strong insight on the balance of Old Testament and New Testament teaching on divorce. And his thoughts on how churches should serve the divorced, and those who are contemplating divorce, are worthy of consideration by churches of all sizes around the country. Implementing his ideas in your community will result in stronger marriages and healthier people who have struggled through this great loss in life.

DUSTY RUBECK

President, Dallas Christian College

It's undeniable: divorce is accelerating in our culture and many people are grasping for hope and perspective. However, in the midst of this disturbing whitewater trend, too many are reaching for rescue shortcuts that, instead of healing, cause further pain and damage. With compassion and understanding, Dr. Barry Ham challenges that tendency by offering a lifeline of both grace and truth. He ignores neither the heartbreaking realities surrounding the issue nor the gracious truth of God's Word. Aiming to help those who are struggling in their marriages, as well as others who are seeking to walk alongside them, he delves below the surface and invites people into a journey of healing as well as rescue.

MATT HEARD

Senior Pastor, Woodmen Valley Chapel

Colorado Springs

CONTENTS

INTRODUCTION

My spouse doesn't love me anymore—what should I do? This marriage is not at all what I thought I was signing up for—how do I get out? I messed up my marriage big time—how do I fix it? How can God even begin to understand my pain? How can He understand divorce? What kind of a dumb title is that anyway? I am divorced—now what? Am I able to remarry? My family members—son/daughter, brother/sister, or parents are going through a divorce—how should I respond? How can I help them? I am watching my best friend's marriage come unraveled—how do I intervene—or should I even try? Husbands and wives are going their separate ways in our church on a daily basis—what can I do? Do we support? Do we confront? Do we counsel? Do we stay out of the way and say nothing?

Questions, questions, questions! These, and dozens more questions around the subjects of marriage and divorce, seem to come at us relentlessly. I know. I have faced them all, as a husband, father, professor, and therapist, which is my reason and my passion for writing this book. It can be an excruciating journey, and I invite you to travel with me down a path that I believe will help provide some support, encouragement, reassurances, and solid biblical answers for the questions and situations you face. And most importantly, I hope you will discover that God does truly understand and He cares.

SECTION ONE

INTRODUCTION

CHAPTER ONE

JEREMIAH 3

"Commitment is what transforms a promise into reality. It is the words that speak boldly of your intentions. And the actions which speak louder than the words. It is making the time when there is none. Coming through time after time after time, year after year after year. Commitment is the stuff character is made of; the power to change the face of things. It is the daily triumph of integrity over skepticism."

—ANONYMOUS[1]

Jimmy and Ellen[2] met in high school. They were in the same grade and began dating their junior year. It was young love, and with it came all of the intensity and proclamations of "forever-ness" that this typically brings. Everyone knew that they were a couple and respected their boundaries. During their senior year, Jimmy decided to join the Navy immediately after high school. This increased the intensity and the pressure of their relationship. If he joined the Navy, he would begin his basic training during the summer following graduation. Ellen would be left at home in California, while Jimmy would be on the other side of the United

States—and potentially out of the country. The thought of separation caused an increased level of anxiousness for both of them. So, acknowledging the many challenges that would lay ahead, they decided to get married before Jimmy began basic training.

Friends and family strongly cautioned them about the challenges of marrying so young. This only increased their determination to take all of the right steps to make certain that their marriage survived. They began to see a premarital counselor in the springtime. It seemed to them that focusing on typical problem areas that couples face would be a protective guarantee for success. Discussions about everything from finances to in-laws were on the table. When the topic of children came up, they spoke with certainty about the fact that they were going to wait a few years so they would have important bonding time together. Counseling seemed to go well as they expressed lifetime loyalty and commitment to one another. In June, just a few weeks after graduation, they were married in a beautiful outdoor wedding with family, friends, and all of the typical adornments—flowers, music, and an elegant reception. With a beginning like this, surely happiness and bliss were on the horizon.

Shortly after the wedding, Jimmy left for boot camp and Ellen remained at home with her parents. While the separation was difficult for these newlyweds, Ellen knew that as soon as her husband received his first assignment, they would be together to begin their lifelong partnership. She was lonely, but it would only be for a short time—then her "real life" would begin. Jimmy was busy with all of the demands of a new recruit. He missed his wife, but he was working hard to keep up physically with his peers and to deal with the flood of emotions that he was feeling. He just wanted this time to pass quickly.

Finally, after the longest eight weeks of their young lives, Ellen traveled to the Chicago area to watch Jimmy graduate. She went along with his parents for a long weekend. Waiting in the hall where the graduation ceremony was to take place seemed to drag on forever. At last, the graduates began their march into the drill hall. She knew that he was in division #133 and she watched intently for his arrival. Finally—there he was. He looked so sharp in his uniform, and she was about to explode with pride. It was all she could do to keep from bursting from the stands and running to hug him. But, she sat patiently—full of excitement—waiting for the ceremony to be over. At last, the "Liberty call, liberty call," order was given, and the graduates were released to be with their families. She ran to her husband, kissing and embracing him, wanting to never let go. He had equally longed to see her and had begun to think that this moment would never come. But, here they were—together—finally. By the end of the weekend, Jimmy had received his orders, and he and Ellen began to make plans for her move to their next assignment.

While they had grown up in far northern California, their new home was San Diego. This was quite different from Redding, but at least it was back in California, and finally in a place they could call their own. Here they were—married and together. Life would be great now!

During the day, Jimmy would be off at work while Ellen remained at home. This seemed terrific at first, but after a couple of weeks, boredom began to set in for her. Ellen wanted to begin taking classes at the local community college, but needed to wait because Jimmy might be transferred again before the end of the semester. She tried to occupy herself during the day, but much of her time was spent just waiting for Jimmy to arrive home. Ellen worked to have a great meal ready for her husband and even tried to make sure that she looked especially nice for him. However, more often than not, Jimmy would arrive home exhausted, barely able to enjoy the dinner and hardly aware of much else. Ellen tried to be understanding, but as the routine became more common day after day, she found herself getting angry. She was homesick;

she had no friends in San Diego, and she was feeling more alone as each week passed.

Weekends were a little better, because Jimmy was home. But rather than making good use of this time, they usually spent it arguing about the rest of the week. It was not a safe or pleasant place for either one of them. They began to question how they had gotten themselves into this situation and secretly began to wonder how they could get out of it. Just when it seemed that things could not be any more complicated, Ellen discovered that she was pregnant. How could this be? They weren't going to get pregnant for several years. They weren't ready for this—not even remotely ready! Yet, here they were. They had to make this work.

Pregnancy was not the glowing joyful time that friends had predicted. Ellen was sick much of the time, and Jimmy was not physically or emotionally available for her. They continued to drift further and further apart. The initial excitement at the birth of their son, Todd, provided a brief respite from the troubles in their relationship. However, within a few weeks they were back into their dysfunctional patterns. Only now, the sleep deprivation and dirty diapers served to amplify problems that already existed.

During this time, one of the young men from the apartment complex began to befriend Ellen while Jimmy was at work. At first, it seemed innocent enough. Eric would just stop by to say "hi." Before long, Ellen would find things that she needed a "man's help" with and call Eric during the day for assistance. Ellen was moved by Eric's willingness and his availability. He never seemed too tired to give her his attention, and he appeared to genuinely listen to Ellen and her concerns. As her feelings began to develop and increase for Eric, she rationalized that she had tried to make things work with Jimmy, but that he just didn't seem to really want her. Now here was someone who did. As might be expected, Ellen and Eric became involved sexually, and soon the affair was in full swing.

At this point, the story becomes a common one—the pattern is repeated daily in this country. Jimmy discovered Ellen's secret. They fight, spewing venom as they each blame the other for the demise of their marriage. The resulting divorce brought with it all of the property and custody issues that are a part of this typical scenario. The impact was like that of a rock thrown into a pond. The ripple didn't stop with just Jimmy and Ellen. It played, and will continue to play, havoc in the life of Todd, Jimmy's parents and family, Ellen's parents and family, and all of their many friends and acquaintances. The effects will continue to be felt in their lives, and in the lives of others with whom they come into contact, for years to come. Lives were changed forever.

Friends and family attempted to intervene with both Jimmy and Ellen, but to no avail. The decision was made. People offered thoughts and opinions, some in support of their decisions and others condemning their choices. Of course, those in disagreement with them simply "didn't understand" what they had gone through. No one really understands the hurt, pain, betrayal, and heartache. Friends from church attempted to get them to examine God's thoughts and desires about all of this, but this too fell on deaf ears. "After all," the couple said, "God may not like divorce, but He doesn't understand what I have been, and am going, through. He is God. He doesn't have any worries, and He certainly doesn't have to live with my spouse. He just orders people not to get divorced. That is easy to do because He has never experienced what I have. He doesn't know how difficult and hurtful this is. He doesn't understand." Therefore, Jimmy and Ellen didn't go to Him for answers. Instead, they went to friends who have perhaps experienced the same hurt and pain that they have. Their friends didn't have any more answers than they did, but they could understand and relate—unlike God.

Well-meaning individuals might conclude that there is merit in this thinking. I mean, after all, what can a holy and sinless God know about a marriage that has gone sour? How can the creator of the universe even begin to understand my feelings when it comes to divorce? The answer is actually quite easy. God understands divorce far better than most may think because God has been divorced.

What? That is impossible. God can't be divorced. He is God. What are you talking about?

God has been divorced!

What is this, some kind of whacked cultic belief in a god who has lots of wives? Is this some kind of Greek mythology stuff?

Not at all. God clearly has been divorced. Let's take a look at the ongoing difficulties that He has had with His bride and the resulting divorce.

Jeremiah 3 presents a clear picture. But before we look at that, let's see what troubles existed leading up to God's divorce.

GOD SELECTS A BRIDE

From the very beginning, God designed people for intimacy with Himself. Adam walked through The Garden in the cool of the evening with God. What an image—the created walks and talks with the Creator. It would be wonderful to have even been just an ear in those conversations—what did they talk about? Were they discussing plans for the future of the world? What kinds of questions did Adam have for God? What an opportunity to be with the Creator! You most likely know what happened in The Garden and the resulting breach in the relationship. This placed humanity in a broken and distant position with God. Yet, God had certainly not given up on people; He had a plan. We see in Scripture the manner in which God's plan unfolded as He chose His bride—by selecting an individual, Abraham, who would become a people—a nation.

God made covenants with humanity—an agreement, a contract. One of those early agreements was made with Noah. The earth had become a very godless and corrupt place. It didn't seem that there was much worth salvaging. Yet, God found one righteous man and gave him very clear instructions concerning what he needed to do to survive the coming catastrophe. Following the flood, God made a covenant with Noah regarding this issue of flooding—He would never again destroy the entire world with a flood.

In Genesis 12, we see God called Abraham. God could have selected anybody that He wanted. He may have even looked around a little to see who would be the best individual for the call. By Genesis 15, God made a covenant with Abraham—a part of which includes this statement: *"Look up at the heavens and count the stars—if indeed you can count them....So shall your offspring be"* (Gen. 15:5). God selected an individual who would become a nation who would become God's bride. This covenant was confirmed again in Genesis 17. The covenant was carried on with Jacob, who literally became Israel, and Israel became the bride of God. Wow! What an awesome privilege and opportunity, to be selected as the favored people of the Creator. Any nation would covet this position, but only Israel was selected. God made His agreement, His covenant, with Israel. In her youth, Israel was devoted to God. She watched God perform miracle after miracle as He loved and protected her. She knew that she had a good deal.

However, it wasn't long before Israel became complacent and self-centered and took the Creator of the Universe for granted. God used Moses to lead the Israelites out of their captivity. Yet, by the time they got to the Red Sea, they were already complaining. In Exodus 15, they grumbled about food; in the next chapter, water; and by Chapter 32, they were ready to forsake God for another. *"Who?"* you ask. *Who could possibly match the kind of Protector and Provider God is?*

A human-made golden calf.[1]

Huh?

I know it seems unbelievable, but that is exactly what they did. Of course there were consequences—many people became sick and died. Israel had been unfaithful to her husband. Yet, even after severe consequences—when you think that she would have seen the error of her ways, when you think she would have learned her lesson—this was only the beginning of her problems.

God loved Israel as His wife. Even when she sinned, if she repented and returned, God took her back time and time again. Yet she never seemed to quite grasp the concept of faithfulness and trust in her Husband. Here are a few examples:

- Numbers 11—the people complained against God.

- Numbers 13 and 14—they didn't trust God and instead feared the Canaanites.

- Numbers 20—they complained about water (they have been here before).

- Numbers 25—Israel was seduced by the Moabites and worshiped human-made idols.

By Deuteronomy 28 and 29, in an event similar to the renewing of wedding vows, God described the blessings and curses in their marriage agreement and renewed the covenant. Joshua renewed the covenant in Deuteronomy 8. However, by the Book of Judges, we see that the pattern of unfaithfulness was running rampant.

- Judges 2—Israel was serving Baal. The covenant was violated and God responded.

- Judges 3, 6, 10, 13—Israel continued to violate her covenant with God.

- 2 Kings 17—Israel was exiled because of her sin.

- 2 Chronicles 36—God sent messengers to Israel to plead for her return, but she mocked the messengers.

- Isaiah 1—we see that Israel became a rebellious and sinful nation.

- Ezekiel 11—God passed judgment on Israel's leaders for disobedience.

- Hosea—the entire book deals in some form or fashion with Israel's repeated unfaithfulness and God's persistent and unwavering love.

- Amos 3—God listed witnesses and evidence of Israel's unfaithfulness.

- Micah 6—the Lord presented His case against Israel.

- Malachi 2—Following the split of Israel and Judah into two nations, Judah was also unfaithful.

What an amazing pattern—Israel continued to sin against and stray from her husband; God punished and yet pleaded for the nation to return; Israel repented and returned; God blessed Israel; and then they walked away again, thus repeating the pattern. It made no sense. They found no fault in God, but they forsook Him. Jeremiah probably presented the case most clearly.

Jeremiah received the word of the Lord and recorded it during the beginning of the reign of King Josiah. He continued until the people of Jerusalem went into exile. As you read Jeremiah's writings Chapter 2, you almost get a feeling that he is baffled, that in his mind, this surely can't be happening. In the Book of Jeremiah, you see the development of Israel as she loved the Lord, but then changed gods. She was likened to a prostitute, to a donkey in heat (see Jer. 2:24). Yet, even after God punished her, no change occurred. Unbelievable! Israel was even so bold, after all of this, to make the statement, *"I am innocent; He is not angry with me, I have not sinned"*(Jer. 2:35). Hello? What planet is she from? How could she have possibly asked this question with a straight face? Yet, she did. Finally, in Jeremiah 3, God lowered the boom.

It is important to understand God's pattern of love for His bride. Notice that He didn't give up on her the first time she was unfaithful—or the second, or the third, and so on. God continued to forgive and take her back. He is a God of reconciliation. This pattern has implications for our own marriages and will be addressed later in the book. But for right now, it is important to see that after a continued unrepentant lifestyle of unfaithfulness, *God gave Israel her certificate of divorce.* This was no arbitrary "in the heat of the moment" impulse. God had dealt with Israel's pattern of unfaithfulness for years and years. He realized that she was not going to change.

So, He filed for divorce. Yet, even in the midst of this, He continued to plead and offer restoration.

> *"Return, faithless Israel," declares the Lord, "I will frown on you no longer, for I am merciful," declares the Lord, "I will not be angry forever. Only acknowledge your guilt—you have rebelled against the Lord your God, you have scattered your favors to foreign gods under every spreading tree, and have not obeyed me" declares the Lord. "Return, faithless people," declares the Lord, "for I am your husband"* (Jeremiah 3:11-14a).

Many people have experienced the pain of an unfaithful spouse. Yet, I wonder how many have experienced repeated unfaithfulness over the span of many years as God did. Some, I am certain, but not most. My point here is that as you read Jeremiah Chapter 3, it becomes quite clear that God was grieved at the loss of His beloved. Not only does He understand divorce, but He also understands all of the accompanying pain. He understands the complications, the anger, the logistical issues, the embarrassment, the betrayal and rejection, the longings, and all of the other associated hurts. He understands it, because He has experienced it. God knows the impact that divorce has on people because it has impacted Him. God even knows what it is like, and how difficult it is to initiate divorce, because He had to initiate it. God understands divorce.

I know—this may be a difficult concept to get your head around. We usually don't think of God having to deal with this kind of an issue. We think that He is busy keeping the stars in place and making sure the earth tilts the right direction. But feeling hurt and pain, understanding where I live day in and day out—we tend to think that God is out of touch with these kinds of issues. Know that He is not.

So, what is your situation? Has your spouse been unfaithful? God knows that pain better than anyone. Has your spouse said one thing and done another? Israel fits there. Have you pleaded and tried everything that you know how to do in order to save your marriage? So did God. Were you the one who had to begin the divorce proceedings because you had run out of options? God knows how difficult that is. Or perhaps your spouse has decided to leave the marriage for no apparent reason. You have been a faithful husband or wife. You have done your best to meet your spouse's needs, offering love and kindness at each turn. Your spouse truly has nothing against you. As a matter of fact, your spouse has had to work to manufacture some twisted justification for these actions. How awful is that? God has been in the same place.

But wait a minute—what about property issues? God never had to deal with dividing who gets what and the unfairness that can accompany this. C. White, author of *Marriage, Divorce, and Reconciliation,* states "Jerusalem is the wedding band of God and Israel. Jerusalem is a representation of the covenant and when God divorced and put away Israel, then Jerusalem is totally destroyed."[3] The very city that God gave to Israel with instructions for His temple, He had to watch be destroyed. This was significant. And what about child custody? *He didn't have to sit with a court mediator and hear His spouse tell lies in an effort to win the kids. He didn't have to see His children upset and torn from the home and people that they loved.* But didn't He? The prophets, God's messengers, went to Israel pleading God's case. These sinful, guilty people lied to the prophets, as we saw in Jeremiah, claiming that they had done nothing wrong. As Jerusalem was destroyed, as the people lived in exile, as segments of the population were taken into captivity, as all of this happened—God had to watch. Israel took her unfaithfulness to a new level, and therefore could no longer be married to God.

Yet in this process, God watched innocent children live in brokenness, pain, hunger, and misery, while they were homeless and lost. This grieved God's heart. This was not what He wanted. These were not the plans that He had for His bride. He had told Israel repeatedly the limitless blessings that He would bestow upon her if she simply remained faithful. He desired to be a loving husband to her. All she had to do was let Him. But regardless of the breadth and depth of His love, she still chose a different course. It made absolutely no sense. Logical or not, it was still the choice that she made. You may have thought up to now that no one understands you, that no one gets what you have gone or are going through. Believe me—God gets it. He understands all of your pain in your situation. He understands what divorce does to people—and more specifically, He understands what it has done to you.

CHAPTER TWO

THE ANATOMY OF A DIVORCE

"We must all suffer from one of two pains: the pain of discipline or the pain of regret. The difference is discipline weighs ounces while regret weighs tons."

—JAMES ROHN[1]

Nearly 90 percent of children lived their first 18 years in homes with two biological, married parents during the early 1960s. During the past 40 years, that percentage has diminished at an alarming rate.[2] It has been reported that by 2001, 18.5 million children under the age of 18 lived with one parent.[3] This is a reflection of the reality that 50 percent of all first marriages in the United States result in divorce[4], with the average length of marriage being just under 8 years.[5]

This current state of divorce is a relatively new one. Until recent years, divorce was considered to be rare and unacceptable in society. Approximately 100 women per thousand married each year in the 1920s. During this time, the divorce rate was about 10 per thousand. However, over the next 70 years, the picture dramatically changed. By 1990, the first-marriage rate of women had dropped to about 80 per thousand each year, yet the divorce rate had increased to 40 per thousand. What this meant was that the number of women getting married for the first time had decreased by 20 percent, yet the divorce rate had also increased by 300 percent.

Going back in history even further, we see that approximately only 5 percent of marriages in the United States ended in divorce just following the Civil War. This number increased to 10 percent by the 1920s, to 36 percent by 1964, and then up to 50 percent by 1990. One researcher refers to this extraordinary increase in the divorce rate as being the result of the "divorce revolution."[6] Now for the shocking statistic that best captures the picture of this progression—from 1865 to 1990, a span of only 125 years in this country, the divorce rate increased by 900 percent![7]

It is encouraging to observe that, even with our high divorce rate, the majority of people in our country are married. In the year 2000, 54.4 percent of our population was currently married, approximately 10 percent were divorced, 8.5 percent widowed or separated, and 27.1 percent had never been married.[8] Yet, that information does little to relieve the staggering knowledge that our divorce has increased by 900 percent, as noted previously. *900 percent!* What does that number do to you?

I often times turn on the evening news, or pick up the daily newspaper, to see what is going on in the world. I read about the latest natural disaster—hurricane, flood, earthquake; the latest series of violent actions—kidnapping, sexual assault, terrorist activity; the current wave of dishonesty—embezzlement, insider trading, price fixing; and on and on. I must admit that my days of getting really upset, or even feeling "righteous indignation," have passed. I have reached catastrophe overload. I even think about mailings that I receive from a variety of organizations—good and worthy organizations—that regularly let me know about starving children, water shortages, and the threat of deadly disease in third-world countries.

Are the issues real? Absolutely. Do they merit our action and support? Of course. But what do I do with that information. I used to feel guilty that I couldn't respond to every request to meet a legitimate need. I used to think, "Well, perhaps if I turn off the TV to save the electricity cost, I could then send that money to sponsor that child." But not anymore. Now, I support what I feel that I can and should, and I pretty much ignore the rest—throwing money requests away without even batting an eye. Is that a good thing to do? I am not sure if that response is better than initially feeling guilty. However, I do know that it is a result of being unable to take in a continuous stream of overwhelming information that is more than I can respond to. Therefore—I become desensitized and just shut down.

The same thing can easily happen when I read a statistic like the one about the divorce rate jumping 900 percent in this country. That feels like an astronomical number. One that is certainly too big for me to comprehend, let alone mount some kind of adequate response. Besides, in this day and time there are so many divorces, single moms, dating dads, latchkey kids, support programs, and a seemingly diminishing stigma, that I began to wonder whether or not it is even important to mount a response. Perhaps we cannot get our minds around, and really grasp, a number of that magnitude—900 percent! But we might be able to better understand it when we see it in smaller, bite-size chunks. And we do see it in these chunks nearly every day. Perhaps we can begin to view the divorce rate, and maybe even address it, at that level.

THE ANATOMY OF A MARRIAGE:
A NEW LIFE IS FORMED

Anatomy—"structural makeup especially of an organism of any of its parts...a separating or dividing into parts for detailed examination."[9]

Jesus clearly indicated in Matthew 5 that when we are married we become one flesh. As Scripture indicates, it is no longer "me" and "her." A husband now loves his wife as he loves his own body. This joining together is not a loss of who we are as individual personalities, but it is the creation of a life that didn't exist before. We have taken all that we are—our strengths, giftings, the manners in which we do things, the ways that we think and process, our insights, as well as our naiveties—and brought them to the mixing bowl. God takes those varied and different, yet complementary, ingredients and makes something new and exciting that did not exist before.

Once we are married, we are no longer two but one. We offer to God, as well as others, a partnership, a life that is a brand-new creation. While this may feel somewhat mysterious, I believe it is a concept that God wants us to understand. He wants us to understand that this is something significant, not to be taken lightly.

I am always amazed when I see a newborn baby. I especially recall when my first son, Jeremy, was born. Seeing him and holding him for the first time rattled me at the core of who I was. Here was this new life. He did not exist before. While God was the one who knitted him together, I had a role and was responsible for his conception. I had been part of the process of bringing this new life into the world and with that came incredible responsibilities—responsibilities that sometimes made my head spin.

Yet, on a daily basis, we see people get pregnant and have babies for all kinds of reasons. Sometimes they simply want to play house. Other times, it is because they just want something, perhaps a hamster, a beagle, or a baby to love them unconditionally, since they feel no one else has up to that point. As we have seen from the trend in abortions over the past 30 plus years, creating a new life is not always viewed with the same awe and possibilities that God would desire. Yet, regardless of how it is viewed, a new life has still been created.

In many ways, a marriage is not unlike the significance of a newborn baby. When two people come together, a new life is created. Many times, I have seen individuals view the matter with this kind of weightiness. However, in our country today, we see kids who get married because they naively believe that another person will fulfill all of their dreams and make them happy. We see cheap assembly-line marriages in places like Las Vegas, where a couple can, whether on a whim or because they are overly intoxicated, get married any time of the day. Have they contemplated the lifelong significance of this "new life?" Hardly. They have simply done what they felt like doing at the moment. (The same way that many babies get here.) Regardless, a new life is created. This "new life" is of life-changing, world-impacting significance. It has even been likened to God's relationship with us, which we will discuss in a later chapter.

So here we are with this "new life." It is not the same as it was. We can even see it in the traditional name change. Our individual friends Fred Cooper and Susan Jones now become known as Fred and Susan Cooper. We talk about them as a unit. We say, "Let's have Fred and Susan over." We ask others about how our friends the Coopers are doing. You have probably known friends who have gone through a divorce and found yourself having a difficult time thinking of one without the other. While I could certainly give additional examples ranging from the legalities of joint ownership to the mystery of how individuals begin to look alike over the years—you hopefully by now understand the concept. When two individuals decide to join their lives together in marriage, they create and become a part of a new life.

Now that we understand this idea of a new life, we need to examine the counterpart to that. And that is a "new death." When a couple enters into a divorce, they begin the process of death to the relationship, a death to this life. I have spoken with hundreds of people experiencing divorce involving all forms of pain. Men and women will frequently say that a death would be easier to live with and deal with than a divorce, because in a death there is at least some kind of finality and closure that one usually isn't able to experience in a divorce. Actually, divorce is sometimes referred to as a "living death" for this very reason.

I want to use the remainder of this chapter to look at the anatomy of divorce, a detailed examination of what this dying process looks like and entails. It doesn't always look the same. It begins in different ways, proceeds differently, and can end with a variety of ugliness. Some people get sick and die of a disease. Others are killed in an auto accident. Still others are killed in an unexpected tragedy. This is also true of marriages. While this will certainly not be an exhaustive examination, we will look at a few examples of what this death can look like. At this point, I have chosen not to address issues involving sexual or physical abuse or drugs and alcohol, but rather those issues common to most couples. You may see your friends, or even yourself, in these real-life depictions.

STRETCH IT TIL IT BREAKS

Most couples that I know have to, at one time or another, address money issues. "We need more. We can't pay the bills. We are never able to take a vacation," and on and on. Individuals often come together with extremely different views of how to handle money and some are even frighteningly creative. Tom and Juli were one such couple. As you might expect, their own parents also had conflicting ways of handling financial issues. Therefore, neither Tom nor Juli ever had the opportunity to see healthy money management modeled or even to acquire information regarding how their parents managed money. As they entered young adulthood, each had his or her financial style. In college, Tom worked very hard to learn thrifty spending habits as he worked part-time and paid the majority of his college expenses himself. He valued financial independence, as this represented to him what responsible adulthood was all about. On the other hand, Juli had always had a bank account in college, and she wrote checks from it whenever she needed money. Her dad deposited money in the account for her. Juli, for the most part, viewed a checking account as something that someone else kept stocked and that she withdrew from as she desired. I don't mean to oversimplify this by making it sound as though Juli didn't understand that someone had to earn the money that went into her account, but she had given little thought to budgeting and financial stewardship.

Tom and Juli dated for about a year as seniors in college before they got married. During that time, Tom always paid for the dates, and Juli had adequate money to pay for birthday gifts and occasional surprises, as she deemed necessary. At this point, neither one of them thought anything was unusual about their financial arrangement and never would have imagined that they would eventually have money problems. You see, both of Tom's parents worked bringing in relatively equal shares of their family's income. While Tom never knew how his parents spent or managed their money, what he did know was that he and his sisters were taught the importance of financial independence with everyone sort of pulling his or her own weight. Therefore, this is how he thought it was done. However, in Juli's household, her dad was the sole source of financial income. She never heard her parents discuss money. She just knew that she and her mom went shopping when they wanted to and the family always seemed to have plenty. In her view, her dad's job appeared to bring in the income. While neither model is right nor wrong, just different, you can no doubt already see the collision that was about to take place.

It wasn't long into the marriage when they each began to realize that they weren't on the same page financially. While Juli had her own job, she never realized that Tom expected her to contribute to the household expenses. Likewise, Tom was appalled to discover that Juli did not see her role in the monthly bills and seemed to think that the checkbook was just an endless supply of check writing opportunities. Tom tried to discuss these differences with her, but the discussion always seemed to end in tears and accusations. Juli felt that if Tom really loved her, he would just "take care" of the finances and not make this into a big deal. However, Tom thought that this was about being a team, and he felt abandoned by Julie in the pursuit of financial stability. At first, they would both leave their discussions about money confused and bewildered. However, as time and further discussion went on, they began to walk away hurt and feeling lonely and hopeless. Juli began to view Tom as a financial tyrant and cheapskate, who had obviously fooled her into marrying him with no intention of really taking care of her. Tom began to believe that Juli must really despise him. Why else would she be out to bankrupt him?

It wasn't long before Tom began to open other bank accounts that he kept from Juli's knowledge. He feared that he couldn't make their money stretch far enough to be responsible and fund Juli's spending at the same time. Juli began to siphon money from their joint account and hide it in a purse in their closet. As this pattern escalated, so did lack of communication, separateness, and mistrust. Without some kind of intervention and change in behavior, this marriage would be in serious trouble. This new life, this body of marriage, was beginning to show early signs of death.

HE'S OBSESSED

Bryan and Linda were in their late 40s and had been married for about 25 years when they entered my counseling office looking despondent. After getting acquainted with them over some general small talk, I asked them what brought them in to see me.

Linda jumped right in to tell me what a good and loyal wife she had been. She told me that she had been the primary force behind raising their two teenage children, one of whom had special needs. She went on to inform me of how well she managed the household finances and even the role that she played in keeping the books and doing all of the invoicing for her husband's business. I could sense the buildup coming and was waiting for the bomb to drop. As she continued to extol the virtues of her wifehood and motherhood, I asked them again what brought them in. She then blurted out, "I do all these things, and yet he never thinks about me. All he ever wants is sex. He is obsessed."

There it was—the "S" word that I hear so frequently.

I turned my head toward Bryan as he rolled his eyes. Being a man of few words he said, "I don't know why I even try to be romantic—she must be the most frigid woman on the planet." It was clear to see that Bryan and Linda's marriage was losing feeling in the extremities of their body—death was setting in.

As I continued to explore with them, I learned that they had a fast and furious physical relationship in high school. Linda had always felt guilty about it, but also felt as though she had to be physical in order to hang on to the relationship. Bryan had never thought much about it, except that he figured that this is what a relationship was about. During college, they saw other people for a period of time, but eventually got back together and married in their early 20s.

Their early-married years were typical of so many young couples. Bryan began his retail business, they had two children, Linda became active in the women's group at their church, and they took the typical family summer vacations to see the relatives. But their physical intimacy just never seemed to take off. Whenever they had a sexual encounter, it seemed to be about pleasing Bryan without much regard for Linda. Following sex, Linda desired to talk and to be held, while Bryan wanted to get up and go watch ESPN. As time went on, sex became less and less frequent, but a continual source of discussion and irritation. Finally, to no one's surprise, there was an affair. Well, actually, there was a surprise. The surprise was that Linda was the one to have the affair. Some might ask, how can that be—she doesn't even like sex? This is where sex can be easily confused and used synonymously with feelings of love and intimacy.

Linda met a father at her daughter's elementary school. They met at a back-to-school night and conversation came easily. He was married, but was also experiencing difficult issues in his marriage. They would find themselves arranging to pick up their children at the same time in the afternoons. Soon this led to coffee meetings and eventually a full-blown affair. Still, you might wonder how this could happen. Even though it broke all of Linda's rules for life, it touched and met needs that she had been longing to have fulfilled. This man gave her conversation and seemed genuinely interested in her. As this interest blossomed into emotional and physical intimacy, Linda found an interest in sex she didn't know that she had, and she was both thrilled and petrified by it. She had let this horse out of the corral, and she didn't know how, nor did she have the desire to, lock him back up.

Eventually, through a chain of events, the affair was discovered, and it ended. While it was a very difficult time, Bryan and Linda managed, with the help of their pastor, to hold their marriage together. As you can imagine, Bryan couldn't understand how his wife could have sex with another man, but didn't desire to have sex with him. Of course, the issue was that Bryan was unwilling to connect the dots between sex and intimacy. He thought they were one and the same and refused to see it any other way. As time went on, Linda continued to retreat into her shell, and Bryan eventually began a relationship with a woman with whom he worked. The death rattle was all over this marriage.

Bryan moved out and lived with the woman that he had been seeing. Linda was at a loss as to what to do. She would talk with her women's group friends and would hear advice such as, "Remember the affair that you had. You just need to let him get this out of his system." Her children would send mixed messages. One would say, "Please let dad come home," while the other would protest, "I want the bum out." Her parents said that he was a jerk and that they never liked him in the first place. They admitted that they knew that sooner or later he would do this kind of thing to her. They encouraged her to move back home with them.

It was only a few months into the affair when Bryan began to experience something very familiar. Initially, the thrill of the affair and the sex caused Bryan to feel that he had finally found a woman who understood him. She seemed to like sex regularly, and he thought that this is what he had been looking for. Yet, after the first couple of months, this woman "who understood him" was beginning to emotionally retreat. She began to refrain from sex and even physical touch. Fortunately, something clicked in Bryan's thinking, and he realized that this was a very familiar feeling. Could it be that this new woman was becoming all of the things that he couldn't stand about Linda? Surely not. Or worse—could it be that this is really what all women were like? As Bryan related this story to a friend whom he trusted, his friend was able to get Bryan to understand that there was indeed a commonality, but it wasn't what Bryan expected. The commonality was Bryan.

In the meantime, Linda had filed for divorce. She hated filling out all of the paperwork required by the court. It asked for so much information regarding her finances, her job, education, and so on. It was tedious, and she thought she would never get it all completed. Each page brought back memories of years of marriage to this man who was a stranger. Seeing their children hurt and long for their father's presence was almost more than she could bear some days. Reading about the formulas that were used for determining amounts of child support and alimony was depressing. Linda felt that her world was spinning out of control and that she would never recover emotionally or financially. Everyone was telling her that this was the best thing, but if it was, why did it feel so devastating? It seemed easy for others to give their opinions, but they went back home to their comfortable families. They didn't have to live her life. She was confused and began to have anxiety attacks. There were times when she truly thought that her heart was going to beat out of her chest and that her head was going to explode. She expected that each day might be her last and that she might be close to death. She was no longer seeing the possibility of death as a bad thing. She welcomed it, because the pain was just more than she could bear.

Once Bryan began to realize that his new relationship was the same old pattern with a new face, he moved out into a small apartment. He too was meeting with an attorney and filling out paperwork comparable to Linda's. It looked as if he was heading to the financial cleaners. He wondered how he worked so hard in his business for it to come to this. The affair had kept Bryan mentally and emotionally occupied for some time, but then, in the small, quiet apartment, he began to realize how much he missed seeing his children daily. And when he did see them, they were oftentimes withdrawn and angry—angry at him. His kids used to look up to him, wanted their dad to do things with them and take them places. They wanted to be like him and receive his approval. He liked that. But oh how things had changed. They seemed to visit him begrudgingly. When they were with him, they just watched television or played video games. They rarely smiled and seemed sullen most of the time. What was wrong with these happy-go-lucky children? He knew what was wrong, and he hated it. Four lives were in a downward spiral with no end to the pain in sight. How did this happen? This "body," this marriage, had just about flatlined.

YOU WANT ME TO WHAT?

Kyle and Wanda had only been married for two years. But during this time they had already been separated twice, and it began to look as though this "life" together was about to enter a coma.

This early-20s couple thought they knew exactly what they were doing when they married right out of high school. Following their brief honeymoon, they began to set up "house." They had decided that Wanda would work full-time while Kyle went to school to earn a degree and then pursue medical school. Similar to Tom and Juli, they each thought they knew the roles and functions in a marriage. After all, they had watched their parents for 18 years. Surely they had learned all of the appropriate tasks during that time. Kyle imagined that he would be a full-time student and commit his time to studies. When he wasn't studying hard, he figured that he probably needed to play hard in order to "rest his brain." So, he spent lots of free time playing video games and hanging out with friends. He figured since he would earn a big paycheck one day as a doctor, his wife would appreciate the hard work he was putting into school right now and that she would, more or less, take care of things at home. He felt that with the educational sacrifice that he was making, Wanda would be thrilled to work full-time, take care of all of the cooking, cleaning, shopping, laundry, finances, and anything else that seemed domestic.

For some strange reason, Wanda's ideas were a bit different. Yes, she had agreed that Kyle would go to school while she supported them financially, but she believed that the separateness ended there. She envisioned that they would blissfully work together sharing all of the other tasks—she would cook meals, while Kyle would clean the kitchen; she would dust and he would vacuum; and she would pay the bills while he did the laundry. What she didn't imagine was that she would head to bed early each evening since she had to get up early for work, while Kyle stayed up into the wee hours of the morning playing his most recently purchased video game.

Wanda attempted to talk with Kyle about her frustrations only to be met with disbelief on his part that she would have any such expectations for him. How could she possibly expect him to go to school, study, and perform domestic duties? Those were the things that "a wife was supposed to do." Wanda suddenly began to feel as though she had inherited Kyle's mother's job and that she was going to have to finish raising, and for all she knew, dressing and feeding him. This is not the deal she believed she had agreed to, and she was determined to have no part of it.

After what felt like continual nagging to Kyle, he actually vacuumed the apartment one day. Wanda came home after a 10-hour day at work, including several stressful client meetings, and collapsed on the couch. Kyle gave her all of about 60 seconds to notice his domestic prowess before launching into how much he sacrificed and how she didn't even appreciate his extra effort and work that day. At first she thought that he must be kidding, but she quickly realized from the vein-popping look on his face that he was in fact quite serious.

At this point, in frustration and exhaustion, she called him a narcissist and told him that he acted just like his mother, always wanting recognition for the most meager of deeds. He responded by saying she had no idea how hard he worked in trying to achieve academically and did not understand the pressure he was under. He made sure that Wanda knew what a spoiled brat she was— "just like when they were dating." Needless to say, they were both so wrapped up in their own isolated and unsupported worlds that neither one could see what was going on in the other's.

Kyle wound up moving back home with his mother, who sympathized and promised to take care of him. She "always knew that Wanda couldn't care for him as she had." While this seemed good to him for a couple of weeks, he began to realize that this was not what he wanted. He didn't want to be a child at home again. He was an adult and wanted an adult relationship—he just wasn't quite sure how to get to it, at least not with Wanda. Perhaps he had just picked the wrong person and needed to find someone else who would better understand his needs and could be more supportive.

Wanda began to question herself—should she have just done all the domestic chores and not questioned Kyle's behavior? Should she not have expected him to help her and give her attention and time? Did she not do enough to "hang on to him?" Her father had always told her that she expected too much of others. Was this true?

They were both miserable, but seemed clueless as to how to "fix" things. So, in order to save face, they filed for divorce. Each felt like an utter and complete failure. Ashamed and embarrassed, they began to pull the plug on any life support. Death appeared imminent for this young, two-year-old, new life. Killing this new life was fairly easy legally, but the ripped-open hearts were certainly not.

CAN WE SELL THEM ON EBAY?

Bob and Roxann were thrilled beyond belief when they had their two children. They had looked forward to having kids and to the opportunity to be parents. Convinced that God had given them the love and compassion necessary to be good parents, they thought they were blessed in a way that would never end. Yet, here they were sitting before a custody mediator trying to decide the fate of their children and, ultimately, the fate of their lives. Submitting to the directions of a mediator, and giving a stranger the power to make decisions regarding your own children, is a paralyzing feeling. How did this happen?

Things began well enough when the children were young and compliant. However, as they got older and more complicated and challenging, Bob and Roxann discovered something rather shocking—they didn't seem to know what in the world they were doing and couldn't seem to agree on anything regarding the kids.

Bob would see misbehavior and respond quickly to punish it. He remembered his own teenage years and all of the things that he got by with. While he turned out OK, he wanted to make sure that his children toed the line, as he should have. In an effort to foresee every possible misbehavior before it happened, Bob made rules and regulations for everything and every situation. The kids began to feel that they lived in some kind of a cellblock and needed to find an escape. Their escape came in two forms—first, to secretively find ways around the regulations by looking for loopholes and technicalities. The second was to plead with mom and exploit her sense of fairness and understanding. Mom, inadvertently but willingly, became an able accomplice.

As Bob meted out a punishment, Roxann would do whatever she could to soften the blow. She thought that Bob was overly harsh and unfair in his discipline, and therefore felt it was her job, as the loving and caring mom, to make amends for his overly strict approach. As you might imagine, the children absolutely loved this. Time after time, situations were framed with dad being the evil tyrant and mom being the savior. Mom was the ally against the enemy. The more that Roxann intervened, the harsher Bob's consequences were for the children. They each saw themselves as the one who had to balance out the other's extreme responses. With each encounter, they grew further and further apart as a couple. Bob felt undermined at every turn and began to micromanage everything he possibly could.

Home became a prison of sorts for everyone in the family. Bob and Roxann no longer consulted the other about permission each had given or prohibited with regard to the children's activities. When a child misbehaved, they each interpreted its intent and impact differently, and therefore responded in completely opposite ways. Bob and Roxann no longer trusted or liked one another. They spent less and less time together. Bob framed the problems as, "If the kids and Roxann would just do the things they should, all would be fine." Roxann, on the other hand, simply summed it all up as, "Bob is a control freak. If he would just quit trying to control everything and everybody, all would be fine." While the kids were oftentimes seen as the source of the problem, they weren't. The issue was about Bob and Roxann getting on the same page, but that wasn't happening. They both had retreated and become entrenched in concrete around their positions. No one was willing to move and look at anything differently. As a result, they came before a custody mediator.

Blame, blame, and more blame—what had it accomplished? Certainly no solutions. They were at the point that they couldn't even be civil. Every encounter involved name-calling and door slamming. Roxann was "spineless and weak," while Bob was "Attila the Hun." And this is the *printable* name-calling.

What was the end result? Primary physical custody was awarded to Roxann, while Bob was given every Thursday night and every other weekend with the kids. The kids were awash with guilt and felt responsible for all that happened. They wanted to get mom and dad back together, but didn't have a clue as to what they should do. Mom and dad used the kids as pawns to lob verbal hand grenades at each other—taking pot shots at every opportunity. With each verbal explosion came new threats and animosity.

Bob had moved into a small one-bedroom apartment that was sparsely decorated, and he hated going home to it. He felt as though he simply existed from day to day. His life that had felt so blessed at one time now seemed more out of whack than he ever thought possible. Bob had never known such a deep sense of pain and loss. He had lost his way.

Roxann felt isolated in the spacious house that she and Bob had built. She was overwhelmed at the prospects of living alone as the kids approached college age. She never imagined that her marriage would come to this. The brokenness was more than she felt she could bear. How had she lost her way like this? What was she to do? While this divorce was not what either Bob or Roxann signed up for when they said "I do," this life, this marriage, was just about dead. They both believed that because of the actions and wishes of the other, their marriage must have a Do-Not-Resuscitate order attached to it.

THE LANDSCAPE VARIES

The reasons can vary as to why people are in these situations. If you are currently facing, or have gone through divorce, it may seem to center on issues of finances, intimacy, expectations, or parenting like the couples we have just discussed. However, your situation may look completely different. Perhaps your wounded relationship has to do with unjust criticism, lack of forgiveness, a void of meaningful communication, or broken trust. Regardless of what seems to have led you to this place, the pain is real, and it runs deep. You never stood at the altar thinking that you would be going through such gut-wrenching agony now. In light of your early love and unwavering expressions of commitment, this is absolutely unthinkable. Yet the unthinkable has happened. We created a "new life" together, one that had not existed before, but that was supposed to last a lifetime. That was certainly your intent, your mate's intent, and God's design.

Yet, it is very possible that as you read this, you are staring at the corpse of your created life together, or at the least, a very, very sick body. Regardless of the situations that arose and contributed to where you are, the result is the same: death of the most significant human relationship in your life. It hurts more than anything you could have ever imagined. The loneliness is overwhelming, and you are honestly not sure that you will ever recover. How can someone survive this? You want to scream out so others will grasp the devastation of your searing pain. Yet, you are convinced that no one can understand. Indeed, perhaps no person really can. But without offering trite platitudes, you must know that God sees every tear, hears every cry, and knows every stab of piercing pain that you experience. He doesn't miss a beat and He truly "gets it." Rest assured—God understands your divorce completely!

CHAPTER THREE

MY STORY

"Where we have strong emotions, we're liable to fool ourselves."

—Carl Sagan[1]

I have waited as long as I can to write this chapter. I am writing it after having written others that follow because this is one that I have dreaded. It is one that is full of difficult memories: memories of confusion, pain, sin, and more pain. Individuals who have experienced the devastating emotions and loss of divorce know a level of gut-wrenching loss that most others cannot comprehend. It is sometimes difficult for these individuals to hear the well-meant sympathies, platitudes, or advice of those who have not walked this dark and shattering road. I write this chapter because I believe it is important that you know that, unfortunately, I have walked this road—not once, but TWICE. So, if in this book you hear me understand and identify with your pain and loss, know that it is because I *really* do. Perhaps your story will mirror pieces of mine.

I have wrestled with just how much information to convey, how much detail and description to give. Sharing every detail would serve no purpose. At the same time, I want to share enough that this will be meaningful and encouraging for you, as you identify and connect with my story. While I want to protect identities and people, I also want you to know my heart, the awesome power of God, and the absolute evil of the deceiver. I will do my best to convey my story with this as the goal and to communicate it in balance.

MY FIRST MARRIAGE

"It all began in a 5,000-watt radio station in Fresno, California." OK—it didn't really, but that is such a great line from Ted Baxter on the old Mary Tyler Moore television show, that I just had to use it. Actually, my marital journey began in Houston, Texas, in the late 1960s. During my junior year in high school, I met my future wife. I was in the marching band and Kaye (not her real name) was on the school's drill team. I remember that I hadn't even met her yet when I turned to my friend in the band and said, "I'm going to marry that girl." No, these were not great prophetic words, but more the foolish ramblings of a 16-year-old. However, we did meet, date, and were actually married three years later when we were sophomores in college.

We were 19 years old when we got married. Oh, yes. I know now all of the obstacles that were against us getting married that young. Certainly people tried to warn us of the dangers. But (see if you have ever said this), we were different than the population at large. We would make it without all of the problems that others have experienced because "we knew what we were doing." As I look back, I realize that at 19, I hardly knew how to blow my nose, let alone tackle the institution of marriage. But no one could tell us anything. We had both come from parents who had married young and were still together, so that was our defense.

Following our marriage in 1971, we worked, finished college and, like most couples, had difficult struggles as well as some wonderful times. As young and foolish kids, we fought over ridiculous things, we played foolish head games, and we would threaten divorce when things got tough. Of course we never intended to divorce, but throwing that word around proved to be a powerful weapon to get one another's attention. We frequently used words to get what we wanted without realizing the lasting damage that we did.

It is no mistake that the Scriptures say that we will be judged by our words (see Matt. 12:37) or that Jesus is called the Word (see John 1:1). Words are powerful in how they impact people and in how they shape lives. We need to weigh our words carefully and run them through a cautious filter before they leave our lips. It is significant that James talks about the power of the tongue to harm and to heal (see James 3:9-12).

In 1980, our first child was born and five years later our second son came along. We loved these boys and found great joy in parenting. However, we were less and less happy with each other. Sure, we knew that marriage wasn't just about our own happiness. But like so many people, what we knew and what we felt were two different things. We espoused all of the right things regarding righteousness, unconditional love, and the sanctity of marriage. But at the end of the day, we allowed our emotions to sit on the throne of our hearts. What a dangerous place to live; yet we did.

During this time, I was actively involved in ministry, and my wife was a stay-at-home mom with the boys. We both found some fulfillment in our respective roles, but we found more frustration than fulfillment with each other. So, what did we do? Did we get great counsel and advice from others couples? Did we find a competent therapist to help guide us through these choppy waters? No. We were in ministry. This was during a time when there was a lot of pressure to appear to have it together if you were in this kind of position. To admit weakness, that you were struggling in your marriage, could most likely cost you your job.

Therefore, to have credibility, you almost had to live deceptively. This is absolutely foolish, but it is a conflict experienced by many in ministry positions. When you can't be aboveboard, what do you do? You go underground. You try to give the appearance of pushing all of the right buttons, and walking all of the right paths, but behind that is a whole other life. And I will tell you, duplicitous living is very difficult. It will suck the life out of you and strip you of all integrity. Jim Tomberlin, who was the senior pastor at Woodmen Valley Chapel in Colorado Springs back in the '90s, once said in a message, "If you aren't transparent, then you aren't authentic. And if you aren't authentic, then you are a hypocrite."

That was us. We hadn't set out to destroy our marriage. We hadn't purposed to sin. But we certainly hadn't put the hedges in place to protect our marriage either. In our unhappiness and aloneness, we sought out the company of others who might help to soothe our pain. We both, at some point, became involved with other people. As I look back, the rationalizations and justifications abounded. Oh not openly. Not verbally. We would never do that because we knew better. But in the secret of our own hearts we tried to somehow make the puzzle pieces fit.

I learned during these years that once you rationalized one inappropriate relationship, it was much easier to do it again and again. The Scriptures state, *"after desire has conceived, it gives birth to sin; and sin, when it is full-grown, gives birth to death"* (James 1:15). I know that my sin led to death in a variety of significant things: the death of my marriage, the death of truth and honesty, and most significantly, the death of me as a person.

It seemed that we were fighting non-stop, and it was wearing us both out. I foolishly decided that I should move out for a period of time so that the boys wouldn't see us constantly fighting. Perhaps then we could find times to talk and work through important issues. Statistics consistently report that when a couple separates, the chances of divorce increase significantly. But once again, I thought that I knew better and that I could beat the odds. Sadly, Kaye had already been considering a divorce, and my moving out was the act that sealed the deal for her.

THE DIVORCE AND AFTERMATH

The next several months were filled with adversarial interactions, attorneys battling over oftentimes insignificant items, mediations, child custody fights, rejections, verbal sparring, and probably most importantly—two innocent boys who were slowly being destroyed. When the dust settled at the end of the day, another marriage, another family, had been destroyed. We both thought we were somehow at least partially justified. We both worked to spin the story to our advantage. But the reality was that we had chosen sin over righteousness, compromising behaviors over protection of our spouse and family, and selfish desires over love. I did not like who I had become—a duplicitous man with little integrity.

By the time we divorced, we had been living in California for seven years, so when Kaye took the boys and moved back to Houston, I was devastated and was left to deal with me and who I had become. It was exactly where I needed to be, and I hated it. Do I blame Kaye for the divorce? Absolutely not! Yes, we both made grave errors, but I take full responsibility for the unraveling. I have often wondered if I had been the husband that God called me to be, would the results have been different? Sure we had taken very different approaches to life, but that is not insurmountable. If I had loved her better, and protected our marriage better, and been the man of integrity that God desired, would the marriage have lasted? Perhaps. I will never know.

If you have ever been to a theme park such as Universal Studios, you may have taken the back-lot tour. It is great fun to see familiar sets where well-known movies have been made. However, what you see, perhaps the front of a building, may only be a façade held up by two-by-fours. I remember having the chance to visit the Ponderosa Ranch near Lake Tahoe in the mid '90s. What a great place. I had spent my Sunday evenings week after week watching Bonanza and the lives of the Cartwrights. I remember touring the house where Ben, Adam, Hoss, and Little Joe hung out and realizing that the stairs went up to...nothing. They just came to a dead end in a wall. I used to watch Little Joe walk up the stairs, thinking that he reached the second floor, because the next scene would show him on the second floor. But it was a façade.

I realized that I was like those stairs. I was a fraud. I was not the same person in the back lot as I was on the stage. I was not transparent. I was not authentic. I was a hypocrite. Oh yes, my pain was real. I never expected to be divorced. I was devastated at the distance of my children. I didn't like the pain I felt, or the pain that I had caused. Seeing the fear and loss in the eyes of my children was probably the worst. Watching their tears, and feeling my own each time I had to put them on a plane, was absolutely heart stabbing. I was alone. I was divorced! I never, ever expected to be there—but there I was. There had been so much hope and promise in 1971 when we took those vows. We had pledged our love and eternal faithfulness, but then failed to honor it. I was staring at an unbelievable, catastrophic train wreck. Where in the world was I to go from here? And the worst part was—as far as I was concerned—I did this. I was guilty.

TRANSITION

Following the divorce, I went back to school to work on my second master's degree. I still recall walking into the book store at California State University, Fresno, and seeing a button, which said the following: "Everything prior to 40 is just rehearsal." This got my attention. Here I was 37 years old, feeling like my life was a disaster movie, and I was unsure of whether I could salvage it.

Some people are amazing in their ability to figure life out at an early age and really get it together. Unfortunately, that is not the majority of people, and it certainly wasn't me. But here was a statement that I was in the rehearsal stage; that in essence, the best was yet to come. Maybe my life wasn't over yet.

I was fortunate at this point to have several puzzle pieces fit together for my benefit. I was on staff at a church that was understanding, supporting, confronting, and loving. I had offered my resignation to my senior pastor when the divorce began, and he had refused it. Bufe was an amazing man in many ways. He was often willing to buck the trends to do what was best for individuals, and this was one of those cases. He knew that I needed to be with my church family and to have a safe place to deal with my stuff and begin to heal. That turned out to be a great move for me on his part.

The second puzzle piece was going to graduate school and getting into a disciplined routine. My life became a steady cadence of regular contact with my kids, planning for and maximizing their visits, graduate school, ministry, church family, and most of all, significant times of aloneness with God. My good friend and worship pastor Dave Schroyer taught me a great deal about worshiping, serving, and living authentically in the presence of God. I didn't go from a man of duplicity to a man of integrity overnight. It was a process and a journey, but one that I desperately wanted to make and was determined to do so. Those next two to three years were tremendous times of growth. And by the time I hit 40, I actually did feel that everything had been rehearsal leading up to a time when I could really possibly be of benefit to someone. But I am getting a little bit ahead of myself.

MY SECOND MARRIAGE

Within about a year and a half following my divorce, my oldest son Jeremy was back living with me, while my younger son remained in Texas. Being a single dad presented a whole new set of challenges, but I must admit that these were great years together. Working two jobs, going to graduate school, and being a single dad made for a full plate of activity, but somehow we were able to juggle it all and make it work.

It was during this time that I met Leaha (not her real name) through a mutual friend. I was immediately attracted to her spunk, wit, and passion for children. She was an elementary school teacher and, therefore, related to my children very well. She had moved back to Fresno to live and work. During that first summer, she would regularly keep my boys for me when I was working. We were only friends at this point, but I appreciated her willingness to help me with the boys, and I enjoyed her company. She was intelligent and a great conversationalist. By the fall, we had become pretty comfortable friends. She decided to take some classes at the university, so we frequently carpooled together. I was attracted to her, and yet I was quite gun-shy. I felt conflicted because I had been burned, and I had burned another person as well. I had two boys who were the apple of my eye, and I did not want to do anything that would make their lives more difficult. They were my first priority, and I was very protective of them. I missed the company of a godly woman and desired to be in a relationship, but I was still growing in my own journey to integrity and wasn't sure whether I was ready for a relationship.

While trying to weigh and balance all of these emotions, I decided to ask her out. We dated for three years before I was ready to propose in 1992. I was extremely cautious in not wanting to make another mistake. I wanted to make sure that I had found a woman who would be a good stepmother to my children. I felt that I had grown, vacated my previously duplicitous lifestyle, and had learned a lot about being a husband and a father. I believed that I was *becoming* the man of integrity that God wanted. I was not a naïve and ignorant 19-year-old. I knew exactly what I was signing up for and committing to by marrying Leaha. We married, and I was convinced that I had found the love of my life. I believed that we were on the same page in thinking that marriage is a lifelong commitment, and I was thrilled.

Over the next 10 years we had some great times. Needless to say, we also had challenges—mostly around parenting/step-parenting issues. We made our share of mistakes and we grew. Leaha was an outstanding schoolteacher. I continued to work in a combination of ministry and counseling positions. We were doing well financially and seemed to be growing the depth of our love. In 1996, we decided to move to Colorado. This was an exciting move as we saw the Lord open doors in truly miraculous ways, and we knew that he had plans for us there.

Our first years in Colorado were exciting. We had new jobs, designed and built a new house, were able to do some traveling, and life seemed to be going well. We had problems and challenges along the way (I don't think that anyone raises teens without them), but I was always convinced that our marriage was intact. I believed that we would weather and work through whatever problems we faced.

I began to notice changes in Leaha when she decided to go back to graduate school and pursue a master's degree. I couldn't pinpoint what it was exactly. On the outside, her behavior didn't seem to radically change, but she began to hint at the fact that she didn't like being married. At a couple's retreat we attended a few years earlier, Leaha looked me in the eyes and said that she knew, and wanted me to know, that no matter what happened, she would never divorce me. Yet, something had started to change, and I somehow felt that the person who had made that statement was not the person I was dealing with now.

In December 2002, we planned a big trip to celebrate our ten-year anniversary. About two weeks before the trip, Leaha announced that she didn't want to go. She didn't love me, didn't want to be married, and she wanted a divorce. I was dumbfounded.

Even though her behavior had seemed different of late, I had not seen this coming.

Unlike in my first marriage, I had worked diligently to be a faithful husband who treated his wife well. This just didn't make any sense. We talked a bit more specifically about particular issues and how we might address them. Leaha agreed to go to counseling, but this didn't seem to make any difference. She continued to grow more distant and cold. It seemed that the more I tried to address her issues of concern, the angrier she got. She continued to ask for a divorce, and I continued to encourage her to work things out with me. Eventually, she decided to separate from me and moved into an apartment. I didn't think this was the best move for us, but I didn't have much say in the matter, and all I could do was respect her wishes. She asked for a month of no contact and didn't tell me where her apartment was located or share her new phone number with me. We agreed to see a counselor six weeks later, after which we could begin to talk and work things out.

After our counseling appointment, Leaha informed me that she had filed for divorce and no longer wanted to work on our marriage. I was blown away. That night I experienced my first panic attack. I had heard other people talk about how they felt, but I had never experienced feeling like I wanted to crawl out of my skin before. I felt instantly abandoned by my wife and everyone I knew, even abandoned by God. It was like being left in a black hole from which there was no return. It was the scariest feeling that I have ever had in my life. Once the attack subsided, my greatest fear was that it would return.

I didn't understand how this could have happened. I knew what those vows meant. I knew what marriage meant. I knew how to be kind and loving to my wife and, while I certainly wasn't always successful, I had strived to do so. I loved this woman with all of my heart and was willing to do whatever we needed to do to salvage this and make it a relationship that honored God.

The next several months were a whirlwind. My oldest son Jeremy was away in the army and seemed to be minimally impacted by all that was going on. However, Jason, the youngest, had a difficult time. Leaha had been the most solid mother figure that Jason had had in his life. She timed her departure two weeks before he was to leave for college, and the loss of another maternal relationship rattled him at his core. By November he was put on anti-depressants as his depression was beginning to have a paralyzing effect upon him. He made attempts to remain in contact with Leaha. But every time he attempted to address what was going on, he was shut down. Ultimately, she cut him off, just as she did our church and all of our friends. By March, Jason dropped out of college and came home to try and get a handle on his own emotions. It was a difficult thing for a parent to watch.

Prior to the divorce being filed, I had only shared what was going on with a limited close group of friends. I kept thinking that Leaha would figure this thing out, stop the divorce, and come back home. However, once she filed, then I knew that I needed to pull out the stops. I contacted a group of about 100 people who had been good friends and who I knew would be good prayer warriors. I asked them if they would be willing to stand in prayer on a regular basis for our marriage. Each week I sent out an update on where things were, and they stood before God with our petition.

There was a part of me that kept thinking, if I just get enough people to come before God, He will have to take notice and change Leaha's heart. I wanted this restored with all that was in me. I sometimes wondered if God was even listening. Yet, friends assured and encouraged me that He was listening and acting. In my mind, His will was never in question; His Word is clear. But we also have free will. He will allow us to make choices whether they are right or wrong. He will not force us.

Leaha had read some of John Eldridge's books about desire and seemed to take them to an extreme. She desired to not be married and believed that God wanted her to have the desires of her heart. This was certainly a perversion of Scripture in my mind. I contacted John and shared with him what was taking place. His response was affirming when he wrote me:

> It grieves me as well to think that because of a misunderstanding of my message, anyone has found reason to dissolve their marriage. Desire is a powerful force for good or for ill; my point exactly. And I believe that our deepest entrance into holiness is through the doorway of desire—especially as we learn to surrender every desire to God in order that we might learn to love as He does. Ultimately, a life worth living isn't found in having our desires met, but in having God and in loving as He does. How sad to think that anyone sees the fulfillment of their desire as an excuse to walk out on a sacred bond. It will not work, of course, for in the end it only adds sorrow upon a vain search for happiness. How can we be happy outside of God's will?[2]

During the coming months, friends and pastors occasionally attempted to contact Leaha, but to no avail. Nothing seemed to make a difference. It was a tremendous time of growth for me. My intimacy with the Lord was stronger and deeper than ever before. My trust and reliance upon Him grew deeper each day. I sought out my own counselor to help to unpeel my layers so that I could make sure I was dealing with my own issues. I wanted no stone left unturned. Regardless of what happened with the marriage, I needed to make sure that I was really dealing with me.

I wish that I could say that all of these efforts resulted in a restored marriage—but they didn't. I stood firm—the wedding ring didn't leave my hand. I waited for the Lord to work—whether that was in her heart for restoration or in preparing me to move on to the next chapter of life. Friends were kind and supportive and they prayed as well. I still loved this woman with all my heart, and I really wanted our marriage to be restored. I wasn't just going through the motions so that I would look like a good guy who was doing the right thing. I truly wanted healing.

As the date for the final divorce hearing approached, one of the pastors from our church agreed to lead a time of prayer for God's intervention into our marriage and family. About 25 close friends in the Colorado Springs area came together in support and prayer. It was a wonderfully affirming time that God used to better prepare me for the days to come. The next day I sent my wife this note:

Dear Leaha,

I am writing you a short note just to check in with you. I guess my question is, are you certain that you really want to go through with this divorce? We have shared nearly 15 years of our lives together. During that span we have had some intensely loving, wonderful, and fulfilling times. We have shared important years of history and growth. Even with all that has happened and all that has been done, I continue to love you with all my heart. I know beyond a shadow of a doubt that God desires reconciliation. He hates what is happening to us and our family. We can do this and God will restore it if we will only allow Him to. It is not too late. God has promised to honor our obedience and He will show us how to do this. He will not just help us restore our marriage, He can make this into something far more wonderful than either one of us has imagined, and the coolest thing is that He will be the One that is glorified by it! We can start again.

Leaha, you are still the woman that I care about unconditionally. I would love to simply have coffee (or
chai tea) and talk.

With all my love,
Barry.

I wish that I could say that this letter did the trick, but it
didn't. The final divorce hearing took place and the marriage was
officially dead.

POST-MORTEM

Now, in case some of you are reading this and thinking "Oh,
what a sad story," or "Poor Barry," please stop. That is not the
purpose of this chapter. I am fine. I am not a victim or a martyr
here. I am simply a person who has been on both sides of the
coin, and *that* is what I really want for you to hear. I have been
through TWO divorces. Some of you can relate. I never thought
I would be divorced. But now, not only am I divorced, I have to
specify which ex I am referring to when I speak. Yuck!

Yet, please hear the important message of this chapter. I have
been on the side of divorce where I was a participant, a pursuer,
an instigator. I have caused hurt and selfishly gone after my own
desires regardless of how it affected others. I was the one who
couldn't look beyond the moment to see how my actions were
affecting others. I have been the "bad guy." I have also been on the
other end of the stick, so to speak. I have worked hard to build and
maintain a marriage. I loved my wife from the bottom of my shoes.
I worked hard to keep growing at being a good husband, and yet I
had the door resoundingly slammed in my face. I have felt the devastation and gut-twisting pain of being trampled on and rejected,
and I have felt the guilt-searing pain of doing that to another.

If you have gone, or are going through, a divorce, you are
probably sitting in one of these two places. For you, this may

absolutely not be what you want. Sure, you have contributed to problems, but you are more than willing to pursue solutions with equal vigor. You do not want a divorce, you love your spouse, and you are willing to do anything in your power to save it. Or, perhaps you find yourself wanting a divorce. You may have gotten to this place in all of the wrong ways, and for all of the wrong reasons, but you are here. You have rationalized and built your scaffolding in order to spin this in a way to lose as little face as possible. You have glossed over your mistakes and your sin and worked to explain them in a way that allows you to live with yourself. In the moment, it might feel doable and even good at times. Of course it is also possible that it is not quite this simple. Perhaps you have been in a marriage that has included such things as infidelity, abuse, or drug addictions and divorce truly seems to be the only option. As you continue to read, know that these issues will be addressed as well.

Whichever place you might be in, I have been there. I get it. I understand. I want you to know this so that as you approach the rest of the book, you will not think I am writing trite, nice-sounding, biblical counsel when I have no idea what it is like to live in these places. I have been there and it stinks!

CHAPTER FOUR

THE CAUSE OF DIVORCE

"That which is common to the greatest number has the least care bestowed upon it. Every one thinks chiefly of his own, hardly at all of the common interest; and only when he is himself concerned as an individual. For besides other considerations, everyone is more inclined to neglect the duty which he expects another to fulfill."

—ARISTOTLE[1]

We have all seen marriages crumble for a variety of reasons. Sometimes we are convinced that the wife has been a skank or the husband a sleezeball. Other situations seem to indicate that children or stepchildren have done all that they can to make life difficult and have maybe even worked to split up the parents. At other times, we attribute problems to everything from stressful job situations to meddling in-laws. For whatever reason, divorces occur.

I want to use this chapter to give you a clear perspective on why divorces occur. There will be a quiz along the way, so tighten up your thinking cap as we briefly examine the most common factors that contribute to couples or individuals making the decision to pursue a divorce. Following each scenario, you get to decide who appears to be at fault for the divorce. Oh yes, I know we have had no-fault divorce laws in place in some states for over 40 years. However, anyone plugging in more than a half a dozen brain cells knows that divorces don't "just happen." Somebody did something; someone chose a behavior, and decisions were made that led to a divorce.

Bob and Diane

Bob and Diane have been married for 20 years. About a year ago, Bob began to spend more time working closely with a female colleague. This frequently included evening business meetings and occasional overnight travel. Diane began to notice changes in Bob's dress, attitude, and priorities. She expressed her thoughts and concerns to Bob, but he always rationalized and explained them away. He said that she was being silly. However, there was a deep gnawing in her gut that told her something was wrong.

Bob enjoyed the company of his colleague. They worked together on projects, she looked up to him and showed him respect, she seemed to really understand him much better than his wife, and she always complimented him on how he looked. Bob found himself finding more and more reasons to spend time with her. As happens more times than I can recount, what began as a close, working relationship developed into a strong, emotional connection and eventually into a full-blown physical affair.

Diane began to discover receipts for lunches at romantic restaurants, as well as charges on their monthly Visa bill for gifts that she didn't receive. She tried to deny the fears she had, but her instincts were overwhelming her. She finally decided to check up on Bob one evening at work, where all of her fears were confirmed. There was lots of yelling and finger-pointing, but ultimately divorce proceedings began. According to McManus,[2] 17 percent of all divorces are the result of infidelity. Bob attempted to blame Diane for never being there to understand and support him. She was always too busy with the kids and her friends, so he had to find someone who would care about him. Diane was devastated that wedding vows seemed to mean so little to Bob and that he would betray her like this. And yet, here they were in what would have been an unthinkable place 20 years earlier. While this may seem like an easy one, who do you think is at fault?

☐ Bob

☐ Diane

☐ Another person

☐ No one

Doug and Susan

Doug and Susan had always enjoyed an active sex life. It seemed that just about any time and any place was the right time for them. Their sexual appetites matched well, and they both found sexual intimacy mutually satisfying. As a matter of fact, their physical intimacy was so good that they came to take it for granted. They would hear other couples complain about frequency, headaches, and all kinds of other problems that they just couldn't relate to. But then it began. On one particular occasion, shortly after the arrival of their second child, as they were in the passions of love making, Doug couldn't achieve an erection. This had never happened, and Doug found it quite unnerving. Susan didn't know what to think, but tried to minimize it and laugh it off. A few weeks later, it happened again. This time, Susan was not as kind in her words and kidded Doug about it.

This really bothered Doug, and he began to worry about whether or not there was something wrong and what would happen if he couldn't perform. As often happens, his fears contributed to future problems, leading Susan to complain more and to ridicule Doug. In no time, it seemed as though Doug had gone from stud muffin to impotent. Neither one of them knew what to do to deal with the problem, so they argued. Needless to say, things grew worse until talk of divorce began. Susan certainly cared about Doug, but she could not see herself living in a sexless marriage, which was the only way she viewed their situation. Doug was crushed, angry, and embarrassed. Proceedings began. Who do you see as responsible for this predicament?

☐ Doug

☐ Susan

☐ The children

☐ Another person

☐ No one

Tom and Sherry

Tom and Sherry met at a party thrown by friends. They were attracted to each other immediately as they began to chat over drinks. Their relationship grew quickly as they began to spend more and more time together. Tom's friends began to show some concern about Sherry and her seeming large consumption of alcohol. Tom was quick to dismiss their misgivings, as he explained that they both enjoyed a few drinks and that she just liked to drink a little more. Things continued to progress well, and the next spring they were married. Early in the marriage, Sherry became pregnant, and they both seemed thrilled.

What Tom didn't know was that Sherry was actually scared to death. Sherry's mother had been emotionally unavailable when Sherry was growing up. Her mother didn't seem to know quite what to do as a parent, and so she drank most of the time. Sherry feared that she wouldn't know how to be a mother either, so she began to drink more. Tom became concerned for the baby's welfare and pleaded with Sherry to stop drinking, at least during the pregnancy. Fortunately, she did manage to stop drinking. But as soon as the baby arrived, she began to drink again and now more heavily than Tom had ever seen. He would come home from work only to find her passed out with the baby crying in his crib.

He talked with Sherry's parents and learned that she had a drinking problem since early high school and actually had abused drugs during that time as well. He was beside himself and didn't know which way to turn. He would talk with Sherry, plead with her, yell at her, and threaten to leave her. The last straw for Tom was when he came home one day and found Sherry smoking weed with a friend. As one might imagine, he blew up, took the baby, and went to his parents' house. Shortly thereafter, he filed for divorce. Drug and alcohol related divorces account for 16 percent of all divorces.[3] Why did this happen?

☐ Tom

☐ Sherry

☐ The baby

☐ Another person

☐ No one

Rick and Karen

Rick and Karen had always had a very passionate relationship. If I could describe a relationship as bipolar, this couple would be it. They seemed to either be together, glued at the lips, having a fantastic time, or they were initiating the next world war. And when they were at war, there seemed to be no holds barred. They would say whatever mean thing that came into their minds. The sharper and more hurtful the zing, the better. And yet, when things could seem to be no worse—they would find a way to make up. Matching the intensity of their fights, their make ups would involve outlandish gifts, cards, flowers, promises to be wonderful forever, and so on. The highs felt great, and the lows couldn't seem to be worse, and there didn't seem to be anything in-between.

One day, it happened. In the middle of one of their biggest fights yet, Karen unleashed a barrage of hurtful words. Rick responded by hitting her. This was a place they had not been before, and for a moment it stopped them in their tracks. Rick apologized and said that it wouldn't happen again. Karen was stunned and uncertain how to respond. Things seemed fine for awhile, but during their next big fight, it happened again. This time Rick gave Karen a black eye. Once again, Rick expressed what seemed like sincere regret. However, with each escalation, the physical abuse became worse. Karen was too embarrassed to tell anyone about what was going on. One day the fighting got so bad that the neighbors called the police. Rick was arrested, and Karen was taken to stay with some friends. Her friends told her that it was obvious that Rick was an abuser and that she needed to leave him immediately for her own safety. While she felt as though she had contributed to the fights, she could see that her friends must be right—he was an abuser and she needed to leave. Soon after, divorce proceedings began. Where does the fault lay with this couple?

☐ Rick

☐ Karen

☐ Other people

☐ No one

Brad and Jessica

Brad and Jessica met while Brad was in the military, just after Jessica had graduated from high school. As is common for many young, military couples, they moved with some frequency, which made it difficult to put down roots. Brad was often away on duty, and Jessica stayed home by herself to raise their children.

Following several years of this pattern, Brad retired from the military and went to work for a civilian contractor. By this time, their two children were in school, so Jessica decided to use her free time to go back to school and get the college education she had not been able to pursue until then. While Brad never expressed direct resistance to this idea, he wasn't a big supporter of Jessica's quest either.

Jessica loved college and thoroughly enjoyed what she was learning and the ways that she began to see herself grow. She found it invigorating and intellectually stimulating. Unfortunately, Brad didn't share her newfound enthusiasm. At every opportunity, he minimized what she was learning and tried to manipulate her back into the "stay at home with the kids" role that she had held before. She felt more and more restricted and stifled. Jessica felt that Brad just didn't understand her, and she became convinced that he never would. She believed that she was discovering her true self and that she needed to be free to grow. She felt that she was outgrowing Brad, and she needed to follow her newfound path. It became obvious to her that Brad would always limit her and that she needed to move beyond him if she were to continue to develop. At the encouragement of her school friends, she finally filed for divorce. Who holds responsibility for this divorce?

☐ Brad

☐ Jessica

☐ The children

☐ Other people

Larry and Denise

Larry and Denise, like most couples at some point, struggled with the issue of finances. There never seemed to be enough money. Sound familiar? Larry was a saver (Denise called him a cheap skate), and Denise was more of a spender (which Larry referred to as a shopoholic). They constantly had battles over exceeding their spending limit on the charge card or overdrawn bank accounts. They never really discussed the subject; they just sort of lobbed verbal hand grenades at each other and built higher and higher walls between each other. Over the years, Larry built a successful business that provided plenty of income and a comfortable living for the two of them. However, this never laid their financial issues to rest. It seemed like the more money Larry made, the more Denise spent. The more Denise spent, the more Larry tried to control the money flow. The more Larry controlled the money, the more resistant Denise became to any spending guidelines, and so on.

One day, Denise bought a new $450 purse, and Larry lost it. She had so many purses in her closet that she never used now, why did she need another one? He told her what an irresponsible child she was and that no matter how many hours he worked, and how much he made, it never was (nor would be) enough. He was weary of pushing this financial ball up the hill each month by himself. He had begun to feel that the only reason she kept him around was to pay all of the bills and to make deposits in her checking account. Denise was crushed by Larry's remarks and felt that he was very unfair in his assessment. Yes, she liked expensive purses, but she did try to watch sales for other things. She was aware that money didn't just grow on trees, something that Larry continued to remind her of. She felt that the pressure that he put on her was just too much. Divorce proceedings began not long after this exchange. Who do you think bears responsibility for the demise of this marriage?

☐ Larry

☐ Denise

☐ Other people

☐ No one

Greg and Bonnie

Greg and Bonnie had three daughters that were such delights—when they were young. However, when the girls became teenagers, they posed challenges that Greg and Bonnie had never imagined. It seemed that if one of their daughters wasn't breaking curfew, then another was being caught smoking at school, or the other was failing three classes. Greg and Bonnie had tried to model responsible behavior and just didn't understand why their sweet, little girls were turning on them like this. They were continually asking themselves what happened? But the answers eluded them.

However, the most difficult problems weren't with the girls' behavior. The most challenging issue seemed to be with how they responded as a couple. Greg's solutions frequently involved yelling, belittling, grounding, and other severe restrictions. This seemed to give Greg the feeling of some control in what was an out-of-control situation. But this perceived control was actually an illusion. Bonnie felt that Greg was so extreme in his responses that she needed to balance it out for the girls. As a result, she would undermine Greg and allow the girls off of restrictions when he wasn't around. He and Bonnie were constantly arguing about consequences and punishments for the girls. They would often wind up each feeling that he or she was the only parent truly present, and along with this came feelings of aloneness and futility. When one of the girls came home and announced that she was pregnant, Larry packed his bags. He said, "I have tried to raise these girls with some discipline, but I am thwarted at every turn. Now look what has happened. I quit! I give up! If this is how you all want to run a family, then go for it. I am out of here!" Who is responsible here?

☐ Greg

☐ Bonnie

☐ The daughters

☐ Another person

☐ No one

Steve and Linda

Steve and Linda had always had a "fun" relationship. During their dating and early-marriage years, they traveled extensively, went to plays, and held season tickets to the symphony. They hobnobbed in the elite social circles and attended major sporting events. Life was good. However, as careers developed, children were born, and parents aged, life became routine and not as much "fun."

While they both were aware of the changes, Linda seemed to have more difficulty adapting. She missed the trips that she and Steve used to take as a couple, but the diminishing social activities were the hardest for her. She was constantly trying to find ways to recapture those moments, but she was disappointed each time because it just wasn't the same.

About 11 years into the marriage, Linda began to talk with her single girlfriends about her feelings of frustration at the things she was missing in life. She just wasn't happy. Shouldn't she be happy? Her girlfriends encouraged her to pursue the things that brought her pleasure. Life is short, Linda reasoned. She owed it to herself to be happy. While she didn't have any specific complaints toward Steve or the kids, she just knew that they weren't making her happy. So, she moved in with a girlfriend for a few months to try and figure out what she needed to do. At the end of three months, she was no closer to figuring it out than when she began. But she reasoned that she wouldn't be happy until she left the marriage and began to build a life on her own. After all, it was when she was "footloose and fancy-free" that she was the happiest. With no animosity, she told Steve that she wanted a divorce. Steve was blown away by this announcement and tried to talk her out of it, but her mind was made up. Steve and the kids were bewildered as Linda moved on to her new life. Was this all Linda's doing? Or was Steve at fault for not continuing to make her happy? Where does responsibility lie?

☐ Steve

☐ Linda

☐ The children

☐ Another person

☐ No one

Dan and Julie

Dan and Julie had grown up in homes that were completely opposite to each other. Dan had lived with parents who were open to different ideas and who were supportive when their children wanted to venture out and try new things. However, Julie's household was one where criticism was the standard method of operation. Her parents had modeled rigid boundaries with little room for variation. As a result, whenever she did anything that was not according to her parent's wishes, she was quickly reprimanded and instructed in "the way" to do whatever it was. It might be the manner in which she answered the phone, the way she fixed her hair, the clothes she wore, even how she held her fork at dinner. The list seemed endless. So, it was no surprise when, after a few months of marriage, Julie began to do what had been modeled for her. It was the very thing that she hated, yet she knew how to it do well.

Dan began to feel that an alien had taken over Julie's body. She had been so kind, considerate, and respectful when they were dating. How could that same person now be so intolerant? She seemed to have a "right way" to do things. She criticized how Dan did the dishes, how he folded clothes, what he watched on television, and yes, even what he wore and how he did his hair. She seemed to have set herself up as the scoffer of Psalm 1, or we might say that she had deemed it her job to "fix" all of Dan's flaws. He needed to become the person that she thought he should be. It seemed that nothing he did met Julie's standards. Needless to say, they fought about these issues, with lots of yelling but never any resolution.

In some areas, Dan knew that Julie had good insight, and he honestly tried to take her suggestions to heart. Yet, he would still be criticized. Dan found himself apologizing all the time, even when he wasn't sure quite what he had done. It just seemed easier to keep peace. Julie readily let him take responsibility. However, the words "I'm sorry" didn't seem to be on her vocabulary list. If Dan did something wrong, he was to be chastised and put in his place. If Julie appeared to do something wrong, it was quickly justified because she only did it in response to some wrong behavior on Dan's part.

If you think that reading this circular illogic is driving you crazy, imagine being in Dan's shoes. He began to doubt his ability to do anything correctly—not just at home, but at work as well. His self-confidence waned, as did his ability to make any solid decisions. One day, his boss sat him down to discuss his sagging work performance. As a manager, this floundering and uncertain Dan was not working. Dan listened intently and began to realize what was happening. Then and there, he made the decision that he could not longer be treated like this and survive. He went home and told Julie about what had happened and that he was tired of the intolerance and would no longer live this way. The surprising result was that Julie left and sought a divorce. What happened here? Who is to blame?

☐ Dan

☐ Julie

☐ Another person

☐ No one

Michael and Victoria

Michael and Victoria were typical of most married couples in that they arrived home from the wedding and began to set up house together only to find that they had differences.

I know that this seems like an obvious point and a bit naive, but keep in mind that many couples really believe that they have found their soul mate—a person just like them—and that life will be blessed and easy. However, most forget that at least *some* of the differences attracted them to each other in the first place. It is important that we have differences that are complimentary. If we are just alike, if we are exactly the same, mirror images of one another, then one of us is unnecessary. Some differences are a good thing.

It has seemed that in earlier generations couples would more readily come to learn and acknowledge their differences, value each other's strengths, support each other through their weaknesses, communicate through these issues, and learn the art of and strength of compromise. However, that began to legally change in 1969 with the introduction of no-fault divorce laws in California.[4] Since that time, most states have adopted some form of law where no one is faulted for the ending of a marriage. So, if a couple discovers their differences, get tired of each other, and just don't want to put in the effort to work it out, they can just say so and get out of the marriage. In some states, this type of couple is just seen as incompatible. Other states will label the marriage as irretrievably broke. Whatever the term, the results are the same. Author and researcher Michael McManus has noted that 57 percent of all divorces are somehow related to failed or poor communication or to poor conflict-resolution skills[5] It seems that people used to value the importance of communication and conflict resolution, but that doesn't seem to be as important to people anymore, as Michael and Victoria have learned.

This couple didn't have any huge, earth-shattering, unworkable problems. They just had differences. They were incompatible. Norman Wright states that all couples are incompatible.[6] Given that fact alone, it is amazing that marriages ever work.

Michael liked to stay up late, while Victoria went to bed early. Michael liked the home cool, but Victoria liked it warm. He used the same washrag for several days, while she used a new one each day. He liked everything in its place, yet, she could allow things to accumulate and become cluttered, only putting things away once a week when she cleaned. As you can see, they had differences. So, availing themselves of their state's no-fault divorce laws, they ended their marriage, figuring that they would do better the next time around. So, is this truly no fault or is the divorce their fault? You decide.

☐ Michael

☐ Victoria

☐ Another person

☐ No one

THE BOTTOM LINE

We have briefly looked at 10 different couples with a variety of struggles. The issues that that have faced encompassed:

- infidelity

- impotence

- drug and alcohol abuse

- physical abuse

- personal growth

- finances

- parenting

- personal happiness

- intolerance and emotional abuse

- incompatibility

While this list is certainly not exhaustive, it does cover the majority of scenarios that people seem to face. So, how did you do on your quiz? Where did you place fault and blame? If you are waiting for the correct answers, I hate to disappoint you, because the answers are not always as simple as checking a box. Sometimes, multiple boxes need to be checked, which I am sure that you discovered. Other times, you may have found yourself wanting to give an answer that wasn't among the choices that you were given.

So, what is the cause of divorce? Well, as we have looked at a variety of situations, it would seem that the cause can be lots of different things—anger, infidelity, and so on. However, I want to submit to you that the cause is much more basic than the scenarios we have examined. You may have found yourself identifying 10 different causes as to why these marriages ended. You may have come up with a list similar to the one above. And yet, none of those items listed are the cause of divorce—they are simply the manifestation of the cause.

You see, in each and every situation the cause of divorce is SELFISHNESS! Yes, that's right. One cause—many manifestations. Take a minute and let that thought settle in.

OK. You may want to take me to task about now, especially if you have been divorced, and you are the one who filed. Am I saying the *you* were selfish? That I don't know. All that I am saying is that all divorce has its roots in selfishness. Now, you may want to scream at me and at this page, but hang in here with me and follow the thinking.

You may be thinking,

> *You have no idea what I went through. My spouse was an unfaithful slob. He didn't just have one affair, but five! I caught him multiple times and each time he seemed repentant, and I took him back. But the reality was that he wouldn't get help and didn't want to change. It was a lifestyle that he was unwilling to leave. I believed that I did what was necessary for the protection of my family and me, and I sought a divorce. Are you now saying that I was selfish in doing this?*

Not at all! I merely stated that selfishness is the cause of all divorce. In this case, your husband's determination to continue his unfaithful lifestyle, his selfish desire to do what he felt like doing without consideration for your welfare and the importance of the family, led to the divorce. Selfishness is the cause of all divorces—not necessarily your selfishness, but selfishness nonetheless.

But what if you were like Brad and Jessica? Who was selfish in this situation? Or maybe a better question is who wasn't? Jessica wanted to grow and felt that Brad was somehow limiting her. She felt that as long as she stayed there she couldn't become all that she wanted to be. I mean, don't we want people to achieve their full potential? Sure we do, but that is not the point. Why do we find that this cannot be done in any other way than a divorce?

Why do people have to polarize their view and see this as either, "I stay in the awful marriage and life continues to be horrendous and never gets any better," or "I get a divorce and all is well"?

Week after week, I see couples come in with this either-or thinking, and I am always amazed that they never see a third possibility. Was Jessica exhibiting selfishness? Absolutely! Of course, she wasn't the only one. Brad tried to contain her in some preconceived mold because of his own fears and insecurities. Was he interested in her personal growth? No more than she was interested in his concerns. His own selfishness contributed to the schism they were experiencing.

Take a few minutes and go back and look at these 10 couples. This time, don't look for blame, but look with an eye to spot the selfishness. Look for who is pursuing what they want without regard for the other person. It may be one individual, or it may be both. See if this filter of "selfishness" changes how you see these situations. If you have been divorced, try to set your own issues and situation aside as you review these couples. This is not the place for you to feel that you are being judged. You may ask, *"But what if I see myself in one of these couples, and it becomes clear that I was the one pursuing my own agenda?"* Save this for later, and we will address it in a future chapter. For now, simply examine each situation objectively and see where selfishness is apparent.

In Matthew 19, Jesus makes it clear that marriage was designed to be lifelong. He responds to the questions of the spiritual leaders by saying that divorce is due to hardness of our hearts. It is important to understand that our selfish desires, if pursued, can only be successful and rational if we adopt a hard-heart position. As you look at these couples, find the selfishness, find the hard heart, and you begin to understand the root of divorce.

SECTION TWO

WHAT HAVE WE DONE?
HAVE WE SUCCESSFULLY
ADDRESSED DIVORCE?

CHAPTER FIVE

THE CHURCH'S POSITION

"Churches all agree with one another about marriage a great deal more than any of them agrees with the outside world. I mean, they all regard divorce as something like cutting up a living body, as a kind of surgical operation. Some of them think the operation so violent that it cannot be done at all; others admit it as a desperate remedy in extreme cases. They are all agreed that it is more like having both your legs cut off than it is like dissolving a business partnership or even deserting a regiment. What they all disagree with is the modern view that it is a simple readjustment of partners, to be made whenever people feel they are no longer in love with one another or when either of them falls in love with someone else."

—C.S. Lewis[1]

Throughout this country, thousands of Christians struggle with the issue of divorce on a daily basis. They receive different and often conflicting information from their friends, their counselors, and yes, even their pastors and their churches. In the midst of their emotional pain and confusion, they now find themselves wrestling with possible intellectual confusion as well. If you fit into this category, I want to assure you that you are not alone.

From the early history of humanity, through the Old and New Testaments of the Bible, to modern times, the message of "what to do" has run the gamut from being clearly understood to garbled at best. Therefore, in this chapter we will examine the Church's position (including the nation of Israel) from past to present. If you enjoy the detail of connecting the dots, you will have fun with this chapter. I have also summarized each section and highlighted these in bold for you.

There are three principles of hermeneutics (interpretation of Scripture), as suggested by Instone-Brewer, that I want to lay out before we start, as I think that they are important to the proper understanding of Scripture.[2]

First, Scripture should be examined through the eyes of the people to whom it was addressed. This takes into account both their language and their culture. When we fail to do this, and simply try to apply what was said several thousand years to a 21st century context, we sometimes get some very strange results. Think about the changes that have occurred even in our short lifetime. Imagine that I give you a set of instructions on how to hook up your stereo system. In the course of the instructions, I make it clear which plugs are for your turntable and which ones are for your 8-track player, but there are none for a CD player. To try to apply that set of instructions from just a few decades ago to today's high-tech system would be confusing at best. Yet, if you understood the context in which those instructions were given, you would probably be able to make them applicable to your system today. This same concept is true for things written thousands of years before us.

Second, the teachings of the Scriptures should be viewed in relation to the culture for which they were written. Because certain concepts are already understood in a particular culture, the Scriptures may not mention a key point because it would be redundant.

Third, Scripture is not so complicated that only the local intellects are able to understand it. The basic meaning of Scripture is the clear understanding that an ordinary person would have in the culture in which it was written.

OLD TESTAMENT

From the earliest of times, namely The Garden of Eden, we see God's clear and simple design for marriage.

> *For this reason a man will leave his father and mother and be united to his wife, and they will become one flesh* (Genesis 2:24).

Two individuals come together and become one. That's the deal. And it worked great—until someone didn't like something that his or her spouse did, something that was said, a repeatedly annoying behavior, and so on. Then people began to look for a way out of being "one flesh."

By the time of Israel's early history, marriage was understood in both Israel and the surrounding societies, to be a covenant. David Instone-Brewer, author of *Divorce and Remarriage in the Bible: The Social and Literary Context,* points out "The primary meaning of 'covenant' [during this time] was an agreement between two parties that was mutually binding."[3] As a part of this covenant or contract, money was exchanged. The groom made payments for the bride, and the bride's father would give a dowry, which was often viewed as her portion of her father's inheritance. All of this was a part of "sealing the deal" from a contractual viewpoint.

So far, so good. But by the time of Moses, things had become messy. During that time, with rare exceptions, men had the right to divorce their wives. Understand that God *never* instituted divorce. But once the people began to practice it, and abuse the reputations of women, God allowed Moses to give the people instructions. It had become all too common for a man to become displeased with his wife and then send her away. Generally, if the woman was sent away, people believed it was because she had been unfaithful or indecent. Therefore, if a woman was sent away, unfaithful or not, her reputation was ruined.

Olan Hicks, author of *What the Bible Says About Marriage, Divorce, & Remarriage,* explains this well when he states:

> By the time of Moses it had become necessary for God to provide legislation on the procedures to be followed in situations where divorce occurs, because men were now practicing marriage destruction. Evidently some were doing so in cruel and heartless ways by putting their wives out without giving them a full legal release. In such a case the woman was not permitted by law to marry another husband. Being virtually without personal legal rights, she was ruined. Many women in that situation turned to prostitution as a means of survival. So God gave instruction through Moses that in the case where a man had decided to put away his wife he must give her a written certificate or "bill of divorce."[4]

We find the instructions for this *"certificate of divorce"* in Deuteronomy 24:1. Unlike the ancient Near Eastern laws, the Old Testament provided a clean end to a broken marriage. The husband had no further claim on her, could not demand that she return, and could not sully her reputation by saying that she had left by her own choice. Once the woman had been given this certificate, she was free to remarry. The only limitation was that "she could not marry her lover or the person with whom she was suspected of committing adultery,"[5] if this had in fact been the issue of divorce.

While we find Moses' instructions for how to handle divorce, we have to remember that God despised what men and women were doing to each other. By the end of the Old Testament, unfaithfulness was rampant, and not just in marriages. People had made unfaithfulness to God, and each other, a way of life. God is more than crystal clear when He spoke through the prophet Malachi, *"I hate divorce"* (Mal. 2:16). He hates Israel's unfaithfulness to Him, and He hates the unfaithfulness in marriages. Malachi even implies that, when we break the covenant with our spouse, God will no longer pay attention to our offering. This will be examined further in a later chapter.

In summary, what we see in the Old Testament is this: God designed a man and woman to be united; in man's selfish desires he began to practice divorce, which Moses accommodated in order to protect women; and God continues to state that His plan is faithfulness to the covenant that people made with Him and each other.

NEW TESTAMENT

During the Intertestamental period, which is the time between the Old and New Testaments, many changes occurred in divorce laws. Instone-Brewer calls it a time of "social revolution."[6] Men and women were both able to divorce at will and needed no grounds to do so.

> A woman would lose her dowry if she was divorced for adultery and a man would have to return the dowry plus a half if he committed adultery, but divorce for other grounds was without any penalty.[7]

As you might expect, all of this contributed to a great deal of instability within the institution of marriage.

In the surrounding Greek and Roman cultures, divorce was almost unknown during this time.[8]

Based on a passage in Exodus 21 regarding obligations in marriage, the rabbis during the time of Jesus generally believed that the following were appropriate grounds for divorce: childlessness, material neglect, emotional neglect, and unfaithfulness.[9] Following what would have been considered a valid divorce, remarriage was generally accepted. However, if it took place following an invalid divorce, it was considered adultery.

The historian Josephus acknowledged that the sole purpose for a Jewish marriage was to procreate.[10] Based upon this premise, infertility was therefore considered by some to be a ground for divorce. Instone-Brewer explains that following this logic,

> Any couple who did not have children within ten years of marriage was expected to divorce. Each party was to remarry someone with whom they might be fertile.[11]

However, there were rabbis who argued against this practice.

The stain of adultery continued in the New Testament. While a person could marry a divorcee or widow, if the woman had been divorced because of adultery, the couple often faced a stigma of shame.[12]

There were two primary rabbinical schools of thought regarding the matter of divorce, and these two schools adopted quite opposite views.[13] As you might expect, this led to great controversy, debate, and, of course, confusion and uncertainty. The two positions were developed primarily from different interpretations of one passage of Scripture, in particular, two words.

Deuteronomy 24:1 states the following:

> *If a man marries a woman who becomes displeasing to him because he finds something indecent about her, and he writes her a certificate of divorce...*

The instructions continue on from there. The two words that have formed the basis for this controversy are *something indecent.*

The Shammai school of thought held that this passage indicated that the husband was displeased because he discovered that his wife had been unfaithful to him. In other words, he found out that she was cheating on him, that she was committing adultery, and he was not happy about it, to say the least. This school said that this was grounds for divorce.

However, the Hillel school took a very different position. While they acknowledged that "indecent" could relate to a wife's unfaithfulness, they interpreted "something indecent" to also include just about anything, including burning his dinner. This meant that a man could seek a divorce for any reason that he wanted. As a result, which shouldn't be a surprise, the vast majority of Jewish divorces sought in Hillelite courts during the first century were, what I would term, any-reason divorces.

Jesus walked onto this stage of debate in Matthew 19 when the Pharisees came to ask Him about this matter. They wanted to know if it was all right for married couples to divorce using the any-reason argument. Jesus' response was a resounding, "No!" We will discuss this important section of Scripture in more depth in a later chapter. But I want you to notice here that Jesus didn't buy into the rabbinical school debate. He was making God's position from the beginning clear, as I quoted from Genesis earlier. He acknowledged that Moses allowed divorce because of people's hard, stubborn hearts but that God's plan was that two people should remain together. He allows for divorce in the case of adultery, but it is interesting to note that even then, it is not commanded but allowed. It would almost appear to imply that the innocent party could forgive the offending spouse and should perhaps only invoke this exception if the guilty party continues his or her sinful pattern, refusing to repent of that lifestyle and embrace one of faithfulness.

Much has been written regarding the idea that if a man divorces his wife for a reason other than unfaithfulness, he *causes*

her to become an adulteress, and anyone who marries the divorced
woman commits adultery" (Matt. 5:32). While we will probably
not solve that debate here, it is important to remember that much
of this may have had to do with perception and reputation. It is
possible that Jesus was talking about how people will perceive this
woman and her new husband. By divorcing his wife for any reason,
he is victimizing her. Others will assume and believe the worst
possible thing about this woman and may even suspect that her
new husband was her lover, and hence the reason for the divorce.
While these facts would be in error, the perception would remain.

The apostle Paul gives us additional thoughts on divorce and
remarriage when he writes his first letter to the Corinthians.

> *To the married I give this command (not I, but the*
> *Lord): A wife must not separate from her husband.*
> *But if she does, she must remain unmarried or else be*
> *reconciled to her husband. And a husband must not*
> *divorce his wife* (1 Corinthians 7:10-11).

At first glance, it would appear that Paul is making a distinction between a separation and a divorce. However, this difference
evaporates when one realizes that in the Greco-Roman world, both
men and women could divorce their partner by separation. It was
considered a legal divorce. As a matter of fact, if Paul were only
talking about separation, then stating that she should not remarry
wouldn't make any sense, because she would still be married. She
could not be referred to as "unmarried." However, since the separation is actually a divorce, then she would be "unmarried." Paul
was writing into this context. If divorce happened by this method,
it was important that believers did all that they could to turn it
around. By remaining single, they were allowing an opportunity
for reconciliation, which we will also discuss later in the book.

Jesus and Paul were both restricting certain types of divorce
in their teaching. Jesus taught that couples could not divorce using

the any-reason argument from the Hillel school. While Paul wrote that the similar method, the Greco-Roman divorce by separation, was also inappropriate and not allowed.

> Paul added that one could not use this procedure even if one was married to a non-Christian. However, if a non-Christian used this procedure, there was nothing that the Christian could to do prevent it.[14]

Paul continued on in this passage by addressing the issue of remarriage. He stated that when a believer is divorced by a nonbeliever against his will, the believer is "not bound" in this situation. Instone-Brewer elaborates on this when he writes,

> Paul cut through this legal problem by declaring "God has called us in peace." The pragmatic solution that he proposed is that all those who have been divorced against their will, and who therefore can do nothing to reverse it should be regarded as validly divorced; they are no longer bound by their marriage contract and are free to remarry.[15]

Of course, the question arises, "What if I was divorced by a believer?" I have found many interesting and diverse thoughts regarding this issue. Some would say that the believer is stuck and cannot remarry. Martin Luther "hinted that a believer who deserted his or her spouse was worse than an unbeliever."[16] Others continue this line of reasoning when they examine the model of discipline that the Church is to follow as discussed in Matthew 18. In this model, the believer who leaves should be privately asked by his or her spouse to return. If he or she refuses, then the spouse is to take a witness with them and make the request again. If the believer still refuses, then he or she is to be taken before the Church and again asked to return. Should the person to continue to refuse, her or she is to be withdrawn from Church membership and regarded as an unbeliever. Instone-Brewer continues:

> If believers are deserted by believing partners, Paul commands the deserters to return. There appears to be no doubt that the believers will obey this command. Paul says that it is not his own command, but that of Jesus (v.10: "not I, but the Lord"). Paul therefore does not even discuss the possibility that believing deserters will not return to their partners. If believers did refuse to obey this command, and thereby refuse to obey the direct command of Jesus, the Church would presumably be forced to excommunicate them."[17]

While this line of reasoning may seem harsh in the 21st century, I wonder if that is partly because we have become afraid of hurting people's feelings and don't want to offend. Therefore, the exercise of Church discipline has become a teaching that resides on a dusty shelf high up in a back closet. Even the Church has occasionally been guilty of adopting a live-and-let-live policy. Yet, Jesus was very clear about the manner in which the Church should respond to blatant disobedience.

Many have asserted that between the teachings of Jesus and Paul, the grounds given for divorce in the New Testament reflect those that were understood previously in the Old Testament. Namely that Jesus referred specifically to adultery and that Paul's allowance for desertion is a reference to the lack of material and emotional support mentioned in Exodus 21. Regarding remarriage, it has been observed that,

> The New Testament teaching on remarriage after a valid divorce, is admittedly, ambiguous and unclear. However, remarriage after divorce was a fundamental right in the first-century world and it was often

regarded as an obligation. Thus, the New Testament writers knew that they would have to enunciate their teaching extremely clearly and unambiguously if they wanted to teach the opposite of this universally held view.[18]

If you wish to research further the teachings and culture of this period, I highly recommend David Instone-Brewer's book, *Divorce And Remarriage in the Bible: The Social and Literary Context.* I have drawn from him in this section in order to give you a brief look into a more in depth understanding of these significant passages.

> As I have come to understand the teachings of the New Testament, I would summarize them as follows. The Jewish culture held two different positions: divorce for adultery only or divorce for "any reason." Jesus addressed these arguments when He said that couples are not to divorce for any reason. He clearly stated that from the beginning, God designed a man and a woman to marry, be united, and become one flesh. Once they are married, God has joined them together, and they are to never be separated! However, if one of the individuals practices a lifestyle of unrepentant continued adultery, then a divorce is allowed. Yet, God's desire is still love, forgiveness, and reconciliation.
>
> Paul continued on by saying that couples are not to divorce. If a couple does divorce, they are to either reconcile their marriage or remain single. However, if the believer's spouse, either a nonbeliever or a believer who refuses to obey Jesus and the discipline of the Church, deserts them, then they are no longer bound and are free to remarry.

Yet, while there seem to be clearly allowed grounds for divorce, I again emphasize that God's desire is not for us to waste our energy looking for loopholes and reasons to get a divorce. The Holy Spirit's continued conviction is that we intently and purposefully look for ways to fix, heal, love, forgive, reconcile, restore, and unite our marriage for the remainder of our lives. That, and nothing less, is the focus taught in the New Testament.

FROM THE FIRST CENTURY TO RECENT TIMES

Following the times and writings of the disciples in the early Church, the Church fathers began to clarify, interpret, expand upon, and attempt to apply their understanding of these matters to believers. Again, the results ran the gamut. The Catholic Church adopted a position that a "true marriage" was a religious sacrament that could not be dissolved by legal means. "Their view is that divorces are merely a form of legal separation, and remarriage is not permitted."[19]

This view in the Catholic Church has continued into the present. One way they have been able to *allow* some divorces is to say that they weren't a *true marriage.* They are able to make this distinction, for example, based upon whether the marriage was performed in the Catholic Church. If it was, the marriage cannot be ended in the eyes of the Church. However, if the marriage was performed in a Protestant Church, by a justice of the peace, or by another means, the Catholic Church may not consider that to be a valid marriage and can grant an annulment. The individuals can then remarry, since they were never really married according to Catholic doctrine.

Swinging to the complete opposite position, Olan Hicks states:

Divorce, in the sense of a formal, legal pronouncement that a marriage was terminated, always meant the end of that marriage, whether it was done for right reasons or wrong reasons. The notion that a marriage broken for wrong reasons somehow continues to live on "in the eyes of God," after formal divorce, is entirely an invention of man and has no basis in Scripture. The explicit statement of God himself is that after the written divorce is given "she may go and be another man's wife." Never in any culture has the divorce decree meant that a marriage remains intact in anyone's eyes. Neither has it ever meant release for one party from the marriage bond but not the other. All such nonsense came on the scene much later, long after the cessation of divine revelation and the completion of the Bible. It grew out of great confusion in a period we generally call the dark ages."[20]

As you can see, the understanding of what is biblically permissible and what isn't didn't become clearer with time, but only more confusing. Even during the 20th century, we have seen a similar swinging of the doctrinal pendulum, just in different ways. During the first half of the century, there was a condescending attitude toward those who were divorced. They were often viewed as second-class citizens in the Church. Even if an individual was perceived as a victim, they were still viewed through a filter or stigma of suspicion and were not seen as equal to those who were not divorced. People would question, *"Can the divorced individual serve? Can they teach Sunday school, sing in the choir, or serve as an elder or deacon?"* Some were concerned that if divorcees were allowed to serve, others would see this as an endorsement of divorce. And, of course, if we extrapolate that, then the danger is that divorce would become epidemic.

Following the advent of no-fault divorce in the 1960s, the '70s and '80s began to see a shift in the attitude of the Protestant

Church toward divorcees. The Church began to offer more grace and understanding. They began to minister to the needs of those hurting because of divorce and examined the specific needs of single parents. Churches realized that these individuals were of value, an untapped resource, and they accepted and created opportunities for divorcees to serve.

However, as frequently happens when the pendulum swings, it sometimes swings to the other extreme. Certainly, the Church's position needed to change. The Church needed to demonstrate grace and see divorcees through God's eyes. Yet, in doing so, the Church began to stop addressing the sin of divorce. Suddenly, the Church took a hands-off approach. The leadership didn't want to ask too many questions lest they be seen as judgmental. Christians began to adopt the world's attitude of progressive acceptance that has often become known as "sloppy agape." In other words, love that is a sham. You see, true love is willing to love in the hard times, speak truth, set boundaries, and hold others accountable. But this blanketed unquestioning acceptance was nothing of the sort. Yet, in the world's eyes, questions and accountability indicated rigid rules and a judgmental attitude. Certainly Christians didn't want to be accused of that, so we jumped on the everything-is-OK, live-and-let-live bandwagon. Christians began to throw everything under the only-God-can–judge bus, absolving those at fault of all responsibility. It sounds progressively good. The only problem is, this is contrary to the teachings of Jesus, the apostles, and even the Old Testament writers. What a wide swing in a short few decades.

CURRENT PRACTICES IN THE CHURCH

In order to gain as accurate a perspective as possible regarding current practices, I have approached this in an objective, global manner as well as in a local, experiential one. I wanted to know what churches are doing across the country. How are they approaching divorcees and their needs? What does their ministry to singles look like? How do they handle moral issues? What is their position on remarriage? Are they doing anything programmatically to address divorce prevention and marriage restoration?

I began by locating 100 churches across the 50 states that offered some type of divorce recovery program. These churches ranged in size from a couple hundred members to thousands. I worked to discover what churches are doing in the arena of marriage, divorce, and remarriage across denominational lines and among both Catholics and Protestants. The results were broad in scope and presented a good picture of what is taking place in our churches. The specifics of the questionnaire can be found in the appendix. I will only discuss here the information relevant to this particular discussion.

From an experiential perspective, I attended and participated in the two largest divorce recovery programs in Colorado Springs, Colorado.

CHURCH QUESTIONNAIRE

We will examine here the responses to a few of the questions I asked on the questionnaire. Many responded with answers that talked about helping people through the pain, networking with others, and reaching out. I will share a few of the responses below that I feel offer healthy objectives, so that you can get a general feel for the perspective that is shared.

What are the specific goals and objectives of your divorce recovery program?

> "To help couples become dependent on God to meet their needs instead of each other in the area of self-identity and self-image."

"1) To provide a support system, education, and biblical counsel. 2) To provide a "safe" door into the Church. 3) To help develop leaders through volunteering."

"To help individuals who are hurting from divorce or separation discover hope, find help, and experience healing. To let them know they're not alone."

"To exhaust every effort to restore marriages. To help individuals come to a point of forgiveness and move on. To instruct, encourage, assist when possible, and help bring people to become all God wants them to be."

"1) To help participants grow emotionally and spiritually as they undergo divorce; 2) to cope with divorce in biblical ways (e.g. avoid resentments and staying stuck in the past), 3) to be an outreach to nonbelievers, to invite them into the Church and if possible bring them to a saving knowledge of Christ."

"To restore God's ideal—to bring healing/correction/restoration."

"To help determine if the marriage they are in can or cannot be revived. By using our divorce care program, we try to help people get rid of past baggage—mainly in the form of forgiveness so they can move on.

"Divorce Recovery—A 9 week workshop equipping those who have experienced marital or relational breakdown with tools to resolve current challenges and identify next steps towards spiritual and emotional health. To accomplish this we help participants understand the pain and healing they are experiencing is a process, and we walk with them through it. We help them discover their part in the relational breakdown, as we all have a part. This is to help them not repeat their same mistakes. Lastly, but most important, is to introduce them to Jesus and/or bring them closer to Him through this process."

While I am encouraged by the position that the Church has taken in recent years to minister to those recovering from the devastation of divorce, I am particularly interested in its approach to those who are still married.

How do you address issues of people that are separated but still married?

This is asked in the context of those attending a divorce recovery program. Many churches responded that they just treat all of the individuals the same without examining who is still married and who might be divorced. Some responded that reconciliation would be nice if it happened, but they were not actively involved in the process of facilitating that. Only about a third of the churches indicated that they specifically try to get involved encouraging and assisting in restoration attempts. Here are a few of the stronger comments.

> "We make every effort to reconcile the marriage. We ask them to not attend singles activities if it would send a negative message to the estranged spouse."

> "We encourage those that are separated but still married to get marital counseling if it is possible to save the marriage."

> "Seek restoration/reconciliation. Seek to reconstruct vital components with relationship."

> "We work to keep marriages. Our church is starting to put pressure on these marriages. We try to show them it can work and it costs too much to divorce."

I would add a thought to these comments. If a person is still married, I would suggest that they should not attend single's activities regardless of whether it would bother the estranged spouse or not, because they are not single.

Some churches adopt a very hands-off process that concerns me. One respondent stated,

> "They are welcomed into the group but we don't counsel couples in the decision-making process. None of our participants have gotten back together with their spouses while the program is in process."

I am not surprised that none of the participants have gotten back together in this church, as they have chosen to stay out of the process. The Church has the opportunity to bring life, hope, and wisdom into the process. If we fail to do that, I wonder if we are not guilty of what Jesus would refer to as the salt losing its saltiness. He says that when that happens, *"It is no longer good for anything, except to be thrown out and trampled by men"* (Matt. 5:13). At many points in history, aspects of the Church have unfortunately fit that description. The Church has the opportunity to intervene and be the light of the world that it was created to be. It is important that we not abdicate that role; if we do, we have ceased to be the body God has called us to be.

Please Describe Your Ministry to Singles

Some churches have watched their singles die a slow death. Others have been able to develop thriving ministries. Some are separated into several age groups, while others, due to size, have everyone together from age 20 to 70. Approximately two-thirds of the churches that returned questionnaires have some types of single's group. They host activities like Bible studies, football and basketball leagues, hiking, Christian concerts, bowling, movies, Sunday school, Saturday night socials, Tuesday night dinners, coffeehouse discussions about relevant topics, dance lessons, Sunday brunches, retreats, and worship teams. One church had several service opportunities, including a program where men worked together to repair cars belonging to single moms in the church.

Does your church have any programs that address divorce prevention or marriage restoration?

Obviously many churches have developed programs for hurting individuals following the marriage train wreck. It is terrific that we have developed programs to meet the needs of people where they are. However, with the divorce rate in the Church mirroring that of the world, I was interested in what we are doing, not just reactively after the disaster, but proactively to prevent the disaster. By the divorce rate, it is clear that we have not done a very good job in this area.

Approximately a third of the churches responding stated that they did not have anything in place to address prevention or restoration. Another 10 percent of the churches reported that their pre-marital counseling program is their prevention program, but they do not have anything in place to address restoration.

Of the remaining 57 percent, the responses ranged from a once-a-year seminar to programs that engage couples on a weekly, or at least a frequently regular, basis. Some of the various programs offered included: "Making Love Last a Lifetime," classes on making marriages stronger; Marriage Encounter marriage retreats; marriage mentoring; a married couples social group; Bible studies for married couples; Crown Financial Ministries classes; blended families support groups and studies; a marriage enhancement and restoration program; a young married's group; a "Love and Respect" seminar; and "Marriage Matters," a program to strengthen and repair marriages.

It is encouraging to see how seriously many churches have taken this matter and the efforts they are making to address this vital problem and need. At the same time, the fact that 43 percent of churches are not tackling these difficult issues is disturbing.

What is your church's position concerning issues of remarriage?

Only about 20 percent of the churches stated that they have no conditions or objections to remarriage. The other 80 percent endorsed remarriage with a variety of conditions. These conditions ranged from the individual having exhausted restoration attempts to having repented and sought forgiveness. Most responses indicated that they would support remarriage if the divorce was what they considered a biblical divorce. Of course, what that means also varied. Some considered it to only be a biblical divorce if adultery was involved. Others considered it legitimate to remarry if the spouse had died, divorce had occurred because of moral unfaithfulness, or if an unsaved spouse had abandoned a person. Some churches have constructed a formalized elder-approved policy regarding remarriage. Below is the current formalized policy of one church.

Elder's Statement on Divorce[21]

The following statement was adopted by the elders of ***** Church as a guide for those considering divorce, or considering remarriage following a divorce.

> Because marriage has been established by God as an indissoluble union, and since it is an earthly copy of the relationship between God and his people, it is to be kept inviolate. However, because of the fallenness of human nature, the Scriptures permit divorce in the following cases as condescension to human frailty for the protection of the innocent party:
>
> 1. Divorce for the cause of immorality with the understanding that the obligation to maintain

or reinstate the marriage may not be imposed upon the innocent spouse.

2. Divorce for desertion—desertion being defined as behavior equivalent to the abandonment of the marriage relationship. In such cases, the offending party becomes subject to church discipline in order to bring about repentance and reconciliation. Should efforts to achieve restoration fail, the innocent spouse is not bound. He or she becomes free to remarry in the Lord.

The remarriage of believers may not be approved when:

1. Divorce is being used as a vehicle to seek a different mate, since such pre-intent makes the divorce adulterous.

2. There is no evidence of repentance and brokenness over the circumstances that caused the divorce.

3. Restoration of the original marriage remains a viable option.

Each case of divorce or remarriage has to be dealt with on an individual basis from the perspective of God's inexhaustible capacity to forgive human sin and restore broken lives.

Does your church utilize church discipline such as described in Matthew 18:15?

Over 90 percent of the churches acknowledge that this is God's plan and that they agree with it. Some take a very intentional and active approach, working to lovingly, yet purposefully, confront individuals for the purpose of repentance and restoration. Others want to follow the model, but are hesitant and uncertain of how best to proceed. I find it encouraging that in the 21st century, this many churches see the value of Jesus' plan for correcting mistakes and restoring individuals to fellowship following sinful choices.

DIVORCE RECOVERY EXPERIENCE

As I mentioned, I attended two different, large divorce recovery workshops. Both churches have been conducting these workshops for many years and have developed well-organized programs called "Starting Over Workshop" and "Divorce & Relationship Recovery Workshop." The workshops run six and seven weeks in length respectively, meeting one evening each week.[22]

"Starting Over" covers the following topics:

1. Myths about Growing and Healing

2. Understanding your identity

3. What's the deal with Forgiveness?

4. Letting Go of the Past

5. How Do I Relate Now?

6. Assuming New Responsibilities.

Participants use a workbook that includes fill-in-the-blank pages for use during the lecture. Each session includes review questions to assist the individual with further introspection.

Also included in the workbook for the "Divorce & Relationship Recovery Workshop" are fill-in-the-blank sections for use during the lecture portion of each session. Session titles include:

1. Moving Toward Acceptance

2. Coping With Loss

3. Emotions: The Slippery Slope

4. Experiencing New Growth

5. Dangers to Avoid

6. Healing the Wounds Within

7. Feeling Good About Yourself.

As opposed to review questions this material utilizes different types of post-session assignments, such as setting goals and objectives, learning to journal, reading an article and writing a response, and so on.

Some common themes exist as both of these workshops endeavor to assist wounded and hurting individuals as they try to make sense of their unique situations and learn to move forward with their lives. Figuring out who you are as a single person, grieving your loss, letting go, learning to forgive, and growing into a strong and healthy individual who can stand and be OK by him- or herself are all common threads that these workshops emphasize. Both of these venues begin with a main session that features a particular speaker. Following the main session, individuals break off into their pre-assigned small groups. Oftentimes, these are designed by criteria that may include age, length of time since divorce, children vs. non-children, etc.

I feel that both of these multi-week presentations do an outstanding job of communicating the value of the person, God's love for the hurting individual, and the church's genuine care and desire to be a resource in the person's life. This approach is so much healthier than the Church of decades ago. It is truly an attempt to meet people where they are, minister to their needs, and help them to grow. I believe that this models Jesus' love in a powerful manner. One speaker I heard at one of these groups made the statement, "Pain is inevitable, but misery is an option."

These workshops give hope to individuals that life can be better and offer the option and opportunity to pursue that.

However, as was reflected in the national survey, my concern here continues to be that we need to be bolder in our fight to save and redeem damaged marriages. These workshops have an opportunity to impact this fearfully neglected area.

In summary, most churches subscribe to an understanding that divorce is not God's plan. While a few simply seem to accept divorce and remarriage as realities that exist, most churches recognize that divorce is supposed to be rare and only for limited reasons such as adultery and abandonment. Most also only endorse remarriage according to how they understand Scripture to allow it.

The Church is doing a better job today of ministering to and validating those who have weathered divorce. However, we are still weak when it comes to our willingness to take a more active role in restoration and prevention. Clearly, in the area of reconciliation and restoration, the Church has demonstrated timidity. Only a third have really been willing to get in the trenches and do what needs to be done to encourage the saving and healing of marriages. While over half of churches are making attempts in the area of divorce prevention, these efforts clearly need to be stronger, more intentional, a higher priority, and bolder in scope. One hundred percent of the Church needs to rise up and be the Church that God has called us to be in a world that is chaotically lost and spiraling out of control. The world should not be the champion of marriage and the family. If the Church doesn't fill that void, then no one will. If marriage, as God designed it, is not to become a thing of the past, the Church must rise up and fulfill her role.

CHAPTER SIX

RATIONALIZATIONS AND OTHER CREATIVE REASONINGS

"One of the most striking differences between a cat and a lie is that a cat has only nine lives."
—MARK TWAIN[1]

I still remember a professor I had during my freshman year at Dallas Christian College, Ronnie Hannah. Ronnie was a man with many pithy sayings. If you said "heck" or "darn," he would stop you and point out what you were really saying. If you got mad and upset, he would respond with, "Don't be bitter; reconsider!" But one of the phrases that Ronnie frequently said if you claimed you had a good excuse for turning a paper in late or missing an exam went like this: "You know what an excuse is? It is the skin of a reason stuffed with a lie." What? I wasn't lying! I really had what I felt was a good reason for not being ready for class. OK. Maybe I had made other choices with my time the previous day that contributed to my paper not being written. But I really thought that my rationale would hold up under mild scrutiny. Hmm...obviously not!

Satan is the master of deception, the ultimate author of excuses, and can weave a rationalization with more twists and turns than

111

the "California Screamin" rollercoaster at Disney's California Adventures theme park. He is amazingly helpful in assisting us in doing the same, and oh how good we have gotten at it. Satan knows the truth, and he knows how to lie. He is the chief crafter of taking an element of truth and shaping it into something that looks reasonable, that makes logical sense if I connect the dots just so, and then stuffing it with absolute heresy.

I love chocolate éclairs. On the outside is the chocolate covered pastry and inside is that delicious Bavarian cream. However, if someone at the donut shop were to replace the cream with broccoli, lawn clippings, or nuclear waste, we would have a very different continental breakfast. At best, it would taste awful; at worst, it would kill me. On the outside it would look like something that I could chew and swallow without doing damage, but once inside, the consequences could be life threatening. We have to know what these stuffed lies look like in order to resist them. It is imperative that we be able to identify how they appear if we are to avoid them. We will examine seven very common "skins of reasons" and the real filling that we find on the inside.

"GOD WANTS ME TO BE HAPPY"

This is probably a phrase that I hear more than any other as I counsel couples and individuals, and it sounds so...reasonable. After all, wouldn't a loving God want me to be happy? If He is our parent, surely He means for us to be happy. After all, I am a parent and I want my children to be happy. There is even an old song that supports this—"Don't worry! Be happy!" Didn't God say that Jesus came to give us abundant life? Surely that means that he wants us to be happy. Happy—happy—happy! I must confess that this mantra in our culture has led to chaos. And it has gotten to the point that when a Christian says to me, *"I am miserable in my marriage, and I know that God doesn't want me to live this way. I am going to get a divorce because He wants me to be happy,"* I just about gag. Look at the shell of truth. Yes, you are miserable in your marriage, and yes, God really doesn't want you to live that way. Now look at the nuclear stuffing: I will get a divorce because God wants me to be happy. Argh! Where did this stuffing originate? Our theology? No. Post-modern relativism? Sort of. Actually, it originates from the father of lies himself—satan.

Satan began this lie quite early in our historical story. Adam and Eve had a pretty good set-up in The Garden, hanging out with God and enjoying the beauty and fruit of The Garden. They were able to live there in the middle of that and didn't even have to weed (or spray Roundup). The Garden of Eden was the time-share resort to end all resorts. God gave them a relatively simple and clear instruction—you can eat of any tree in The Garden, except the Tree of Knowledge of Good and Evil. Why couldn't they stay within these boundaries?

God gave Adam and Eve every tree and fruit they could possibly want with but one restriction. God said that the consequence would be death if they ate from that tree. So, what happened? Satan came along and had a conversation with them. He asked them how things were going (a bit of a paraphrase here), what they had been up to, and how the sampling of the fruit buffet was going? They related to him that they could eat of any tree in the garden except the Tree of Knowledge of Good and Evil. Satan asked them what was up with that. They related the consequences that God warned them about. Satan responded, scoffing in disbelief that they would be so stupid as to buy such a line. He appealed to their sense of getting what they wanted and being happy.

Now here comes the construction of the poison éclair.

> You've got to be kidding me! [Paraphrasing again.] Did He really tell you that you would die? That's not going to happen. Take a bite and see. Besides He is just

trying to keep you from being happy. Listen, if you will eat from that fruit bar, you will become smarter than you ever imagined and life will really be great for you.

Is there a component of truth in this rationalization? Of course! As we know from a hindsight perspective, satan was correct in that they didn't actually die as soon as they ate of the tree. We also know that their eyes were opened and there was an increase in knowledge and awareness. The outside chocolate looks pretty good. But what was the filling on the inside? After eating the forbidden fruit, they began the aging and dying process that would eventually culminate in their actual death. Yes, they gained knowledge, and with it came a loss of innocence that they could never regain. They were kicked out of The Garden, and life became a pretty intense journey with lots of hard work and pain from then on. The cream filling was their undoing and destruction. They thought that they would be happier if they did what seemed best to them, even though it was in direct disobedience to God. However, they quickly realized that obedience to God's instructions would have left them in a far better place than they found themselves after the Original Sin. In other words, had they obeyed, they would have been happier.

Scripture is very clear that God's priority for us is holiness, not happiness. For some reason, this seems to be a difficult concept for us to grasp. And yet, if we could learn to wrap our brains around this, we would find that by choosing holiness, happiness has a much better chance of following. Please don't misunderstand me though. I am not saying that you will always be happy if you do the right thing. That is oftentimes not true. But I will say that if you choose what appears to be happiness over holiness, you will ultimately be very dissatisfied.

Happiness is such a fleeting feeling. Yes it is nice to feel happy, and it is great to enjoy those moments. But it is amazing how much effort and focus we place on something that is so brief, and how little attention we give to the things that have long-term consequences. When are you most pleased—when your child gets drunk and enjoys a few moments of seeming abandon and "happiness" with his or her friends, or when your child makes the right and responsible choice that you know will benefit him or her long-term? Our Father is no different. He loves us and wants our absolute best. When we take away the "excuse," we will discover the truth.

- The Skin—As a believer, God promises me abundant life.

- The Lie—God's highest and best desire for me is that I be happy.

- The Truth—Yes, I may be miserable in my marriage, and yes, God doesn't desire for me to continue to live like this. What He does want is for me to be obedient to Him, to seek holiness and righteousness, and to begin to take the steps necessary to change the dynamics of my marriage.

Now I know that for some, your initial thoughts are

Yeah right! I have already tried to change things, and it didn't work. So, my obvious choices are to either stay here, and be miserable for the rest of my life until I finally die, or get out of this marriage and make my life better.

I am very, very aware of the complexities of marriage, how badly things can hurt, and how alone you can feel. As you saw in chapter four, I know that marriages can be more than challenging. So I assure you that I am not offering some platitude such as, "Just stay and be good and all will turn out happily ever after." If only it were that simple. But I am telling you the truth when I say that God desires your obedience over your focused pursuit of happiness. (We will look at some strategies and resources in later chapters.) I believe that God's Word confirms that the only actual chance that I have for long-term satisfaction (far superior to short-lived moments of happiness) will come as a result of my intentional decision to obey Him in the most difficult of situations.

Obedience is work. If my son loves ice cream and wants to eat it at every opportunity, and I order him to eat ice cream, how difficult is that to obey? Not at all. It is when I tell my child that dinner is in 30 minutes and that he can't have ice cream right now. That is more difficult. Obedience involves trusting God's love enough to obey Him even when I don't understand. I can tell you that I have never regretted making the decision to obey. However, when I have disobeyed because my logic seemed to have a better idea of how to achieve happiness, it has come back to bite me without fail. God desires a relationship with us based upon love and trust. He doesn't need us to do great deeds of service nearly as much as He needs us to live an authentically obedient relationship. The Scriptures say, *"To obey is better than sacrifice"* (1 Sam. 15:22).

"I DESERVE..."

You don't have to spend too much time today watching television to get a sense that you are entitled. Whether it is a commercial for shampoos or stereo systems—the world tells us that we deserve the best. At every turn, you are told that you shouldn't have to put up with an inferior product or make-do with something that is less than perfect. So, just dispose of that old car and get a new one. That washer and dryer aren't the latest models, so you better hurry down during the weekend sale and get a new one. Why? Because you deserve it. Really? Well, of course. I mean, you work hard at your job, you have sacrificed for your kids, and you deserve nothing less than the best. And if you carry this logic through, one might conclude that since I should have the very best and not have to make-do with the old vacuum cleaner or microwave, why should I have to make-do with this old, difficult, flaw-ridden marriage? Hmm—great question. I guess I deserve something better than a spouse who doesn't appreciate me 24/7. I deserve a spouse who is better looking, more attentive, makes more money, and is more masculine or feminine. Life is too short to settle for less. I need to jettison this man or woman and go find the best because, well, I deserve it.

Beginning with Adam and Eve's kids, we see a similar flaw in thinking. Cain and Abel had an issue surrounding their sacrifices to God. Actually, in reality this was probably more of a heart issue. But the bottom line was that God was pleased with Abel's offering, and He was displeased with Cain's. Well, for Cain this just wouldn't do. He felt that he had worked hard and brought an offering like he was supposed to. So, he deserved better. God should be pleased with him too. He didn't see this as his issue to correct, but he saw it as God's issue. Therefore, he would solve this by removing the one with whom God was pleased, then Cain would somehow get what he felt he deserved. As we know from the incident, killing his brother did not even begin to get Cain what he wanted. As a matter of fact, this logic basically ended his role in the story, relegating him to a place of irrelevance.

- The Skin—I have worked hard, invested a great deal, and tried to do the right things.

- The Lie—I deserve better than what I have in a spouse. I deserve the best. Hmm—the Scriptures state that, *"all have sinned and fall short of the glory of God"* (Rom. 3:23). Because of that, what I deserve is *death*. It is only by the grace of God that I don't get what I truly deserve. But I can keep believing the lie if I choose.

- The Truth—I have received far better than I deserve. Out of my love for God should pour a heart of gratitude and a desire to honor Him and commitment to love my spouse better than he or she deserves. I deserve death, but I have been given an opportunity to create a life of love and forgiveness, blessing my spouse, blessing God, and putting myself in a position to be blessed in the process.

"I AM CLOSER TO GOD NOW THAT I HAVE LEFT THE MARRIAGE."

Every time that I hear these kinds of statements, I cringe. This kind of deception is nothing new. People work very creatively in their logic to please themselves, keep the heat off of themselves, and avoid working on – *themselves.*

In Exodus 20, we find that the children of Israel had come to a very significant place in their covenantal journey with God. He was about to give them His laws to live by, which would deepen their special relationship. God had called Moses to come up Mount Sinai to receive what we know as the Ten Commandments. Moses spent significant time there with God. But it wasn't long before the people got restless. They were convinced that Moses had died, that God had forsaken them, and that they needed some other kind of spiritual connection. Wanting to please the people as well as to feel more spiritual, Moses' brother Aaron instructed the people to bring their gold and jewelry to him, which he then melted down to fashion a golden calf for the people to worship. Now once again, they felt spiritual. However, as we know, God was displeased and many people died that day. *Wait a minute—how could God be displeased? They felt more spiritual than they had in a while. Isn't that what is important?* I don't mean to complicate the picture, but could it be that obedience to God is necessary for a truly genuine spiritual connection? Or does God contradict Himself by saying, "Obey, but if you choose not to, no problem. We will be even closer and more on the same page than ever." Scripture says that God draws close to those who love Him. Jesus says in John 14:23 that the one who loves God is the one who obeys Him.

- The Skin—"I am closer to God..." Wow—who can argue with that? When someone makes that statement, we are afraid to disagree because it sounds so appropriate. We always want people to be closer to God. However, there is a huge difference between "feeling" closer to God and actually "being" closer to God. Feelings are about as dependable as the weather.

- The Lie—if I do what I want and what I feel good about, even if it is disobedient to God, I will be more connected and have a much closer relationship with Him.

- The Truth—when my child is obedient to my instructions, our relationship is better. When he is willfully disobedient, our relationship is strained and distant. In the same manner, when I believe and trust God and take Him at His Word, my obedience enhances our relationship and closeness. When I disobey, doing what I want instead, we are less connected and live further a part. That is reality. My feelings may or may not reflect that reality.

"I NEVER ASKED GOD IF MY MATE WAS HIS WILL FOR ME."

I forgot to ask God if I should marry you, and now I have determined that this was a bad choice, and I am not sure this was His will. Therefore, I will be obedient now and get out of this and go find the person who really is His will for me.

The Israelites tried to use this very logic. You may recall in Numbers 23 that the leaders sent 12 spies to check out the land of Canaan. When the spies returned, their reports were mixed. Ten of the spies relayed that the land was full of giants that they could never defeat. They explained that the situation was bleak; they might as well give up this idea of the Promised Land and settle for a trailer park in the swamps. (Yeah, I know. A bit of paraphrase again.)

However, the other two spies reported that the land was indeed all that God had promised. It was ready for the taking. All they needed to do was to trust God, and it would be theirs. Well, the people listened to the fears of the ten spies and started looking for doublewides. Their lack of faith displeased God. He responded by telling them that they were obviously not ready to inherit something this lavish, so instead they would have to hang out in the desert for 40 said, "Ah, you know, we really didn't consult God about this decision to be scared and not take the land He promised. We didn't seek His will as we should, so we will change our position now and get out of this desert situation and do what we should have done in the first place." Not a good idea. Doubting God and having to hang out in the desert may not have been God's initial desire for you. However, once you made that choice, then He made it pretty clear that waiting four decades for the promise land was now His will. But rather than obey, the Israelites continued to take things into their own hands and rushed in to take the land. What happened? They were soundly defeated and suffered a great loss.

- The Skin—I never sought God's will with regard
  to you and this marriage. Therein is an element of

truth. Perhaps I didn't check in with God before I committed my life. It would have been best had I done that. This is true.

- The Lie—I should divorce you and seek God's will next time. This argument is not from God, but from the very pit of hell. It contradicts everything we find in His Word.

- The Truth—When a couple is married, God has joined that relationship. Whether this was God's best match or not becomes an academic question only. Once I have married my spouse and God has joined this relationship, as He always does, this is now indeed God's will for my life. To decide to vacate my vows is as foolish as it was for the Israelites to rush in to Canaan.

"IF I AM HAPPIER, MY KIDS WILL BE HAPPIER."

The Scriptures state that, *"There is a way that seems right to a man, but in the end it leads to death"* (Prov. 14:12). Jesus recalled, as recorded in Luke 12:19, a story about a rich man who had plenty. No problem so far. There were all kinds of things that this man could have done with his wealth. He could have helped the poor, contributed to worthy projects, or any number of other things. However, in his own narcissistic logic, he concluded that the best thing to do was to tear down his barns and build bigger ones in order to have a place to store all of his stuff. It just made good sense to him. He would certainly be happier with this arrangement so surely it was the right thing to do. Of course, we read that God took the rich man's life that very night. Perhaps his way wasn't the best after all.

- The Skin—We have probably all heard the statement—"If momma's not happy, nobody's happy." Using that same logic, if I am happy, then those around me, even my kids, should be happy. It sounds reasonable; it sounds true.

- The Lie—research has shown repeatedly that children are typically not happier following a divorce. We will discuss that in greater detail in Chapter 8. But for now, suffice it to say that just because a parent may be seemingly free of conflict, may be having more fun engaging in a new relationship, may feel happier, does not mean that children are happier or benefit positively from the divorce. This is a lie that is espoused by secular, social scientists. It may sound reasonable, but it is nonetheless most often a lie.

- The Truth—If I am happier, I am happier. However, that does sound rather self-centered, and I certainly don't want to appear that way. I cannot deal with the guilt of knowing that my desire to be "happier" may be detrimental to my children. So, I will try and twist this in a manner to free me of guilt. But it doesn't change the truth. If I divorce because I want and choose to do so, my kids may be unhappier and wounded deeply. Ouch!

"I MARRIED FOR THE WRONG REASONS."

I had one client recently share with me that she had married her husband for the wrong reasons. As a matter of fact, she was mad at God and partly married this man to get back at God. It reminds me of a student who completes his homework only to not turn it in so that he can somehow get back at his parents. The student receives an "F" and the parents are unaffected. This is flawed logic.

It is true that people sometimes marry for the wrong reasons—to get away from parents, because of a pregnancy, because they are afraid that if they wait they won't have anyone, because they need a person to attend functions with them, and many other such reasons.

We read in Genesis 37 about Jacob and his 12 sons. Competition and jealousy were a way of life for this family. Joseph was obviously Jacob's favorite, and this caused all kinds of problems. Everything from Jacob presenting Joseph with a colorful coat to Joseph sharing prophetic dreams of his successful future fostered hostilities between Joseph and his brothers. Eventually, Joseph's brothers decided they had had enough and plotted to kill him. However, his older brother Rueben stepped in and convinced the others to sell Joseph into slavery, which they did. Knowing that their father would never understand, they concocted a story about Joseph being killed by a wild animal. Needless to say, Jacob was devastated and heartbroken to learn that his favorite son had been killed.

Fast forward a few years later. Joseph had risen to second in command in the land of Egypt. (If you are wondering how he went from slave to such a position of power, you may want to read Genesis 39—41.) His brothers had gone to Egypt during a famine to buy food, and guess who they ran into? Yep, you got it—Joseph. Things were tense for a bit, and there were some interesting mind games being played. But in the end, it became clear that what the brothers had meant for Joseph's destruction, God had used to bless and benefit Joseph and his brothers.

- The Skin—I married for the wrong reasons. This is very possibly true. Therefore, it makes a great skin of a reason.

- The Lie—since I married for the wrong reasons, I need to divorce this person and start again with someone else and marry for the right reasons. Oh, how we creatively work to connect distant dots. This is absolutely not what God desires. Sure, He would have liked for us to marry for the right reasons. But the fact that we didn't doesn't invalidate the marriage. Much like rationalization number 4, what I may have done for the wrong reasons, or without proper heavenly clearance, does not mean that the right thing to do now is run.

- The Truth—I may have married for the wrong reasons. But I am now married for the right reason—what God has joined together, humanity (man, woman, husband, wife, attorney, judge, parents, in-laws, etc.) is not to separate. God desires for us to now do the things that will build this marriage on the right reasons. Regardless of our reasons for originally marrying, obeying, loving, and honoring God, and loving, respecting, and supporting our spouse, God's child, are great reasons for remaining married. It is God's desire.

"I WILL BE ABLE TO SERVE GOD BETTER IF I HAVE A MORE SPIRITUAL MATE."

I am reminded of a story that Bill Cosby told about a 2-year-old wanting a cookie. The child got into the cookie jar only to be stopped by the parent. The mom told the child that he is not to have a cookie at that time and then proceeded to place the cookie jar out of the child's reach. When she was not looking, the child constructed a way to climb up and get the cookie jar. As the mom heard a commotion, she came in to find the child with cookie in hand. The mom said, "What are you doing? Didn't I tell you that you couldn't have a cookie?"

The child responded affirmatively, "Uh huh."

"So," she said, "then what are you doing?"

This 2-year-old then replied, "I was getting the cookie for *you*."

The mom said she didn't want a cookie, so the child said, "Then can I have it?"

How noble sounding this child was, going to all of that effort and care in order to get Mom a cookie. Fortunately, we are able to quickly and clearly see through this smoke screen to what was really going on—the child wanted a cookie. Likewise, how religious it sounds to say that I want to serve God better and need a more spiritual mate to do that.

In First Samuel 16, we read about the plight of King Saul. He went gone into battle with orders from God (through the prophet Samuel) instructing him to leave all spoils behind. He was not to take any livestock, CD players, RVs (I know—paraphrasing), no nothing. However, Saul disobeyed and brought back stuff from the conquest. As the prophet approached and heard the bleating of sheep, he questioned Saul as to what he had done. Saul responded by saying he only brought back animals so that they could be an offering to God. In other words, "I was getting the cookie for you."

- The Skin—I want to serve God better. This sounds great: so holy, righteous, and pious. Surely no one would disagree with this religious desire. What a perfect skin!

- The Lie—therefore, I should divorce my spouse because it is only by divorcing him or her that I can best serve God. Excuse number 3 stating that "I am closer to God now" is a very similar argument. How can I serve God better by disobeying, by making decisions that are clearly contrary to His stated desires? Wouldn't the exact opposite be more likely true? Yep.

- The Truth—Paul writes in First Corinthians 7 that if a believer and unbeliever are married, and the unbeliever agrees to remain married, then the believer is to remain married. This sounds very different from "I will be able to serve God better if..." As a matter of fact, Paul was saying that I will be able to serve God better by remaining married to my unbelieving spouse. The truth is that our argument is in blatant contradiction to God's Word. Serving God is not about doing some great mission trip or performing a sacrificial task. It is about a relationship with the Creator. It is about understanding His Word, His desires for me, and faithfully and diligently walking with Him. The truth is that I will be able to serve God better by pursuing and remaining in a submitted relationship with Him. By living a life of commitment to God and His truths, my testimony could ultimately be the puzzle piece that enables my mate to become the more spiritual mate that I am looking for.

As we discovered in the beginning of this chapter, the skin looks terrific. The chocolate is spread evenly and looks extremely inviting. I want it. But I can't bite into it and escape the poisonous waste inside. It will erode and destroy who I am in Christ. No matter how artfully I craft the excuse, it is still an excuse, an ill-conceived attempt at connecting the dots in a manner that is straight from the deceiver of deceivers. No matter how I might dress up the skin, it doesn't change what is inside.

Each rationalization has a common element—it is meant to get me off the hook. It is an effort to shift the responsibility of work and effort from me to someone else—most frequently, my spouse. To examine the truth of what is inside this excuse, to genuinely lay it out for honest examination, will ultimately require that I do the hard work of dealing with me. It will require that I submit to God's desires for humility, confession, forgiveness, authentic openness, sensitivity, kindness, and place the care of my spouse above my own self-centered interests.

I frequently teach my university students that they need to study, pursue, and arrive at their theological positions and decisions out of conviction, not convenience. In other words, they can study and discover God's clear desires and then choose to follow them. Or they can decide what it is that they want to do in the first place and work backwards to construct a creative theology that will act as shaky scaffolding to support their desires. Conviction in my understandings and beliefs will result in an intimate journey with the Author of Life. Convenience will lead to a conflicted and disjointed journey depending on how far I walk apart from the Lord.

It is imperative that we expose the excuses and lies for what they are. It is time to dump the rationalizations that support our conveniences. While God understands divorce, he also understands our marriages, our weaknesses, and even our excuses. He loves us through them, and yet, He calls us to live above the excuses. As believers, it is essential that we walk forward with honesty, stripped of faulty excuses, intent on pursuing God's desires and honoring Him with our choices.

CHAPTER SEVEN

WHAT'S THE BACKUP PLAN?

"God's Word contains the only genuine blueprint for successful relationships, both with Him and others."

—GARY SMALLEY[1]

The National Football League is a wonderful sport to watch, especially if your favorite team is winning. Football is a game of well-planned skill and strategy. The NFL is nothing like the football we played as kids, where we drew the plays in the sand but generally said, "Joey you go long, and I will hit you in the end zone." In the NFL, great planning goes into each game. As a matter of fact, each team has often already scripted the first 15 to 20 plays. Coaches spend time looking at film, analyzing the other team's strengths and weaknesses, and then they develop a game plan. They begin the game with this plan. If the game plan is working, they will stick with it. However, if they find that this well-tuned plan is not accomplishing what it is supposed to, they will deviate from the plan and try something else, all in hopes of finding a combination that will work against their opponent. Plan A, the thought-out strategy, is well defined. Plan B is frequently a patchwork of pieces, is not as well-thought through, and its outcome is more uncertain. When it comes to God's thoughts, desires, and plans for marriage, there is a well-designed, guaranteed-to-work plan A. It is not fuzzy or uncertain, and there is no guesswork involved. It is a clearly-defined plan. Let's take a look at it.

PLAN A

J. Carl Laney does a good job of building a concise list that describes the essentials of God's marital design for humanity. In his book, *The Divorce Myth,* he writes:

1. Marriage was instituted by God (see Gen. 2:21-24). He created a wife for Adam and ordained marriage because He deemed that it was "not good" for man to be alone. God created a suitable helper to assist Adam in ruling the earth, raising a family, and worshiping God.

2. Marriage is to be a monogamous relationship. God gave Adam just one wife (see Gen. 2:22). Polygamy was practiced during the Old Testament era, but this never made for happy homes and was not in keeping with God's original design.

3. Marriage is to be a heterosexual relationship. God created Eve (a female) for Adam (a male) (see Gen. 1:27; 2:22). There is nothing in Genesis about Adam and Bill! The command for procreation (see 1:28. points to the fact that God ordained the institution of marriage to be heterosexual.

4. Marriage involves formally and publicly leaving one's own parents in order to establish a new family as a married couple (see Gen. 2:24). The customs,

ceremonies, and formalities differ from culture to culture, but there must be a public recognition of the couple's intent to marry. This seems to be inherent in the concept of "leaving."

5. Marriage is a relationship that binds a couple until death. This is implicit in the concept of cleaving—being glued together or bound in a one-flesh relationship. Jesus and Paul explicitly taught that the marriage relationship can only be broken by death (see Mark 10:9; 1 Cor. 7:39; Rom. 7:2-3).

6. Marriage involves the headship of the husband over the wife. This is suggested by Adam's priority in the order of creation and in the naming of Eve. The apostle Paul clearly spells out the headship of the husband in Ephesians 5:23 and First Corinthians 11:3.[2]

It is quite interesting to see the events that lead up to the first-recorded marriage. God created Adam and placed him in The Garden of Eden with the assigned task of taking care of it. God very quickly recognized that it was not good for man to be alone and said, *"I will make a helper suitable for him"* (Gen. 2:18). But notice what happened next. God gave Adam the task of naming all of the animals. *Wait, I thought God was going to make Adam a helper?* That's right. But first, God brought all of the animals before Adam. Adam named them and looked for the helper that God had mentioned. After seeing all of the animals, Genesis recorded that *"no suitable helper was found"* (Gen. 2:20). The Hebrew word that is used here says that no animal "fit" Adam. The word conveys a sexual concept. None of the animals were a sexual fit for Adam. The word *helper* in the Hebrew literally means "one who matches him, one who complements him."[3]

So, God took a rib from Adam and created the first woman, Eve.

For this reason a man will leave his father and mother and be united to his wife, and they will become one flesh (Genesis 2:24).

There you go—the first wedding ceremony. These are simple, clear expectations that are easy to understand. This could be a very short chapter, as this should be the end of the discussion regarding God's plan for marriage. Of course, we know that humanity has a difficult time leaving well enough alone. If we could really grasp this concept of "one flesh," we could revolutionize marriage.

I like what Laney says when he writes,

The "one flesh" that the couple becomes in marriage is beautifully illustrated by the offspring that God is pleased to give them. A child partakes of the flesh of both the father and the mother, and the two are absolutely inseparable![4]

Contemporary research confirms the importance of "becoming one." It has been reported that the most important indicator of how long a couple will remain happily married is how well the individuals emotionally connect and develop a close attachment.[5]

So, there you have it—God's design for marriage. His well-thought-out and carefully-constructed plan. When the Pharisees questioned Jesus about this design in Matthew 19, He restated the same exact plan that God had given in Genesis 2. He added just one more one statement to it when He said, *"Therefore, what God has joined together, let man not separate"* (Matt. 19:6). There is no doubt in my mind that He added this statement because humanity had been making such a mess of the design, trying to find loopholes to fit their own selfish desires. Jesus made it clear that God alone has the "right and power to appoint the beginning and end of marriage. Until a marriage is broken by the death of one of the partners, the couple should heed the words of Jesus."[6] But other than the additional statement, note that the plan had not changed since the creation of the world. Plan A was still plan A. It was still about a man and a woman leaving their parents and uniting, becoming one flesh, for a lifetime of companionship.

Regardless of this, we find ourselves in the 21st century where divorce is an everyday reality. While divorce was uncommon during the mid-20th century, it is an accepted, almost expected, form of family structure today. So, I guess we best address it head on. Just because we may not like it doesn't mean that we should stick our heads in the sand, put our fingers in our ears, and say "La, la, la, la, la." We might as well acknowledge it and see what God says about it.

PLAN B

Have you ever looked at a troubleshooting chart in the back of an owner's guide for electronics or your car? You will notice that it states a possible problem that you might have and then tells you what to do about it. Then, depending on whether or not that step works, you progress to the next step, then the next, and so on. This is where the subject of marriage and divorce gets a little tricky as we examine God's Word. We have examined what God says about Plan A. But what happens when we negate Plan A? What happens when we decide that we have had enough of the other person, and we no longer want to be married? What happens when we find ourselves divorced and want to consider remarriage? When we have children from a previous marriage, and we choose to remarry, how do we prioritize the relationships? These are very important questions to which we must have answers. Surely we can go to the Scriptures and find crystal clear guidelines—or so we hope. Yet, when we go to the Scriptures to research this subject and look for the blueprint for plan B, we are typically disappointed that there is almost no information.

This lack of material has spawned numerous books as authors try to glean a few truths from subtle implications in Scripture. Many have tried to take general principles and interpret and devise a Plan B. As one might imagine, the result is a host of opinions that range from one extreme to the other with little concrete, scriptural support. The frustrating reality is this: God's Word spells out a very clear plan A. That is His plan. There is no plan B because He has clearly told us what He desires us to do—plan A. Anything else is against His design.

Some individuals have adopted a position that if they divorce their spouse, and just remain unmarried, then all is OK. They figured that the marriage was not good, and that an unhappy, incompatible marriage was probably a greater sin than divorce. Sorry! Scripture does not support this conclusion. Instead, it teaches a core principle that marriage is right, and the disruption of marriage is wrong. A pretty simple and clear principle! Without getting into a discussion of remarriage at this point, I do want to emphasize what God emphasizes. Olan Hicks states, "Clearly then, Jesus did not forbid marriage to divorced people but rather forbade divorce to married people."[7]

One of the reasons that it would be very difficult to have a plan B is due to the design of plan A. The bond that Scripture talks about between a husband and wife is significant. When Jesus says that the two will be come "one flesh," He is using the Greek word that literally means that the two people are glued together (see Matt. 19). I like the visual that John P. Spliter gives us in his book, *The Complete Divorce Recovery Handbook,* when he describes this bonding.

> Imagine two smooth pine boards glued together and
> pressed in a vice for twenty-four hours. To drive them

apart, even using a sharp chisel, you will rip and tear the boards, with parts of each remaining forever attached to the other. Similarly, in marriage, when people have been melded to each other, possibly for years, they have shared the most intimate aspects of life. Their identities have become intertwined. They are bonded—glued together. The ripping and tearing that occurs in the dissolution of this marriage is massively painful. People exhibit many of the symptoms of a human organism under deep stress.[8]

Is there any evidence or information that might constitute pieces of a backup plan? Yes, there is some, but even this is geared to maintain the original marriage not to pursue something else. You can see this as Carl Laney notes in First Corinthians 7:11, "if a divorce or separation should happen to take place, Paul leaves the believers two options: (1) remain permanently unmarried—the present tense of 'remain' emphasizing the permanent condition, or (2) be reconciled to one's partner—the aorist tense emphasizing the attainment of the end of the reconciliation process."[9] In others words, even if the marriage is disrupted, Paul said that the goal is to restore it back to a glued and bonded state. Any elements of an alternate plan are never for the purpose of ending a marriage and moving on to the next.

We will look in greater detail in the next chapter at some of the problems encountered as a result of divorce. I want to mention here that second marriages (and third and fourth marriages) don't seem to fix the problems encountered in the first. In this country, we see a divorce rate of approximately 50 percent in first marriages. If subsequent marriages were the answer, we should see a much lower divorce rate. However, instead we find a 60 percent divorce rate in second marriages, and it is even higher in third and fourth marriages.[10] One of the leading causes of failure in remarriage is the effect on the children. According to Gary Richmond, author of *The Divorce Decision,*

> Children always remain loyal to their birth parents. They will inevitably cause trouble for stepparents. It is difficult for the children to get their parents back together. But they try...[11]

In her book, *Divorce Busting,* Michelle Weiner-Davis says:

> I have heard too many disillusioned individuals express regrets about their belief that their ex- spouse was the problem only to discover similar problems in their second marriages or, even more surprisingly, in their new single lives. They admit to re-creating the same unproductive patterns of interacting in new relationships, repeating old mistakes or discovering that they are still miserable....Research shows that except in extreme cases of abuse children want their parents together....I've heard too many divorced parents say, "I wish I knew then what I know now." Gradually, I have come to the conclusion that divorce is not the answer. It doesn't necessarily solve the problems it purports to solve. Most marriages are worth saving....I've grown increasingly convinced that most marriages are worth saving simply because most problems are solvable.[12]

As I have stated, God has not given us a plan B. So, like the Israelites constructed the golden calf when Moses didn't return from Mt. Sinai on their timetable, we have created our own plan B, and it hasn't worked out too well. In the 1960s, Americans initiated a great experiment in this country by making divorce easier. Adults, in their pursuit of pain-free, comfortable happiness, may not always realize that most children see divorce as the most pivotal, central event of their lives. Weiner-Davis points out that

"Children who grow up seeing their parents run away from home, have a different relationship with marriage then those who saw parents hang in there."[13]

Marriage is a relationship that we commit ourselves to with lifelong permanence. Yet, as problems arise (and they will), the seeming permanence quickly morphs into conditional commitment complete with a bailout clause. Can you imagine how this would look if we applied this exit strategy to other permanent relationships—namely our children? I love the following example.

I found it curious that most parents do not question their lifelong commitment to their children. Divorcing our children is not an option even when they thwart our goals and plans, even when they behave in ways we never would have dreamed of. Imagine an overwhelmed parent announcing, "I'm divorcing my son on the grounds of extreme mental cruelty," or "I'm leaving—my daughter and I are simply incompatible." Sounds absurd, doesn't it? Instead, we learn to readjust, to modify our expectations, and roll with the punches. We become grateful for the good times and learn to expect the hard times. "My son is in the terrible twos; no wonder I'm a basket case," reasons the harried parent. We enroll in courses entitled "Surviving Adolescence" to make life tolerable when their hormones are raging. But, where are the courses entitled "Survival After the Honeymoon Period" or "Dealing with His Midlife Crisis" when he loses twenty pounds and buys a red sports car?

Parents often quip, "Too bad babies don't come with instructions." Not knowing what to expect makes parenting a nerve-racking business. But babies aren't the only things that arrive without instructions. Marriage vows are also taken without marriage manuals. Entering marriage with unrealistic expectations can eventually kill the relationship, and it often does. Unlike the committed, all-forgiving attitude we have toward our children, when our mates fail to live up to our expectations, we consider divorce as an option.[14]

While the example of divorcing our children may sound absurd, in light of God's design for marriage, divorcing our mates should seem just as absurd to us. Yet, in our skewed thinking, it seldom does. We appear determined to have a plan B and equally determined to make it work. When it doesn't work, we sometimes continue to push through and pretend that it is working even when we know better. It is easy to forget that "What you are, as a parent, will to a large extent be what your children will become....[How you handle your relationships with your spouse and your children] will teach them how to handle major difficulties in their own lives."[15]

If you find yourself having difficulty with plan A, I want to strongly encourage you to search God's Word for His answers and to seek godly counsel. I have seen too many individuals, who are in a trying marriage, simply "get out" because it is what their feelings dictate that they do. Seeking the Lord, studying, trusting, and submitting are all too difficult. So, they fall back on,"I didn't know better. A friend at work steered me wrong and gave me bad advice. It wasn't my fault." We can't shift the responsibility to someone else. If we obtained poor counsel, we are responsible. We are not excused. Eve tried this approach in The Garden by blaming her sin on the serpent, and it didn't work.

As Christians, we like to talk about our loving God, who is full of grace for His flawed, and often failing, children. God is all of these things, and we are grateful that He is. If He weren't, we would ultimately be eternally lost. At the same time, we like to talk about tolerance, acceptance, and not judging each other.

However, we often want to wrap these principles in a way that makes God into a tolerant, non-judging, milk-toast entity. But this is contrary to His nature. He gives us absolutes that we can hang our hats on, and He makes bold statements that are judgments of behavior. I sometimes hear Christians talk about not judging each other. Someone will say "It is wrong to lie, steal, commit adultery, practice homosexuality, and so on," only to have someone else say, "It is not our place to judge; it is God's." That is true. But when one makes a statement such as that presented, is it a judgment? Of course not! God is the one who has proclaimed absolutes of right and wrong. It is absurd to think that quoting God's Word is judgmental! The Word is filled with God's pure and simple judgments.

Our God is indeed a God of love and grace. He is also a God who draws boundaries of right and wrong, can be displeased, and hates certain things. Below are a few examples.

- God hates haughty eyes. (See Proverbs 6:17.)

- God hates a lying tongue. (See Proverbs 6:17.)

- God hates hands that shed innocent blood. (See Proverbs 6:17.)

- God hates a heart that devises wicked schemes. (See Proverbs 6:18.)

- God hates feet that run rapidly to evil. (See Proverbs 6:18.)

- God hates false witnesses who utter lies. (See Proverbs 6:19.)

- God hates one who stirs up dissension among brothers. (See Proverbs 6:19.)

- God hates it when sacrifices are burned to other gods. (See Jeremiah 44:4-5.)

- God hates a man's covering himself with violence. (See Malachi 2:16.)

- God's hates divorce. (See Malachi 2:16.)

This last passage in Malachi is significant and enlightening regarding the importance that God places on marriages and relationships. Let's look at this amazingly clear and powerful section of Scripture.

Have we not all one Father? Did not one God create us? Why do we profane the covenant of our fathers by breaking faith with one another?

Another thing you do: You flood the Lord's altar with tears. You weep and wail because He no longer pays attention to your offerings or accepts them with pleasure from your hands. You ask, "Why?" It is because the Lord is acting as the witness between you and the wife of your youth, because you have broken faith with her, though she is your partner, the wife of your marriage covenant.

Has not the Lord made them one? In flesh and spirit they are His. And why one? Because He was seeking godly offspring. So guard yourself in spirit, and do not break faith with the wife of your youth.

"I hate divorce," says the Lord God of Israel, "and I hate a man's covering himself with violence as well as with his garment," says the Lord Almighty. So guard yourself in your spirit, and do not break faith (Malachi 2:10,13-16).

Wow! What a phenomenal passage. It is obvious that God considers it a major disaster when we break faith with our spouse. He considers this a sacred bond that is not to be broken. When it is, it doesn't just affect our relationship with our spouse, but God indicates that it impacts our very relationship with Him. We break faith with our spouse, then, in our pain, loneliness, and confusion, we come before God with tears. We cry out when He doesn't seem to pay attention to us. We seem confused and don't understand why He seems so far away. In our pain, we cry out *"why?"* I think that God must shake His head at our seeming inability to connect the dots and understand why our relationship with Him has changed.

In Matthew 19 Jesus said, *"What God has joined together..."* Here God says that He is a witness. God is an integral part of the joining of a husband and wife. He determines the beginning by the commencement of the marriage. He stands as the witness to our proclamation of lifelong "faith" to the other. He is at the heart of the glue that binds us together. And He is saying, ever so clearly, "I have witnessed this covenant. The manner in which you treat and love your spouse is so important that it will impact your very relationship with Me." This principle reminds me of what John wrote:

> *If anyone says, "I love God," yet hates his brother, he is a liar. For anyone who does not love his brother, whom he has seen, cannot love God, whom he has not seen. And He has given us this command: Whoever loves God must also love his brother (1 John 4:19-21).*

I don't think that it is a stretch, or out of context, to combine these thoughts. If we do, I think it might look something like this.

> You are to love your spouse and be faithful to maintain that intimate, covenant relationship. If you say, I will choose to break a lifelong commitment to my spouse, whom I have seen, but I will keep my faith to God, whom I have not seen, I am a liar. Whoever commits

himself or herself to God must also honor his or her lifelong commitment to his or her spouse.

Now, I know that someone will want to take me to task over the liberty I have taken here, and it may be justified. However, I challenge you to consider, in the light of these Scriptures, if there is not merit to my thinking. God expects us to love our brother in order to be able to truly love Him. He also expects us to maintain our commitment and faith to our spouse if we are to be able to keep such with Him as well. I believe that is clear. I think this is consistent with the spirit of God's Word.

God doesn't just hate divorce because of what it says about our ability to keep our word and our commitment. John Splinter, author *The Complete Divorce Recovery Handbook,* comments,

> It's not that God hates it because it represents people stepping out of a rigid cage he constructed and in which he demands us to live. Rather, God hates divorce because of what it does to people he loves! He hates the deception, the breach of faith, the long-lasting agony that is part and parcel of divorce. He hates what it does to the children too....If you're a parent, imagine watching your child go through an experience that would tear at the child's soul and cause deep and lasting pain. Wouldn't you hate anything that would hurt your child this badly? Most parents would.[16]

After reading much of this chapter, you may feel like the disciples in Matthew 19. You may find yourself saying, *"If this is the situation between and husband and wife* (if there is no plan B), *it is better not to marry."* Jesus responded that we do have a choice. We may indeed decide that if there is no plan B, we don't want to run the risk of a divorce and the impact that could have on our relationships with God and others. But if we decide to marry, then we do so understanding that next to our commitment to God, our marriage commitment is the most important and significant relationship in which we will enter. It will require consistent work and an understanding and acceptance of certain principles. David and Jan Stoop, authors of *The Complete Marriage Book,* explain:

> The challenge in Christian marriages is for couples to appreciate their need to know God's Word, submit to the authority of Gods Word on each and every issue to which it speaks, and look to the Lord for the spiritual empowerment that will enable them to practice a style of obedience that imitates the way of the bondservant. Building a strong spiritually based marriage requires a willingness to bring every thought into captivity and conform every behavior to the standard of God's Truth.[17]

Remember—*God understands* us, and He does not give us, or ask of us, more than we can handle (see 1 Cor. 10:13). He only gives us a single plan for marriage, because He knows that with His help, it is a doable plan. Engaging in and maintaining a plan A marriage requires a no-turning-back mindset. The Stoops give a brilliant example of this type of irreversible commitment.

The covenantal seal is meant to designate the irrevocable nature of the relationship. It requires of couples something of the spirit of Hernando Cortez, who in 1519 landed his troops at Vera Cruz, Mexico. When Cortez set fire to the vessels that had brought them from Spain, there could be no retreat. More than 6000 men were irrevocably committed to their task of conquering the new land for their mother country. That kind of no-retreat commitment in marriage is at the heart of the leaving, cleaving, and weaving pattern and is so critical to the building of spiritual foundations in marriages that it is repeated three times in the biblical record. (See Genesis 2:24; Matthew 19:4-5; Ephesians 5:31.)

An irrevocable commitment to covenant-keeping and a moment-by-moment guarding of the seal are absolute prerequisites for those who wish to place and keep their marriages on a solid spiritual foundation.[18]

This is plan A! If you haven't set the escape vessels on fire, it is time to do so!

CHAPTER EIGHT

GOD UNDERSTANDS DIVORCE

Spotted on a sign near a Salt Lake City court-house: "Love is grand. Divorce is 50 grand."[1]

GOD'S DIVORCE

I gave faithless Israel her certificate of divorce and sent her away because of her adulteries (Jeremiah 3:8)

As we discussed in the very first chapter of this book, God has been married and divorced. C. Bruce White, author of *Marriage, Divorce and Reconciliation,* comments:

> Therefore, He can understand and appreciate the kind of feeling, the kind of experience, through which people go in those matters. But we also want to point out further on that God's interest was always in reconciliation. God did not divorce Israel because of one simple act of idolatry. The mercy, the tenderness, the forgiveness, and the desire for reconciliation was in the heart of God with Israel. It was not that Israel made a momentary mistake nor made a slip in the relationship that motivated God to divorce Israel.[2]

145

It was God's desire to remain married to Israel. He gave her chance after chance after chance to come back to Him and remain faithful, but she refused. She demonstrated an unending pattern of unfaithfulness that continued until God said "no more," and He then divorced her.

Ezekiel 16 provides us with a parallel look at God's desire for Israel. You will need to go and read this lengthy passage in order to appreciate the full effect of God's persistent love. However, I will give you a brief synopsis of the early part of Chapter 16.

God begins, as He does many times in Scripture, by going to the prophet and filling him in on what Israel is doing and where she has fallen, strayed, and sinned. The prophets find themselves in a position not unlike marriage counseling, "trying to get Israel to repent, turn around, to be reconciled to God."[3]

Ezekiel narrated the story of God's love for Israel from the beginning. Ezekiel said that on the day that Israel was born, no one had pity or compassion on her; she was like a newborn thrown out into a field. God found her kicking in her own blood. He took her in and said, "Live!" He helped her grow and develop until the time that He made a solemn oath and entered into a covenant with her, and she became His. He took care of her, adorned her with clothes, jewelry, and crowns. Her food was the best. She was beautiful and became queen. She had the best and was the best. She had it made. No one could be a better husband to her than God was. This sounds like a set-up for a happily-ever-after ending, and it should have been. Instead, we find a bride that began to trust in her own beauty, and used it along with her fame to become a prostitute, giving herself to any and everyone.

God took Israel from the depths of nothingness, healed her, helped her grow, married her, and lavished His riches upon her, and she became an unfaithful wife, who quickly developed into a prostitute. As we see in the writings of Ezekiel, Jeremiah, Hosea, and numerous other passages, God was brokenhearted. He sent counselors to persuade her to return. He offered love and forgiveness and begged and pleaded all to no avail. Finally, after all avenues had been exhausted, in the face of a proud and unrepentant heart, when there was nothing left to do, God divorced His bride. This was not what He wanted, but His bride had left Him no choice. God was grieved.

Reflecting back for a moment to the first chapter in this book, I must emphasize again that God understands divorce. He understands the feelings of betrayal, the pain of having to initiate divorce, the issues of property, and the broken lives of innocent children. If you have gone through a divorce, then you know the devastating, gut-wrenching pain that is unlike any other, and God understands it as well. He has been there and is equipped better than any other to get in the trenches with you.

"I HATE DIVORCE"

Many individuals have spoken these words; those who have gone through divorce, those who have had to address the aftermath of divorce (such as teachers and counselors), but most notably, the Creator Himself. As we read in the previous chapter, God hates divorce. He hates it in part because it is the result of broken covenants and abandoned promises. But why else does He have an intense hatred of this act? I believe it has a great deal to do with the wreckage that results from divorce, the shattered lives, and all of the other heart-piercing, logistical pieces. Let's take off our politically correct, rose-colored glasses for a few minutes and examine quotes from interviews, shared by Ron Durham in *Happily Ever After,* from a variety of individuals and just what they are facing when they encounter divorce.

"Sally, an eighteen-year-old, speaks frankly to an interviewer: 'You never get over it; that's the thing. I mean people are real worried about you at first, but then they figure it's been a couple of years and you must be adjusted....But it never goes away. It always is part of you, and it affects things you do.'"4

"I can't tell you how painful it was to have to leave my kids, both initially and then at the end of visits. After a period of five or six weeks when I wasn't able to see our little one-year-old, she didn't recognize me. She didn't know who I was! The blank look on her face..."

"And to leave my children after an extended weekend visit—the way they cried—it was like I was ripping their arms off or something. I would drive away crying and screaming. The frustration that built up was excruciating. I can understand now, someone kidnapping their kids."

"Jock's anger came out in kicking and hitting—just tantrums. And he couldn't express it verbally. I knew what was driving him crazy, but I couldn't help him put it into words. But the minute we got back together he was fine."5

"The fact is, with the permissiveness of the 1960s, divorce assumed a positive reputation that is out of all proportion with the blunt negatives experienced by many who try it. It is a step taken with the culturally supported belief that it enhances life, when in fact, it often impoverishes it."6

DIVORCE'S IMPACT ON PARTICIPANTS

After nearly four decades of this social experiment that has led to runaway divorce statistics, have we found that divorce is not a good thing? It is way beyond that—divorce is dog awful! The negative impact of divorce runs the gamut from issues of health to those of finances. Let's briefly touch on a few of the more prevalent ones and look at some things that we have learned.

- Divorce has been shown to contribute to health problems for many of the individuals involved. It led the authors of a book for medical students to write: "It is wiser to improve marriage rather than dissolve it, and physicians should encourage marital therapy for troubled marriages."[7]

- Chronic loneliness, social isolation, and the sudden loss of love have been identified as "significant contributors to illness and premature death." While on the other hand, physical health is actually enhanced by an intimate relationship in marriage.[8]

- "Emotional loneliness springs from the need for intimacy with a spouse or a best friend. A person who is emotionally lonely feels that there is no one he can absolutely count on. Symptoms include feelings of tension, vigilance against possible threat, restlessness, loss of appetite, an inability to fall asleep, and a pervasive low-level anxiety."[9]

- Working to avoid loneliness can become a monumental relentless task. Yet, another paints the picture accurately when he states, "You need to know that divorce leads to loneliness as sure as Saturday leads to Sunday."[10]

Michelle Weiner-Davis points out that research has revealed:

As compared to single men, married men are better role models, better providers and, in general, make better fathers.

When examined in relation to single, divorced, or widowed individuals, those who are married "have better sex lives, engage in fewer high-risk activities such as substance abuse, live longer, and are happier! [11]

Weiner-Davis goes on to state: "depression is three times as prevalent in women who divorce once, and four times as prevalent in women who divorce twice, than in women who have never divorced."

- Married individuals are more productive employees.

- Significantly decreased standard of living is frequently apparent in single-parent households. [12]

Richmond, author of *The Divorce Decision,* has added to this ongoing list the following:

- The carnage is never over for anyone completely.

- People wonder if being a Christian makes any difference.

- It produces so much pain and damage to the people involved that it does anything but demonstrate God's glory.

- Families are broken up for generations to come.

- Divorce places families in a state of confusion and insecurity.

- Children's loyalties are torn between the two people they love the most.[13]

Divorce is the ripping apart of a couple and a family that was never designed to be taken apart. It doesn't affect everyone the same. For some, the consequences may seem minimal, while for others they feel suffocating. But for the most part, if you have been in the middle of it, or journeyed with a friend through it, you know the pain that feels like it could stop life. And if you know that pain, you have a glimpse of what contributes to God's statement, "I hate divorce."

DIVORCE'S IMPACT ON CHILDREN

Numerous authors and researchers have written about the ways that children are impacted by the decision of divorce. Below are just a few highlights from those studies.

- Children of divorce are nearly 10 percent more likely to develop health problems, both mental and physical, than other kids.[14]

- Some of the extremes that are seen developmentally in children are: "helplessness, typical of babies and toddlers. Guilt, typical of preschoolers. Sadness, in children ages six to eight. Anger among children nine to twelve. False maturity, among teenagers."[15]

- Divorce creates havoc in relation to a child's self-identity and self-esteem.[16]

- "Divorce will leave your child with the inner feeling that his or her world is uncertain and unpredictable."[17]

- Children from divorces are much more likely to commit suicide than children from intact homes.[18]

- They are also more likely to spend time in jail.[19]

- They are at a greater risk for having their own marriages fail.[20]

- It can lead to a greater mistrust of the opposite sex.[21] This can lead to fears of marriage.

- Children from divorced homes have lower grades and poorer attendance in school than students from intact homes.[22] "It is probably far more than coincidence that the US divorce rate, which had been in a slow decline during the 1948-1962 period, rose sharply in 1963 and continued to rise sharply after that during almost exactly the same period as the standardized test score decline."[23]

- "Your child may go through a period of wondering if he or she will ever be happy again." [24]

- "Recent research is concluding that there may be no end to the pain experienced by children as their parents divorce. To a greater or lesser degree, the kids will hurt for the rest of their lives because of the divorce. That's the bad news. The good news is that with the passage of time, the pain will slowly begin to subside, and what may today be a sharp throb will someday become a dull ache. As rough as that is to accept, it's better to deal with the truth than to tell the kids that someday they'll magically understand and will accept the divorce."[25]

- "If parents don't rejoin in marriage, the children's faith is often at risk: 'God didn't hear me.' 'God doesn't love me,' 'There is no God.' 'I'm too bad a person for God to care about.' Another faith issue is sometimes even more destructive in the lives of children in divorcing church families. Especially if Mom or Dad has been involved in some aspect of church leadership, service, or ministry, the children have probably learned that divorce is not God's wish. As these kids watch their parents divorce, they begin to question their parents' faith or commitment to it in very personal terms. 'This faith isn't for me; it sure didn't do much for you.'"[26]

- "Children [from intact families] are more likely to finish school and avoid problems such as teenage pregnancy, drug abuse, and delinquent behavior. Plus, they are more likely to have good marriages themselves."[27]

- "Even if a parent is happier as a result of divorce, there is no 'trickle down effect.' Children will struggle emotionally regardless of how the parent feels."[28]

- "They will be subjected to the repeated tuggings of two parents fighting for their time and emotional support, and they will usually be compelled to take sides, even though that is the last thing in the world that they would want to do."[29]

LIVE IN PEACE

The apostle Paul writes in First Corinthians 7 and reiterates Jesus' words that we are not to divorce. In his discussion of marriage, divorce, and unbelievers who leave a marriage, he states that *"God has called us to live in peace"* (1 Cor. 7:15). We oftentimes would like to force the other person to do the right thing. Yet, we find this technique to be quite unsuccessful. Therefore, Paul is saying, "Do what you can, but you can't force anyone to do anything. So, even in these situations, live a life of peace."

Yet, divorce typically leads to increased conflict, negative emotions, increased stress, and anything but peace. Following a divorce, spouses frequently assume, or at least hope, that the other person will just fade into the sunset, leave them alone, and be out of his or her life. Yet, this is rarely the case. You may be appalled at how your ex-spouse continues to come at you, attacking at every opportunity. If you have children, you will have little choice but to continue to talk with your ex-spouse. You have to schedule visitations, address vacations and holidays, deal with doctor's appointments, soccer games, and any number of other circumstances. If anything goes wrong while you have the children in your custody, then you may hear accusations of incompetence and irresponsibility. A child of a recent client in the middle of a nasty divorce, fell and hurt herself while running and playing. The mother took the child to the emergency room to make sure that all was OK and called the father to let him know what had happened. While she thought that she was doing a good thing in keeping the father informed, upon arriving at the hospital, he called the police to make a child-abuse charge. Fortunately, upon discovering that a custody battle was in process, the police were able to see through the manipulative ploy and dismissed the accusation. Yet, this is a prime example of just how destructively ugly divorces frequently become.

As Richmond points out,

> The sad truth is that if you decided to divorce your mate, you will need a lawyer and you will need a judge. Most people cannot make the important decisions necessary without their help. You will be paying lawyers by the hour, so it is in their best interests to prolong the proceedings. They have no real incentive to do their job quickly or expeditiously. The judges, on the other hand, are hard-pressed for time, and your case is not likely to be given the time needed to make a fair and prudent or wise decision. The judges may also

be bitter, sick and tired of hearing two people cut each other to pieces with words.[30]

If you or your spouse has remarried, then there are issues of a new spouse and perhaps stepchildren as well. Parents are frequently more closely knit to their children than they are to their new spouse's children. Some spouses complain when stepchildren come to the house because he or she is treated almost as if he or she didn't exist and he or she feels completely left out. As much as people may want to be inclusive, people rarely feel the same way about another's children as they do their own.

Richmond relates that by pursuing divorce, many people have missed God's best.

> I have interviewed several people who were initiators and all of them reflected that they had not improved their life situations through divorce. They all shared the common perception that they would, but none of them did. I fully realize that there are probably some who feel better divorced or remarried, but I assure you that the vast majority don't, and studies support this statement.[31]

OUCH—STOP IT!

If you have, or are, contemplating divorce, what you have read may feel overly harsh, bleak, and downright overwhelming and even legalistic. Like Sgt. Friday from the television show "Dragnet," I have tried to present "just the facts." I know they seem hard, but it is essential that I "truth" to you in this area. It is essential that you know.

Why does God so clearly state that He hates divorce? For all of the reasons listed above and many more. God is in the business of redeeming and restoring lives, not in destroying them.

Yet, destroying is exactly what divorce does to lives, relationships, churches, and communities. This is why Jesus says, *"Let no man separate what God has joined."* God understands, more than anyone, the heartbreaking pain of divorce. And even in the face of blatant unfaithfulness, God still desires restoration. While God divorced Israel, He still desired for her return. He said that if she would return, *"I will not be angry forever."* He said that if she would just acknowledge her guilt and return, then things would be good again, *"for I am your husband"* (Jer. 3:11,14).

God understands divorce, and it is because He understands it so well that He says, "I hate it. Stop this unfaithfulness. It is unfaithfulness to your spouse, your children, and to Me. Stop it!" *"But wait a minute,"* you say. *"What if it is too late? What if I am divorced, and I or my ex-spouse is already remarried? I can see what it does to people; I have experienced many of the things you have talked about, but it is too late for me. What do I do now?"*

Praise God that He is full of grace. He knows that we regularly learn needed lessons only after we have destroyed something, and it is often beyond repair. Yet, God still loves us and still redeems us. So, what does God say to those of us in this situation?

Borrowing from the spirit of several passages, I believe God would say something to us like this:

> If you are still married, then take the necessary steps to begin to redeem that marriage. Be the husband or wife that you have been called to be—especially in and during difficult times. Love your spouse with the love described in First Corinthians 13, and love your kids by first loving their mom or dad. If you are divorced, and neither you or your spouse is remarried, be patient, wait, and seek the restoration of your marriage. This is honoring to me. If you are divorced and are remarried, then become the best husband or wife

that you can be to your spouse. Love this spouse with the intentionality that you should have the first time around but failed to do. I hate divorce! Redeem this marriage so that no one experiences another divorce. I have given you My Spirit to lead and fill your every need. I will give you what you need to be the spouse that I have called you to be. Therefore, honor Me in this marriage.

Things I discuss in later chapters will help you in your pursuit of this.

By sharing facts, statistics, and Scriptures with you, please know that I do *not* do so from a high and separated, lofty tower. I do so recognizing your pain of possible betrayal, abuse, or any other number of emotions that push us toward divorce. Remember, I have been there. More importantly, God has been there. All of the pain and brokenness are wrapped in, and around, these truths. When our marriages seem the bleakest, remember that God's Word and eternal truths were given for these very times. In our darkest days, let us acknowledge that He knows what He is talking about and honor that with our choices. If we do, His blessings in our marriage and relationships just might surprise us.

CHAPTER NINE

DIVORCE CAN LIMIT OUR POTENTIAL SERVICE

"Doing the best at this moment puts you in the best place for the next moment."

—OPRAH WINFREY[1]

The list of prohibitions that we encounter on a daily basis, regardless of our stage of life, is endless.

"You can't listen to that kind of music."

"Don't touch."

"Remember—you must be home by curfew or else you will be grounded."

"Don't eat that—you will ruin your dinner."

"Keep off the grass."

"No parking."

Rules and regulations seem to be a necessary evil. Yet, in many cases, even as much as we hate them, we know that they are there for our protection and welfare. The city establishes a speed limit on a particular road because they have deemed that a safe speed at which to drive. We may disagree with the particular limit that is set, yet we know that driving 80 miles per hour through a school zone could have grave consequences. Even still, there is something about our American, John Wayne, I-am-an-individual-and-can-do-whatever-I-want mindset that haunts us. We rebel as teenagers, and we try to skirt laws and policies as adults. Then the funniest (or most pathetic) thing is that we act surprised when we are caught! But the absurdity doesn't stop there. Not only are we surprised, but we are in disbelief that someone went so far as to impose consequences for our violation.

I have worked with teenagers who have been expelled from school for a variety of offences ranging from drug distribution to theft of teacher property. Yet even when students are caught red-handed, I have still had parents argue that they can't believe that the school would dare to kick their loving child out of school for the offense. I recently read about another NFL player who had once again violated the league's drug policy. He was originally suspended for a few games. However, after this additional offence, he was suspended for a year. What do you think—did he accept responsibility and take the suspension in stride? Of course not. He appealed the suspension because he didn't like the consequences. I am not quite sure when we as a society began to adopt such a disconnected attitude; we don't want our behaviors to connect to consequences. From the very beginning in The Garden of Eden, Adam and Eve wanted to pass blame and avoid responsibility for their actions. So, I suppose that we come by it quite naturally.

If we could get our heads around the fact that consequences are connected to behavior, we might be able to make some changes. It is pretty clear that if I rob a bank, I will go to jail. Hmm—I wonder if maybe I don't want to go to jail then—hmm—let me think—I *shouldn't* rob the bank. I know that you are laughing at my profound ability to grasp the obvious. But you have to understand that our seeming inability to get this is exactly the reason that we are surprised by repercussions to our actions. We have occasionally seen men and women go to prison for some heinous crime and then find Jesus. While I am certainly not questioning the sincerity of their repentance, I want to point out that, even if they are truly remorseful for their actions and even receive forgiveness from the victim and from God, they still have to serve their time. Being sorry doesn't remove the sentence. I may truly regret the fact that I hurriedly walked too close to the edge of a cliff and fell off. I may desperately wish that I had walked slower and would certainly do it differently given another chance. I have learned my lesson. Yet, while that is all well and good—my leg is still broken and will still take weeks to heal. The bottom line is this (get ready, it will knock your socks off!): disobedience often results in unwanted consequences.

So, why do I elaborate on all of this? Because there are often repercussions to divorce that we never considered until we were on the other side saying "Oops!" when it was too late. In this chapter, I will use two examples from Scripture, as well as some modern examples, to illustrate two important concepts: 1) God is full of grace and forgiveness, and 2) there are absolutes in what God expects and disobeying His instruction will have life-long implications.

IT'S COOL TO TALK TO ROCKS

Charlton Heston played Moses in the 1956 film, *The Ten Commandments*. Moses was the leader of the Israelites. He was the one who went before Pharaoh to demand the release of the Hebrew captives. God used Moses to divide the Red Sea and lead the nation across, so they could escape the armies of Egypt. Moses climbed Mount Sinai to receive God's Ten Commandments for his people. He acted as a judge for the people and was God's established authority for His nation. I could list many more accomplishments from his resume, but I think that you get the picture: Moses was an outstanding, powerful leader who was on intimate terms with God. That is a pretty cool place to be.

Yet, even with those credentials, Moses was not above repercussions to disobedience. Numbers 20 relates an important event in Moses' life that had lifelong implications for him.

You may remember from Chapter 6 that Moses sent 12 spies to check out the land of Canaan and report back as to what they discovered. Unfortunately, the report back was not unanimous. Only two spies recognized the power of their God and encouraged Israel to take the land that was promised to them. The other ten spies cowered at what they saw: powerful people, well-fortified cities, and even giants. Upon hearing the report, the community rebelled against Moses and God. The nation was then destined to wander for 40 years before they were allowed to enter the Promised Land.

So, that is the backstory to Numbers 20. The people were hanging out in the desert, unable to reach their desired goal for 40 years due to their disobedience. Miriam, Moses' sister, had just died, and now there was no water and the people were thirsty. The people came as a group to Moses to voice their discontent. They argued that they would have been better off if they had remained in Egypt. Moses and Aaron went before God to ask Him what they should do about the water crisis, and God clearly responded,

> *Take the staff, and you and your brother Aaron gather the assembly together. Speak to the rock before their eyes and it will pour out its water. You will bring water out of the rock for the community so they and their livestock can drink* (Numbers 20:6-8).

The instructions were easy to follow—at least one would think they were. But read what happened in the following verses.

> *So Moses took the staff from the Lord's presence, just as he commanded him. He and Aaron gathered the assembly together in front of the rock* [so far so good]

and Moses said to them. "Listen, you rebels, must we bring you water out of this rock?" Then Moses raised his arm and struck the rock twice with his staff. Water gushed out, and the community and their livestock drank (Numbers 20:9-11).

What a minute—didn't God tell Moses to "speak to the rock," and instead Moses struck the rock? In our 21st century mindset, we might think this was a small variation. Moses did other things right, so it couldn't be all bad. Yet, in God's eyes it was simple disobedience. We might consider this to be no big deal, but God responded in this way:

Because you did not trust in Me enough to honor Me as holy in the sight of the Israelites, you will not bring this community into the land I give them (Numbers 20:12).

This man with the superior resume that God had used in powerful and amazing ways, this man who had given his life in service to God to lead these people to the Promised Land, this man who had endured verbal abuse from the people while praying on their behalf, this man who was chased by the enemy in perilous circumstances made this one little mistake and was banished from the place that he had sacrificed everything to get to? What a reminder that God desires obedience—not sacrifice!

It is important that we notice two things here. First, God's grace extended over Moses' life. Even though Moses disobeyed God's instructions, God never renounced him. Moses continued to lead Israel, to make decisions, and he was involved in the transfer of leadership. Moses continued to be involved in the lives of his people, but he was not allowed to enter Canaan with them. This had to convey a lame-duck element to his leadership that resulted in a major loss of influence. How sad and how avoidable this was!

The second thing to notice is that the consequences for bad choices were still intact.

> *Then the Lord said to Moses, "Go up this mountain in the Abarim range and see the land I have given the Israelites. After you have seen it, you too will be gathered to your people, as your brother Aaron was, for when the community rebelled at the waters in Desert of Zin, both of you disobeyed my command to honor me as holy before their eyes"* (Numbers 27:12-14).

I still remember watching Charlton Heston look across the mountain top to the land he worked for decades to get to, and yet this was as close as he would ever get to tasting of it.

Clearly Moses' disobedience limited his effectiveness as a leader. His goal and dream for years, to enter the land that they had all worked so hard to get to, would never be realized. Moses' potential for positive influence had been limited by a simple choice of disobedience.

BLEATING IS NOT A GOOD THING

Do ever remember a time as a kid when your parents gave you specific instructions?

> Come straight home from school! Do not give anyone a ride, and don't make any stops. You are to come directly home!

So, you got home and your parent asks, "Why did it take you so long to come home?"

You respond with, "Well... My friend Ray needed a ride to work. I know you told me to not give anyone rides, but his car broke down, and if he didn't get to work he would be fired. And we just learned in church last week about the deeds of the Good

Samaritan, so I knew that this was the Christian thing to do. And since his job was right on the way home, it's not like I actually stopped somewhere. I mean, it was almost a slow roll while he jumped out." While the answer seems somewhat logical, your parents didn't buy it, and you lost the car for a week.

This is exactly what happened in our second example in First Samuel 15.

> Samuel said to Saul, "I am the one the Lord sent to anoint you king over his people Israel; so listen now to the message from the Lord. This is what the Lord Almighty says: 'I will punish the Amalekites for what they did to Israel when they waylaid them as they came up from Egypt. Now go, attack the Amalekites and totally destroy everything that belongs to them. Do not spare them; put to death men and women, children and infants, cattle and sheep, camels and donkeys'" (1 Samuel 15:1-3).

While these instructions may seem a bit harsh, we will leave that for a discussion at another time. The point that I want you to get here is that God made His will very clear. It was well-defined with not a lot of margin for error.

So, King Saul gathered an army of over 200,000 soldiers to attack the Amalekites. An army of this magnitude certainly should have done the trick without much difficulty. But Saul quickly forgot his instructions.

> Then Saul attacked the Amalekites all the way from Havilah to Shur, to the east of Egypt. He took Agag king of the Amalekites alive, and all his people he totally destroyed with the sword. But Saul and the army spared Agag, and the best of the sheep and cattle, the fat calves and lambs—everything that was good. These they were unwilling to destroy completely, but

everything that was despised and weak they totally destroyed (1 Samuel 15:7-9).

Notice that it doesn't say that the Israelites were in a fierce battle that they had a difficult time winning. There is no indication that this was a difficult battle at all. As a matter of fact, it would seem that the Children of Israel were the heavy favorites and they didn't disappoint. No, King Agag and the best animals didn't struggle and escape. The passage indicates that King Saul and the soldiers knew exactly what they were to do, but they were "unwilling" to follow through. At first, you might think that they were somehow being merciful, but keep in mind that they had no trouble killing all the people; they kept the animals for themselves.

God filled Samuel in on what had happened. Samuel was pretty disturbed by it all and was actually grieved that he had played a role in making Saul king. The next morning he set out to find Saul to confront him with his deed.

When Samuel reached him, Saul said, "The Lord bless you! I have carried out the Lord's instructions" (1 Samuel 15:13).

Doesn't Saul seem just a bit too eager to please Samuel by saying the right thing, even though he knows better?

But Samuel said. "What then is this bleating of sheep in my ears? What is this lowing of cattle that I hear?" (1 Samuel 15:14).

Get ready! Here comes the greatest excuse, rationalization, and blaming shifting that will ever witness.

Saul answered. *"The soldiers brought them from the Amalekites"* (1 Samuel 15:15).

I guess Saul was hoping to convince Samuel that the soldiers had suddenly taken control. But just in case that excuse didn't fly—Saul tried to spiritualize things.

The soldiers took sheep and cattle from the plunder, the best of what was devoted to God, in order to sacrifice them to the Lord your God (1 Samuel 15:20).

Of course! First it was the soldier's fault, and then it was God's fault. *We only did this because He needs a sacrifice! We totally destroyed the rest!*

You can hear the frustrated parent in Samuel when he tells Saul to Stop! with the lame excuses—to stop with the lies. As you read the ongoing exchange, you can see that Saul was absolutely unwilling to deal with his sin. Samuel reviewed with Saul his selection as king, God's specific mission, and Saul's disobedience to God. Saul continued to assert that he did obey, to make excuses, and to blame shift. Samuel responded with powerful words that we would do well to heed.

Does the Lord delight in burnt offerings and sacrifices as much as in obeying the voice of the Lord? To obey is better than sacrifice....Because you have rejected the word of the Lord, He has rejected you as king (1 Samuel 15:22-23).

In the remainder of the chapter, we find that Saul finally got it. He acknowledged his sin and worshipped God. He remained king for a time, but God already had someone else in mind. Saul would never be the great king that he could have been. He would lead a lame-duck administration and die in humility. Disobedience has consequences and can limit our potential for leadership and ministry.

PROWLING AND ROARING

If we are naïve, we may try and chalk up examples such as Moses and Saul to unique, abnormal situations. But that would be foolish. Peter wrote, *"Be self-controlled and alert. Your enemy the devil prowls around like a roaring lion looking for someone*

167

to devour" (1 Pet. 5:8). Satan is no respecter of persons—he will take down anyone!

"But, I go to church every Sunday and know the Bible pretty well." Jimmy Swaggart was a well-known national television evangelist. He also went to church every Sunday and knew his Bible very well. He had a very successful ministry, but it crumbled around him, as his sin of soliciting prostitution became public knowledge. Satan prowled and found himself a victim. Jim Bakker, one of the elite among televangelists, led a ministry and unrivaled broadcasting network. While it looked as though this ministry would just continue to grow under his preaching and leadership, satan roared. Bakker had issues ranging from adultery to inappropriate financial dealings, and this ministry virtually disappeared when Bakker served prison time. Satan took down another one.

In 2006, I was stunned to watch as Ted Haggard, the pastor of the largest church in Colorado Springs and president of the National Evangelical Association, was confronted about a gay relationship. I had sat under this man's teaching and initially refused to believe that this could be true. But in the next few days, his ministry—a church that started in his basement and grew to 14,000 attendees— ended in the blink of an eye. I had never met a pastor that I believed had more integrity than Ted. Yet, because of the deception of a dual life, the man that God had used in magnificent ways to touch people's hearts and minds was rejected from his appointed position.

Will these men serve again? I am confident that, if their hearts are right with the Lord, they may very well have opportunities to impact people's lives. However, I do not believe that we will ever see them in respected positions of leadership such as those they once held. Ted Haggard used to repeatedly say, "Sin will take you places where you don't want to go; it will keep you longer than you ever want to stay, and you will pay a price higher than you ever wanted to pay." In an eerie sort of way, he foretold his own leadership demise. Satan devoured another one. It is sad, gut wrenching, and senseless—but it is reality! Sin limits our potential to impact people in positive ways for the Kingdom.

CARNAGE

It is important that we understand what disobedience and divorce do to our relationships with God, our family, and those around us

First, when we make decisions that are in contradiction to God's expressed will, He is displeased. This is not unlike what we experience with our children. We love them to pieces and would do anything for them. Yet, when they disobey us, when they do the exact opposite of what we requested of them, two things happen. First we are disappointed and grieved. Second, we don't trust them and are hesitant to rely on them to do future things that we ask. We may even remove privileges and responsibilities from them. This is exactly what God does. He doesn't love us any less; we are not any less His children. But He can't trust us and may have to remove us from positions of influence until He can trust us. Our response to our sin will determine whether we will be trustworthy again or not.

Once we have distanced ourselves from closeness with God, we do the same thing with those whom we love. We made life-long vows of love and commitment to a person whom we are now divorcing. We have brought children into a home that should have been permanent for them, but is now shattered, uncertain, and fraught with fear of the unknown. How will our children view us? Can they really trust that we love them when we place our desires ahead of their welfare? Gary Richmond, wrote:

> *You will find that it will be some years before the people who took you seriously previously will again take you seriously. Not only will self-respect be a problem, but disrespect will be a problem.*[2]

I am a Marriage and Family Therapist; relationships are my business! Yet, I find it interesting that at times my grown boys are still a little hesitant to accept words of advice regarding their relationships from me. My divorce compromised my credibility in their eyes. I don't like it, but it is the reality that I must accept. The carnage is still sometimes evident.

My relational decisions continue to affect those around me. Whether it is with my co-workers or close friends, issues of trust and dependability can be at the forefront. Paul wrote to Timothy about the importance of having our act together in relationship to our family if we are to be respected leaders. In First Timothy 3, we read about the qualifications for church leaders.

> He must manage his own family well and see that his children obey him with proper respect. (If anyone does not know how to manage his own family, how can he take care of God's church?) (1 Timothy 3:4-5).

And believe me, making decisions that will lead to breaking vows with my spouse through a divorce certainly indicate that I have some issues in managing my own family. How then can I lead in God's Church? That is a significant question that hopefully leads me to wrestle with my issues and myself.

We often think that we can just divorce our spouse and that this decision will be isolated from the rest of our lives. However, this is certainly not the case. This decision to break faith with my spouse is pervasive and will seep into every area of my life. It builds walls and damages my intimacy with God. It creates mistrust with my children. They will wonder if I will really be there and if they can trust what I say. It creates doubt among my friends. They will question if I bring dependability to the table, and whether they want me speaking into their lives. It brings overwhelming credibility issues to the forefront in any place where I might be in a position of influence—whether that is church or work. My choice to divorce will impact every relationship in my life. With much work, these relationships can be rebuilt. It is critical to understand that, while they will never be the same, they can be healthy once again.

DIVORCE LIMITS AT A PERSONAL LEVEL

In 1981, I moved from Dallas, Texas, to Fresno, California. I had been involved in a ministry to youth in junior high, high school, and college campuses for eight years in Dallas. This had been a creative and fulfilling time of trying innovative techniques in reaching young people for Christ. However, after the birth of my first son, it seemed time to make some ministry changes so that I would not be traveling and could be home and involved in the parenting of my child on a daily basis. I knew that this was going to be an important time, and I didn't want to miss it. So, I accepted a ministry position with a church in Fresno.

I'll never forget the comment that an acquaintance in Dallas made to my good friend Mark. He said to Mark, "Barry is going to go to California and will do significant things in youth ministry." I think this person had observed my passion for ministry and for kids, my willingness to think outside the box and try new things, as well as my energy and commitment to a task, and believed that all of these things would combine to result in a ministry that would have a far reaching impact on both kids and youth leaders. These are not the ramblings of an egomaniac, but merely the observation of one person.

So, what happened? Yes, I did go to California and led youth ministries in a couple of churches. But nothing that this individual had foreseen on a wide scale came about. Why? I loved being in the ministry and touching people's lives on a daily basis. This is what I wanted to do for a lifetime. I believed, and continue to believe, that there is no higher calling than to be used in church ministry. But something happened.

You will recall from an early chapter that in 1988 I went through a divorce. Was this divorce preventable and avoidable? Absolutely—they nearly always are. But the choices, the sin, the self-deception, and all of the things that go into the making of a divorce impacted me, my family, and all those around me to whom I would minister. I went on to minister in part-time ways in a few churches, but it is important to see that my ministry never came close to being the kind of ministry that was foretold by the acquaintance in Dallas. Divorce limited my potential and my high calling in this field.

Please don't misunderstand me here. Did God give up on me? *Never!* Did He throw me in the trash heap never to use me again? *No!* Did He relegate me to doing nothing more than sitting and watching with no chance to participate in the game? *Of course not!* However, I do believe that he removed me from that particular type of ministry.

Yet, I want to again emphasize God's immense love and grace. As I said, God didn't throw me away. However, He did leave me in a place for a season to learn and grow from my stupid mistakes. At that point, I was at a crossroads. I could continue on in my disobedient, self-focused approach to life and perhaps never be heard from again (certainly not in a forum such as this), or I could listen closely as God spoke and taught me through other people and the workings of His Spirit.

I chose the latter route, and I discovered two important concepts. First, as a result of my divorce and the accompanying life choices, my positions of ministry and leadership were removed. I was no different from Moses or Saul. My choices had consequences. And in this case, the ministry to which I aspired and loved was taken away from me. I might get to sit on the mountain and see the Promised Land, but I would not lead the people into it.

Now, let me pause here for just a moment. You may be thinking, *"Wait a minute. I know people who have gone through a divorce, and they haven't seemed to experience any negative conse-quences."* Certainly this may be the case. Please also keep in mind that divorces happen for a myriad of reasons with different areas of culpability. We don't always know all of the details and have all of the insight that God does. We don't always see the loss of cred-ibility among friends, the damage to relationships with children, and so on.

Also, keep in mind that as I speak of consequences, for our purposes, I am speaking primarily about consequences as they relate to positions of leadership, especially within the Church, and our ability to have widespread positive impact on people's lives. You may find yourself resisting this idea simply because you don't like it. If that is the case, I understand. I don't like it either. But the longer I observe the lives and ministries of others, the more convinced I am that it is true. As I said before, the first thing that I learned was that my ministry was removed. Fortunately, the second thing that I learned was that God is *full* of grace. No, He hasn't thrown me away. Quite the opposite was true. As I have been willing to repent, submit in obedience to God, and stead-fastly work for authenticity and integrity, God has redeemed my life. Please grasp this critical statement. *As I am willing to repent, submit in obedience to God, and steadfastly work for authentic-ity and integrity, God has* **redeemed** *my life.* Does this mean that Moses, Ted, or I get our positions of leadership and ministry back? Sorry, but I don't think so. However, I do believe that God will take us with our scars and our brokenness and will use us again in an appropriate venue to impact the lives of hurting individuals.

Sometimes we are like a teenager who comes in an hour after curfew. He wants to be able to say, "I am sorry," and immediately get permission to borrow the car for the next weekend with no additional restrictions. So, when the parent says, "I appreciate your apology, but please understand that trust must be regained. Therefore, you will not get the car next weekend," the teenager is upset. He doesn't want consequences for his actions. We are that teenager. There are consequences. We can kick and scream and throw a tantrum all that we want because we don't like it. It doesn't change anything. Or we can face our flaws, own our mistakes and poor decisions, allow God to redeem our lives, and then wait with anticipation to see how He will use us. Instead of waiting to see if God will give us our toys back and use us the way that we want to be used.

The Scriptures are full of encouragement that reminds us that God will use us if we will give Him free reign.

> *The Lord will fulfill his purpose for me; your love, O Lord, endures forever—do not abandon the works of your hands* (Psalm 138:8).

In my office, I have a plaque with this Scripture on it:

> *For I know the plans I have for you,' declares the Lord, 'plans to prosper you and not to harm you, plans to give you hope and a future* (Jeremiah 29:11).

Yes, the Lord has plans for us from the very beginning of our lives, plans that we frequently usurp and make shambles of. I have an amazing ability to take God's plans for me and rework them and fit them into the shape of what I want. Inevitably when I do that, the result is chaos. Do I believe that God may have had plans for me in areas of ministry very different from what I am now doing? I believe that is very possible. Those plans were scrapped, because I made choices that were incompatible with God's purpose and plans for my life. Those opportunities, in their original form, are gone. But again, because of God's grace, if I will humbly and truly submit my heart at His feet, He will redeem my life.

As Psalm 138 states, He has not abandoned the work of His hands. The Lord will indeed fulfill His purpose in me. I have a choice to get hung up on what I wanted, and could have had, before my divorce in 1988, or I can choose to embrace my brokenness and, more importantly, embrace a God who will pick up those pieces and put them back into a form that fits His purposes. He may use me in very different ways than I had originally hoped, but He has plans that will give me a hope and a future. I gladly embrace that.

SECTION THREE

Essentials for Marriage Survival and Growth

CHAPTER TEN

ALL YOU NEED IS LOVE— BUT WHAT IS IT?

"The most important thing about love is we choose to give it...and we choose to receive it. Making it the least random act in the entire universe. It transcends blood, it transcends betrayal...and all the dirt that makes us human."[1]

—CHAOS THEORY

In the 1960s, we heard the Beatles postulate the answer to the world's problems with a song, "All You Need is Love." You may remember other song titles such as "Love is a Many Splendored Thing," "Love is Blue," "A Groovy Kind of Love," or "I Just Called to Say I Love You." And while the songs may be romantic, sweet, well meaning, and even sometimes funny, they fail to adequately explain what love is.

Yet, it is amazing what people will do in the name of love. I don't know that I can think of a word in our language that is more misused, misunderstood, taken for granted, and yet invoked as much as love. My hope is that, by the end of this chapter, we will have a much clearer understanding of what love is actually all about.

THIS THING CALLED LOVE

I have taught a class for a number of years at Colorado Christian University that is simply titled "Marriage and Family." During one class session, we tackled the topic of love. We usually begin by looking at a variety of words and phrases that people associate with the concept of love. The following is a list of words that a recent class came up with to describe love.

- Commitment

- Unconditional

- Kindness

- Makes me laugh

- Trust

- Patience

- Dependable

- Share

- Lust

- Loyalty

- Similarity

- Sacrifice

- Thoughtful

- Romantic

- Hard Work

- Kissy Face

- Passionate

- Mutual Respect

- Support

- Strength

- Encouragement

- Forgiveness

- Reciprocal

- Eternal

- Bonding

- Edification

- Tenderness

- Freedom

- Financial Independence

- Mercy

- Giving

- Receiving

- Maturity

- Compromise

- Acceptance

- Tiring

- Unfailing

- Adoring

- Exciting

As you can see, these words are all over the board. Depending on a person's background and experiences, different words resonate for different people. But do any of these words singularly capture the concept of love?

Some might say, *"Well, I know love when I feel it. I know what it is like to fall in love."* While I am certain that, at one time or another, most of us have fallen in love, we have also probably made the mistake of thinking that this was the same thing as loving someone. As a result, we often use *love* and *falling in love* interchangeably. Yet, they are very different. Actually, I personally feel that this idea of *falling in love* has created a great deal of confusion and done us a huge disservice. *Falling in love* connotes that something just happened to me. *"It was completely out of my control, and I was just swept away by it."* I guess I would then liken it to hitting a pothole with my car or a tornado ripping my house off of its foundation.

> Well, I was just sitting there watching television when all of a sudden there was this sound and kablooey!—the house was gone.

I know that sounds a bit ridiculous, but it truly is not much different from the way we talk about falling in love.

> I was at a barbeque with a bunch of the singles from church, and then I saw her. Wow! (Translation for Kablooey.) One look and my heart jumped. I knew she was the one. It was love at first sight. I was smitten.

In other words, he wasn't looking for it; it just happened to him. So, if I accept this account at face value, I am to believe that he somehow loves a person whom he has never met and knows absolutely nothing about. Hmm. A more accurate word for this is *infatuation*.

Brennan Manning reminds us that "The root meaning of infatuation derives from the Latin in-fatuus, 'to make foolish.'"[2] Need I say more? Gary Chapman refers to this experience of falling in love as having the "tingles."[3] As I tell my class, you have to be careful that you don't confuse the feelings of a melting popsicle running down your back (the tingles) with the deeper feelings that may be associated with genuine love. And believe me, many people confuse those two feelings on a regular basis.

The media has not been much help in this area. From movies to romance novels, we find this idea of hitting a pothole—oops, I mean falling in love—and with that comes everything from trouble free, no-work-required relationships to perfect, guilt free, uncomplicated, always-simultaneously-orgasmic sex. Of course, when you leave the theatre and go back to your real world and find that it isn't like this at all, you then feel flawed, deficient, broken, and inadequate. Let me reassure you that while you may indeed have flaws and areas that need work, many of your negative feelings come from believing the media's lies. What they have presented is *not real*! I still remember the 1970s film *Love Story*. For years people quoted that movie: "Love is never having to say you're sorry." It is a great example of a feel good story that is not based on truth; it is full of media-created, ridiculous lies.

I remember having a conversation with a Christian psychologist in California back in the 1980s. We were discussing marriage and the permanence that we express in marriage vows when he said to me,

> I think that when we use the phrase "as long as we both shall live," it really means as long as our love will live. Therefore, if our love dies, then it is OK to end the marriage.

I don't know if my jaw actually fell on the floor, but it sure felt like it. What an amazing way to twist and rationalize to fit an agenda. Yet, I suppose that if love is not much more than a melting Popsicle, I guess this comment might not be that inappropriate.

I remember when Jeff came into my office a few years ago. He acted as though he wanted marriage counseling with his wife, but in reality, he said that his love for his wife had died and that there was nothing left to do but get divorced. He had already gotten involved with someone else and wanted my approval of the situation. Unfortunately, Jeff didn't get the response from me that he was hoping. As we look further at gaining some clarification about love, I think you will understand why.

"I love my wife, I love my car, I love to watch football, and I love pizza." These are just a few examples of things that we say that we love. But do we mean the same thing with each one? Do I love my wife in the same way that I love pizza? I certainly hope not. However, you can see how we use a singular word in a variety of ways that would certainly seem to imply a multitude of meanings.

One of the things that I appreciate about the New Testament is that it was written in Greek, which offers several words that we translate into love. I just want to briefly focus on three of those words and how they are often used.

Eros love refers to passionate, sexual love that is typically focused on pleasing oneself. The English word *erotic* is derived from eros. *Phileo*, from which we get the word *Philadelphia* (city of brotherly love), is used most often to describe human-to-human relationships. This could refer to warmth, kindness, friendship, and so on. The third word, which we talk about most often in the Church, is *agape*. *Agape* indicates choice and a covenant relationship. It is the kind of love that God has for humanity, that we should have for God, and that a man has for his wife. This kind of love speaks of devotion. Agape denotes a greater sense of duty, behaving in a certain manner because of a choice that has been made, self-sacrificing, and seeking to benefit the other. It is the ultimate and highest form of love.

FIRST CORINTHIANS 13

This text, written by the apostle Paul, is commonly referred to as the love chapter. We think of it when we discuss the virtues of love, and we often include it as a part of many wedding ceremonies. While it frames nicely and looks good hanging on our wall, I wonder if we really know the significance of what these words convey.

Just prior to First Corinthians 13, Paul discussed the importance of the various parts of the body that we call the Church, and the various spiritual gifts that help to complete the functioning of that body. He concludes Chapter 12 by encouraging believers to desire the gifts, especially the greatest gift, which is love. He begins Chapter 13 by emphasizing that agape love—the highest form of love—is essential. It doesn't matter what other gifts I have, what great works I can perform, or what feats I can accomplish if I don't have love. If I have all of these other things but not love, I am no more valuable to the body than a clanging cymbal.

Following this, Paul tells us what love is.

> *Love is patient, love is kind. It does not envy, it does not boast, it is not proud. It is not rude, it is not self-seeking, it is not easily angered, it keeps no record of wrongs. Love does not delight in evil but rejoices with the truth. It always protects, always trusts, always hopes, always perseveres* (1 Corinthians 13:4-7).

You may have read these words dozens of times and each time seen areas where you dropped the ball. "I was rude and impatient last week." "I still get easily angered with my spouse." But I want you to reread the passage and, as I tell my class, look for what all of these things have in common. As you reread this passage, I want you to find the commonality shared by these words, as well as what is missing. In other words, there may be some thoughts that we typically have about love that we do not find in this description.

After a few minutes, at least a couple of people in the class usually spot something obvious that they may have never seen before. First, all of the words or phrases used are action words or behaviors. They are things that we are to either do or not do. Secondly, and this is usually the bigger surprise, there is not a feeling word in the bunch. Yes, I know, your brain just said, "What?" and you looked back at the passage again. But that is right—there are no feeling words. Now, if you are like a lot of people, the air horns have just gone off in your brain, and it is going into emergency lockdown. Because, if my two previous statements are correct, it may require on your part either complete denial of those statements or a radical change in your approach to love.

I want to look at the thoughts of a couple of authors. In thinking about this passage, Jim Talley, author of *Reconcilable Differences*, states:

> As I look at God's standard, I see a lot of hard work. Love is not so much a warm puppy-like feeling inside your life, the feeling of being on a cloud of ecstasy, as it is an ongoing process of doing and acting in love in order to be in love. Unfortunately, in our society most of us have been taught only to feel love, so once that feeling is gone we give up and then we wonder why things did not work out.[4]

Gary Chapman builds upon this in his book, *Hope for the Separated*:

> Many will say very sincerely, "I just don't love him/her anymore. I wish I could, but too much has happened." The thesis of that statement is that love is an emotion, a warm bubbly, positive feeling one has for a member of the opposite sex. You either have it or you don't. If you don't, there is nothing you can do about it. You

simply move away and hope that you may find it with someone else someday, somewhere.[5]

Michelle Weiner-Davis, author of *The Divorce Remedy*, continues this thought when she says,

> People just fall out of love. False. Some people believe that they need to divorce their spouses because they've fallen out of love. To them, love is a feeling that is either there or it's not there. If it's there, you get married. If it's not there, you divorced. This is one of the silliest ideas I have ever heard. First of all, people don't just fall out of love. If love dwindles, it's because the marriage wasn't a priority. Love is a living thing. If you nurture it, it grows. If you neglect it, it dies.[6]

As we ponder the significance of Paul's words in First Corinthians, our minds have to grapple with the understanding that love is not a kablooey, outside-of-ourselves event. It is not the tingly feeling. Love is a choice. It is an intentional decision. Love does not knock us down by surprise. It is something over which we have complete control.

Now please don't misunderstand me about feelings. I love ecstasy and butterflies and all of the wild feelings that we typically attach to the idea of love. It is wonderful when those feelings accompany love, and they often do in the early stages. That is not where we usually run into problems. It is later on, when the feelings have dissipated, that we get into trouble. Then we have to deal with the fact that feelings are nice, but they are not love. The decisions and choices that I make about how I determine to treat another are what love is about.

Looking back at Jeff's conversation in my office, you may be able to see how he and I were speaking the same words but might as well have been speaking two different languages. As he said to me, "I don't love her anymore," I replied with, "Then you had better start today." This made no sense to him. If love is an emotion that happens to him, that he has no control over, my statement would seem to be asking the impossible. How can he make something happen when he has no control? On the other hand, since the Scriptures teach that love is a conscious and intentional choice, you might understand that a person's response to Jeff's "I don't love her anymore," could be, "So what?" If he is indeed in control, then he is in essence saying, "I have made a decision to not love her any longer with my behaviors," In that context, my reply, "You need to start today," makes perfect sense.

I hope you see that this is not mere semantics. It is a crucial, philosophical shift from our western-culture mindset. Some cultures have understood this concept much better than we have for a long time.

If you like musicals, you may have seen the classic *Fiddler on the Roof.* This tale involves a Jewish family living in Russia. The father is very traditional in his thinking and has plans to hire a matchmaker to find appropriate husbands for his three daughters. However, one by one, each daughter finds and "falls in love" with her own selection. The father is beside himself and just cannot understand how his daughters can do this to him. When he asks them about it, the daughters respond with how they love their man. They are telling their father about how they feel, and it just doesn't compute in his brain. His marriage was arranged, and he has always accepted it. As he ponders what his daughters have told him, he goes to his wife and asks her if she loves him. He might as well be speaking a foreign language because she doesn't understand what he is talking about.

He is trying to ask her if she loves him, if she feels for him as his daughters do for these men. He is asking a feeling question to which she responds with a behavioral answer. She replies by saying things like, "For 25 years, I have fixed your food, darned your socks, raised the kids," and so on. He still presses to know if she loves him Again she breaks into song and talks about what she has done for 25 years. Finally, they conclude that these behaviors, these choices of being committed to and supporting one another, must be love. She loves him! In this tale, we see a wonderful example of what God means by love.

GREAT! SO NOW WHAT DO I DO?

If you are like most of us, you have felt *love* for as long as you can remember. From the time that you first became acquainted with cupid and gave your first valentine to a boy or girl in your kindergarten class, love was about feelings—or at least so we thought. It can take a while for us to understand that the kind of love God talks about is much, much more than a feeling. Yet, it is essential that we do just that. Consider a few choice comments from various authors.

> "...feelings are determined by actions—not the other way around. If you behave as if you love someone, the feelings will inevitably follow in a short time."[7]

> "It's important to realize too that this life-changing attitude doesn't start with a feeling—it's a decision, and the feelings of 'awe' eventually follow."[8]

> "For loving God—like loving one's spouse and children—is first, last, and always a decision."[9]

> "For a man, actions are primarily what dictate feelings, not the reverse."[10]

> "Don't worry about feelings. They're like a caboose following a locomotive."[11]

What Jesus, Paul, and the other New Testament writers teach is that love is an action, a choice, an intentional behavior. When we begin with the conscious decision, the feelings will follow.

However, when we begin with, and continually search for, that elusive feeling in and of itself, we seldom find one that remains through the good and bad times. Love is an act of the will. Not only is love not a feeling, but love can happen even when my feelings are anything but loving. Because love is a choice, I can love my spouse in spite of my feelings. Think about when Jesus taught us to love our enemies. We certainly don't have good feelings toward our enemies, but we can love them anyway. Sometimes you may see your husband or wife as the enemy. You may wonder what you should do when your spouse says that he or she hates you. Jesus teaches us to love him or her in return. In order to do this, we have to put the other person's interests above our own. I know that this can be difficult, especially when everything that you see in the other person makes you want to jump out of your skin. You may need to spend some time looking for the traits or assets that this person has to offer. I know you may think there aren't any. But at one time there certainly were, and as buried as they may be in him or her, they still probably exist. Take some time to rediscover them.

Perhaps your feelings are non-existent because your spouse has wronged you. Gary Chapman makes this suggestion:

> We need to follow God's example in the treatment of our spouses. Yes, we have been wronged, but we have the power to forgive. If your mate confesses and asks forgiveness, you must never again bring up the past.[12]

I appreciate the words of Michelle Weiner-Davis when she wrote:

> Most people assume that spending more time together will be the logical result of feeling better about each other. Therefore, they wait for the hostile feelings to be replaced by positive feelings before doing those

things that once gave them joy. However, the reverse appears to be true: when couples engage in pleasant activities together, it triggers pleasant feelings, which in turn breed a cooperative spirit.[13]

IT'S TOO HARD. I CAN'T DO IT.

Undoubtedly, whether you feel this way right at this moment or not, there has probably been a time in your life when you did. It might have been in relation to a friend, a sibling, or a spouse. You may have felt that loving someone was just too difficult. Their abrasive edges, their mean spiritedness, their callous insensitivity was just too much. Surely God doesn't expect me to aim my "loving behavior" gun at them. It is too hard. It seems impossible.

Even the disciples struggled with understanding this during their days with Jesus. You may remember that after Jesus corrected the Pharisees' understanding of the permanence of marriage in Matthew 19, the disciples responded with, *"If this is the situation between a husband and wife, it is better not to marry"* (Matt. 19:10). They also perceived this as a task that was just too tough.

Yet, we have to remember that anything God has commanded is not beyond our ability. Would He ask of us what is not possible? Of course not. He knows our weaknesses and our seemingly insurmountable challenges. But the coolest thing is that God supplies us with the strength to do what He asks. He knows every marital obstacle before we hit it. He is aware of the rollercoaster of emotions that we will experience. He desires for our relationship to be full of depth and intimacy, and He recognizes that this doesn't come without our working through the most difficult of times. While He expects us to do that, He gives us His grace and strength necessary that comes through the Holy Spirit. His strength is bottomless if we will just go to the well and drink from it.

Learning to rely on His enduring power as we love our spouse does not mean that we are to just be a door mat and allow our spouse to walk all over us. As Chapman so aptly puts it,

> Love is caring so much for their well-being that you refuse to play into their sick behavior. Many people are healed when someone loves them enough to stand up to their inappropriate actions. It is true that God loves us unconditionally, but it is not true that His approach is the same whether we obey or disobey His commands. We do not receive God's blessing unless we are willing to live responsibly. [In the same manner], we cannot have the benefits of a warm, loving relationship unless we are willing to be responsible in our own behavior [with our spouses].[14]

I want to share with you the story of Ron. Ron was a pastor at a church in California. He and his wife, Denise, had been married for nearly 20 years. During that time, they had experienced the typical struggles of most married couples. Of course, theirs were amplified with the glass-house pressures of ministry. Denise continually felt that Ron was not emotionally available to her. He was caught up in his ministry and often failed to see the needs that existed in his own family. Denise attempted to get his attention in a number of ways but it usually made little difference. That is until she told him that she didn't love him anymore, that she had met someone else, and that she was leaving.

Ron's world crumbled overnight. His wife began a torrid affair that ripped his heart to the core. He couldn't sleep and would lay tormented through the night with his imagination and emotions running the gamut. Fortunately, Ron had an understanding and supportive pastoral staff. He also wisely sought therapy. He had never seen himself needing a counselor before, but he became desperate for one. He allowed the counselor to peel him like an onion so that he could begin to see the layers upon layers of stuff he needed to deal with, and he did. He worked hard and learned to be the husband and father that his family needed. The only problem was that it was too late.

Denise had filed for divorce and resented most everything about Ron. Ron's senior pastor told him that as a part of his healing, following his pending divorce, he needed to commit to not dating for at least two years. Ron agreed. And then something interesting happened. Ron figured that since he couldn't date anyway, he might as well try to use the things he was learning with his wife. He determined to be kind to her at every interaction. He chose to take her dinner occasionally when she worked late. He made himself available to just listen when she wanted to talk. He offered invitations with no strings and no pressure. His wife was still very much caught up in her new relationship and usually rejected any overtures that he made.

Yet Ron remained constant and didn't get angry when she didn't respond as he had hoped. As he grew emotionally healthier and stronger, he became a better pastor, a better father, and even a better husband to his distant and estranged wife. He knew the divorce was proceeding and the marriage was probably over, yet he continued to choose loving behaviors toward his wife. He knew God was his source, and he was learning to fully rely on Him. This process lasted over a year. Don't think that all of this was easy. Ron was often dealing with emotional volcanoes inside. Her continued rejections hurt more deeply than anything he had ever experienced. But he had learned that this wasn't about feelings. It was about a choice to act in very intentional ways that demonstrated love to his wife. Even though she usually appeared cold and unfeeling, his actions weren't going unnoticed.

Five days before the divorce was finalized, Denise called it off. The unthinkable had happened. She noticed his behaviors toward her, and they melted her heart. While "happily ever after" didn't happen overnight, she did end the affair, and they began couples therapy. Yes, it took a long time to rebuild trust and put the pieces back together, but I can tell that, as they did the hard work of learning to love each other, they found their marriage to be better than it had ever been in 20 years. It had a new depth and intimacy that they had always longed for but never had. And it came about because Ron chose to love his wife, not with a Hollywood perspective, but with the love we have come to understand from First Corinthians 13.

WHERE YOUR TREASURE IS

In Matthew 6:21 Jesus said, *"For where your treasure is, there your heart will be also."* What He is saying is that what we place value upon is where our feelings will be. Whether that is in our finances, our business, our boat, or our golf game. Where we invest our time and energies—what we treasure—is where our heart or feelings will be. This is just as true in our relationship with our spouse. If this is where we spend our creative energies and place our primary focus, we will be amazed at the outcomes. If I treasure my spouse, my loving feelings about him or her will begin to develop accordingly.

We live in a generation where people are more concerned about their "rights" than they are commitment. Some will read Ron's story and certainly say that he had the "right" to divorce Denise and be done. But what Ron discovered was that he was able to finally break through to Denise by laying down his "rights."

If I will refocus in determining my treasure, it will change everything from my expectations to my marital security. Even as you think about demonstrating loving behaviors toward your spouse, do you find yourself wanting to change him or her? Gary Smalley wrote:

> The more we place our expectations on another person,
> the more control we give them over our emotional and

spiritual state. The freer we are of expectations from others—and the more we depend upon God alone—the more pure and honest our love for others will become.[15]

We need to keep our focus on ourselves. I am sure that most of us have focused our expectations on our spouse and worked to change them into what we think they should be. My question is, how well has that worked? And if we keep doing the same old thing, it will continue to not work. We need to focus on our own shortcomings and learn to love as God has instructed us to do, *regardless* of what our spouse does. Only then can we give our marriage the opportunity to experience genuine transformation. When we begin to pursue this, we create a place of safety and security in our marriage. As Gary Smalley stated so well,

> What many husbands and wives don't realize is that an absence of security in a relationship is like sentencing a person to live on an ice-covered sidewalk. Security results when a man and a woman say to each other, "You're so valuable to me that no matter what happens in life, I'm going to commit myself to you. You're so valuable, I'm going to spend the rest of my life proving to you my pledge to love you." In short, it's a reflection of the kind of security we have in our relationship with Christ....Every enduring marriage involves an uncon-ditional commitment to an imperfect person.[16]

CULTIVATING HEALTHY MARRIAGES

I used to have a vegetable garden when I lived in California. I enjoyed eating home grown tomatoes, green beans, cucumbers, and especially okra (fried of course). Over the years I learned that if I spent the time properly preparing the soil, planting the seeds as instructed, keeping the weeds out, and watering appropriately, I would have plenty of my favorite vegetables throughout the summer. But if I didn't, I would have a puny little garden that yielded little, and what it did produce would be pretty scrawny. If I treasured the garden enough to invest the time and energy to take care of it, the produce was great. If I didn't treasure it, what I received was pretty pitiful. Our marriages respond in the same manner.

I recall when Ted and Rose walked into my office a few years ago. They were on the brink of divorce because of an affair Ted had nearly 10 years earlier. Rose had just learned about it. The mistrust was great, and they had learned to live without much interaction. Like the poor garden, there had not been any weeding and watering taking place for a long time.

Ted suddenly realized what was at stake, and he didn't want to lose Rose. I knew it would be an uphill struggle, but if he was willing to do the work, this marriage had a chance. Of course, after years of neglect, there was no way that Rose believed Ted would respond like she needed him to. She knew where his treasure was, and it wasn't her. Ted began to work to refocus his attentions, to build trust, and to rebuild security. He began to intentionally choose loving behaviors even in the face of a wife who resented him and saw little hope in his ability to change.

I was pleased with how diligently Ted worked, and the results were phenomenal. In a matter of months, Rose's walls were coming down as she was able to see that she was of value to Ted. She was his treasure. As a result, his feelings followed his investment, and as she was able to slowly respond to his bridge building, her feelings followed as well. They now have the best marriage they have had in years, and they are excited about it.

JOLEE GETS IT!

Many of you have or have had a "Jolee." Jolee is my golden-doodle (half Golden Retriever and half Standard Poodle). She is a brilliant and beautiful dog, but that is not what is most impressive. Like most dogs, I am convinced that God has given her the ability to love unconditionally. There are many things she can't do as well as me. But she does this one thing far better. Think about it. She doesn't dictate to me that she will wag her tail and lick me only after I have fed her or taken her for a walk. When she gets in trouble for chewing up something she is not supposed to have, she doesn't get mad and not "talk" to me for the rest of the day. Instead, whether I have just returned from vacation or from a trip to Wal-Mart, she is thrilled to see me. She doesn't complain that I am an hour late. She is just glad I am here. And after being scolded for misbehavior, she is eager to rebuild bridges. As Gary Smalley commented, "Nonverbally, dogs honor their owners with massive doses of love and enthusiasm."[17] He went on to say, "Honor doesn't cast pearls before swine—but neither does it mean that you treat a person like swine until he measures up to your standards."[18]

When we are hurt or upset and want to be loved and comforted, it is easy to go to man's best friend, because they love us unconditionally. While this is a great commentary on the faithfulness and loyalty of dogs, it doesn't necessarily paint us intelligent humans in the best light. I am thankful that my dog can be so unconditional in her love. But I am sad that I struggle so much with doing the same. Don't think that I am naïve. I certainly know the differences in complex issues between dogs and people. But we can certainly learn from them, as we are called to a higher standard. I am called to love my spouse *unconditionally.* That means whether she has met my standards or not. It means regardless of what goof ball things she might do. It means no slippery, ice-covered sidewalk of conditions. It means choosing "love behaviors" in the face of whatever she might bring to the table. Jolee gets it; now can I?

SUMMARY

Understanding God's concept of love is critical to our understanding of life. God's love for us demonstrates what love is to be about: His for us, ours for Him, and ours for each other. I want to attempt to summarize God's love in a concise and portable form—in other words a useable form that you can carry with you daily.

First of all, love is not something that happens *to* us, that is out of our control. It is something that is very much in our control, and we choose it.

Second, as taught in First Corinthians 13, love is not a tingly feeling but an intentional action and behavior. If we will do the action consistently, with time the feelings will follow.

Third, when it seems too taxing to do, we find that God supplies the ability. With Jesus' love at the heart of who we are, we can do it.

Fourth, love breaks down strongholds. Where we invest ourselves, what we make important, our heart will deem as a priority and our feelings will match that.

Finally, the love God teaches us to have is an unconditional love. I am committed to loving my spouse (even when he or she is unlovable), just as God wants him or her to be committed to loving us. There are no exit clauses to unconditional love. Love just is, and it is unending.

Are you up for redefining your love for your spouse? If you are, it can revolutionize and revitalize your life.

CHAPTER ELEVEN

STANDING AND WAITING

"The strongest of all warriors are these two—
Time and Patience."

—LEO TOLSTOY[1]

It was a Sunday morning when Malcolm Tucker's car quit running about two miles outside of town. He walked to town looking for assistance (actually demanding assistance) from just about anyone he came in contact with. The problem was twofold: it was Sunday, when life slowed to a crawl, and a slower pace was already the norm in the town of Mayberry. Mr. Tucker owned Tucker Enterprises in Charlotte and he had to get there that day. Sheriff Andy Taylor was accommodating and took Mr. Tucker to the gas station, and then to Wally, the gas station's owner and mechanic, but Mr. Tucker's impatience did not seem to convince anyone to operate at his pace. Andy took Mr. Tucker home with him and offered him dinner, but he didn't want any. Mr. Tucker wanted to use the phone, only to find that two sisters, who spent three or four hours every Sunday talking, tied it up. (You have to think back to the middle of the 20th century, when small towns still had party lines, to understand this). In frustration, Mr. Tucker said to Andy, "You people are living in another world."

After dinner, Andy and his deputy, Barney, sat out on the front porch. Andy played guitar, and they both lazily sang and relaxed the afternoon away. As Mr. Tucker paced nervously, you could see his pace began to slow. He leaned against the post listening, and it wasn't long before he was singing along with them: "No place is so dear to my childhood as the little brown church in the vale." Mr. Tucker's mind began to think back to a slower and a happier time. He began to reminisce about what it was like to be patient, to wait, and to enjoy the quality things in life. Life had become so busy and complicated that he was missing out.

Ultimately his car was repaired that afternoon so that he could leave. However, as he prepared to depart, Gomer from the gas station wasn't willing to take any money for the repairs, Aunt Bee had packed a lunch for Malcolm for the road, and Opie, Andy's son, offered Mr. Tucker his lucky penny that had been run over by a train. As Mr. Tucker looked at each individual, he realized that the last thing that he needed to do was get to Charlotte. No, he needed to spend the night there in Mayberry. This "man in a hurry" had been getting places fast, but missing what was important as a result. His desire was to stop, wait, and recapture an element of peace, quality, and contentment. And he did just that.

This episode of "The Andy Griffith Show,"[2] is an appropriate reminder to us of what we miss when we are in too big of a hurry to stand and wait upon the Lord.

One of my favorite series of books is C.S. Lewis' *The Chronicles of Narnia*. In this series, four children magically find their way to the land of Narnia. Aslan is the Majestic lion King of Narnia and is representative of Jesus. During the course of the second book, *Prince Caspian*, Lucy sees Aslan, who tells her that they need to follow him. However, no one else sees Aslan, and they seem to doubt that Lucy has either. Peter says, "I know Lucy may be right after all, but I can't help it. We must do one or the other."[3] She is, therefore, out voted and they travel a more treacherous way with unpleasant outcomes.

A little later, everyone has gone to sleep except Lucy. She is drawn to leave the area where they have camped, and she finds Aslan. It is a joyous reunion, and she is thrilled beyond words to see him. Then the following interaction occurs.

> For a time she was so happy that she did not want to speak. But Aslan spoke.
>
> "Lucy," he said, "we must not lie here for long. You have work in hand, and much time has been lost today."
>
> "Yes, wasn't it a shame?" said Lucy. "I saw you all right. They wouldn't believe me. They're all so —"
>
> From somewhere deep inside Aslan's body there came the faintest suggestion of a growl.
>
> "I'm sorry," said Lucy, who understood some of his moods. "I didn't mean to start slanging the others. But it wasn't my fault anyway, was it?"
>
> The Lion looked straight into her eyes.
>
> "Oh, Aslan," said Lucy. "You don't mean it was? How could I—I couldn't have left the others and come up to you alone, how could I? Don't look at me like that...oh well, I suppose I could. Yes, and it wouldn't have been alone, I know, not if I was with you. But what would have been the good?"
>
> Aslan said nothing.
>
> "You mean," said Lucy rather faintly, "that it would have turned out all right—somehow? But how? Please Aslan! Am I not to know?"
>
> "To know what would have happened, child?" said Aslan. "No. Nobody is ever told that."

"Oh dear," said Lucy.

"But anyone can find out what will happen," said Aslan.[4]

You are probably thinking to yourself, *"These are two nice stories, but I am not quite sure how they apply to my situation."* If you currently find yourself in a life-depleting marriage, are currently separated, are waiting for a divorce to become final, or are even recently divorced, then the messages from these two stories are more than applicable.

In the first story, Malcolm Tucker learned that his impatience had caused him to miss out and that waiting could be a good thing.

The second story reminds us that frequently God calls us to follow Him and to take an unpopular stand. As it is much easier to listen to and do what the majority of people advise, we may find ourselves in a position of going along with the popular vote in disobedience to God. If you find yourself in one of the aforementioned situations, I believe that God's call to you, and the message of this chapter, will be, "Stand and wait."

GOOD VERSUS GOD'S BEST

First Corinthians 7 is a chapter of Paul's writings that is abundant with helpful instruction regarding many aspects of marriage, particularly when it comes to separation, divorce, and restoration. For our purposes here, I just want to recall verses 10 and 11.

To the married I give this command (not I, but the Lord): A wife must not separate from her husband. But if she does, she must remain unmarried or else be reconciled to her husband. And a husband must not divorce his wife.

Truly, this disciple of Jesus is writing about standing and waiting. We are in such a hurry to move on and get our emotional needs met today. Standing and waiting does not work well at all with our seeming need for immediate gratification, which we are all about.

I still remember the comments of a well-meaning friend after I was separated from my second wife. She had only been gone for a couple of weeks when he said, "Well she has left; how long until you will just move on?" That pretty much sums up our feelings: you leave me today, then I should find someone else tomorrow. However, Paul says that we are not to find someone else tomorrow. Instead, we are to do the exact opposite. Tomorrow we are to wait, not find someone else, and work toward reconciliation with my spouse. As long as I wait and remain unmarried, reconciliation is still possible.

I understand that you may be separated and experiencing the first no-conflict-days in years. It feels, and it seems good. However, God's desire for reconciliation with the power He will provide, is far better than just "good"; it is God's best.

When we were first married, we had dreams and plans for a wonderful relationship and life together. Those first longings are still worth fighting for. My guess is that the deep longings you originally held are still buried somewhere deep down inside, and with some work are still accessible.

Jim Talley, author of *Reconcilable Differences*, has likened the work that we have put into a marriage to the preparation and work that goes into a garden. He raises the question as to the wisdom of taking on a new relationship as opposed to reconciling the current one.

> Suppose you had arrived one spring as he was beginning to dig. You noticed he was working over a fresh patch of grass instead of turning over the previous

year's plot. What would you have said? I suspect you would have called him foolish, at the very least. That is exactly what many formerly married singles do over and over again. They prepare new "soil" for another relationship when they have an older soil (a former relationship) with a lot less rocks buried underground. A lot of effort has gone into removing rocks in the former relationship, making it a lot easier to become fruitful again.[5]

So why do we have such difficulty with this wisdom? Get ready for the answer; you may not be thrilled with it. If I just jettison my old partner and meet someone new, I can have (in my own mind) a clean slate. In other words, I don't have to work on me or tackle my own issues. The new person doesn't know about all of the rocks buried in my garden, and for a while I can do a pretty good job of hiding them. If I stay in my current or old relationship, I will have to deal with my own stuff to bring about true reconciliation. Yuck! I don't want to work that hard.

I remember a student who relayed to me the story of his brother's *seventh* divorce. His brother's comment was, "I just keep picking the wrong women." Hmm—it seems to me like there might be another common denominator that isn't being addressed here.

Following a separation or divorce, as I mentioned earlier, we may experience a reduction in conflict, which is no surprise since we are no longer around the person who pushes our buttons. We then mistakenly label this lack of conflict as "peace." But in Scripture, peace is much more of an active, assertive reconciliation than it is an absence of conflict. I see couples experience this in therapy. They come in screaming at each other daily and ready to throw each other out the window. As we begin to work, they may have a week in which they only had three days of yelling and didn't want to toss the other one through the front door. And with this realization, they think that their marriage is healed. Hardly. But, again, it is a misunderstanding to think that reduced conflict is the same as an active, reconciled peace.

Just as "peace" is active, so is "waiting." Oftentimes, people get away from each other, have reduced conflict (which is nice), and then think that they will just wait until their feelings change before considering reconciliation. Chapman wrote,

> Many couples feel that a trial separation will help them get their feelings straightened out. They want to separate and have no contact to see if time apart will cause the warm feelings to return. Such a process is futile. Attitude and action must precede positive emotions. Distance alone will not turn emotions around.[6]

HOW DO I WAIT?

Waiting is not something that we come by naturally in our culture. Whether we are in a line at the grocery store, caught in construction traffic, waiting our turn at the Department of Motor Vehicles, we don't like to wait. We want to be waited upon quickly and efficiently. Yet, here I am asking you to wait. If you are a type A personality like me, waiting can seem not only difficult but also illogical. Since we have established that "waiting" can be an active endeavor, let's look at some ways and valid reasons to use this time for our active benefit. Let me suggest six areas that you can focus on during this time.

Honorable Behavior

First, we want to examine our behavior and make sure that it is honoring to both God and our spouse and not retaliatory in nature. I have seen Christians who have managed to justify cruel, venomous, spiteful behavior because of something that their spouse has done. Yet, there is never anything that our spouse can do that can make that behavior OK. As Talley states, "All these circumstance reveal is the real you—the kind of person you really are inside."[7] You may believe that your spouse has done all kinds of awful things to hurt you. But as soon as you respond with hateful behavior, you may actually discover where the real problem lies. Who is the real you? Use this time to find out and to focus on loving behaviors even when it is hard. God is not in the business of asking you do something that you cannot do. He knows that you are capable of loving the unlovely, and this is your opportunity to do just that.

Building A Healthy Community

The second item that you want to be aware of is that you need others. When we are hurting, our natural tendency is to withdraw into our shell. Yet, this is counterproductive to what we need. We need others for support and care. We need safe people who we can lean on. I am speaking here of people of the same sex. The last thing that you need to do is to find support in someone of the opposite sex. It is too easy for that to go from "crying on the shoulder" to "comfort in the arms" of another. That is exactly what you don't need. But you do need reliable and faithful friends who you can count on; Friends who will listen, hold you account-able, comfort, and speak truth into your life. My good friend Al spent many lunch times at Carl's Jr. with me doing just that over a Western Bacon Cheeseburger.

As odd as this may sound, this is also an important time for you to reach out and help others. I remember a client who was going through a divorce who spent time with other guys repairing cars for women who had limited resources. This was a reward-ing time, and helping others is a part of God's healing process for all parties.

Practicing the Art of Forgiveness

The third item on our "waiting agenda" is to address the issue of forgiveness. In Matthew 18, Jesus teaches us about forgiveness in the parable of the unmerciful servant. In this narrative, we find that a servant was in great debt to his master, probably equivalent to millions of dollars. The servant could not pay the debt and begged for additional time to take care of it. Instead of just granting more time, the master actually cancelled the debt and allowed the servant to go. This man, whose debt had been forgiven, then went out and found someone who owed him a few dollars. This man also couldn't pay and begged for additional time. Yet, this man who had been forgiven so much was unwilling to waive the small debt owed to him. As the story got back to the original master, he became enraged and threw the servant whose debt had been cancelled into jail to be tortured until the debt was completely repaid. Jesus then said, *"This is how my heavenly Father will treat each of you unless you forgive your brother from your heart"* (Matt. 18:35). Our Father has wiped away a million dollars worth of sins, granting us complete forgiveness and redeeming our very lives. Yet, I have seen many separated or divorced individuals who are completely unwilling to forgive their spouses for the few dollar wrongs that have been committed against them. How will God respond?

This is a time of learning to understand the breadth of God's forgiveness in our lives and in turn learning to extend that to the person for whom we may feel such animosity. This step may take some time, so it is a good thing that we have some while we are "waiting."

Managing Emotions

Our fourth step is to address what are frequently "overwhelming emotions." The feelings that we are experiencing toward our spouse, about ourselves, with regard to our hurt, and our fears about the future seem to take on a life of their own. It seems to be way more than I can even begin to deal with. So, I don't. I may shut down, become paralyzed, and crawl into a hole. Yet, this is not productive. Remember, we are determined to "wait" in an active, productive manner. So what can we do? I really like what Chapman suggests when he says,

> Concentrate on small, attainable goals at first. Do not look at the rest of your life as one great unknown. Make plans for today. What can you do today that will be constructive? As you fill your days with meaningful activity, hope for the future will grow. As you come to understand yourself, develop yourself, accept yourself, you enhance the prospects of reconciliation with your spouse.[8]

Certainly every day will not always be emotionally easy and productive. But it is a game plan that will slowly prove to be more beneficial than not, and with time and effort it will grow more consistent. Don't beat yourself up over the bad days. Cut yourself some slack. Chalk the bad days up as a learning experience and become more healthy and productive tomorrow.

Finding a Solution for Loneliness in God

God has designed us for intimacy, especially intimacy with Him. As we become involved with our spouse, our kids, and our friends, God frequently gets relegated to some kind of Sunday ritual or morning routine. As we lose an important spousal relationship, we may find ourselves experiencing incredible, gut-wrenching loneliness. While I don't want to sound insensitive to your pain or overly spiritual, I want to make a point that loneliness is intensified because we have tried to use our spouse to meet needs that only God can. This may mask the void, but it never fills it. When our spouse is gone, our lack of intimacy with our creator is amplified. This "waiting" is the perfect opportunity for us to begin to truly get to know and connect with God in ways that we may never have before. Filling your need for intimacy with God frees you to cultivate relationships with your spouse and others from desire, as opposed to neediness, which is a much healthier place to be.

Mastering the Steps that lead to Stability

My final suggestion of how to "wait" is also where these other steps are leading and that is to becoming stable. As you go through a time of separation or divorce, you may feel as though your life is founded on quick sand. There is no stability, and the Colorado weather forecast is more stable than your life. If that is the case, then you know just how unstable and unpredictable that truly is. Becoming stable involves making good choices about behavior, enlisting the support of others, forgiving my spouse who has wronged me, tackling my out of control emotions in bite size chunks, and building an intimate, unshakeable relationship with God Almighty. It also requires being able to face yourself each day, acknowledging your situation, and stating, as Talley says,

> I am going to make it work. I am going to balance my life out. Frankly, you are not ready to be married until you are content to be single, that is, until you get both feet on the ground and establish yourself.[9]

As I have stated, "waiting" is an active process, and it is not always easy. Talley also calls us to reality when he says,

> The fact is that none of us has the inner resources to park for long on the line of reconciliation. We need a support system, and the best support system is Jesus Christ living in us through the Holy Spirit.[10]

He goes on to suggest that as we read Paul's letters to the Ephesians, Philippians, and Colossians, we learn to say with Paul, *"I can do everything through him* [Christ] *who gives me strength"* (Phil. 4:13). Again, I am not offering some trite spiritual platitude here. I am suggesting that you embrace life-changing, biblical truth.

FACING REAL ISSUES

Acceptance

In the ongoing process of "waiting," there are some realities that need to be acknowledged. I often overhear people refer to a situation and say, "Well, it is what it is." While I am the first to respond with "Duh—you think?" because of the obviousness of the statement, it does have a place when it comes to accepting the reality of the way things are. Individuals going through an unwanted separation or divorce will often have great difficulty accepting what is taking place. They will fight it and deny its reality until the cows come home. So, the first reality in facing issues is to accept your situation, whatever it may be, and determine a plan of action to move forward to the next step of your life. I am not talking about giving up and finding another relationship, but I am referring to the need to move forward in your own healing and growth. According to Chapman,

> Marriages fail...for three primary reasons: (1) lack of an intimate relationship with God, (2) lack of an intimate relationship with your mate, or (3) lack of an intimate understanding and acceptance of yourself.[11]

Acceptance

Reality number two is accepting the truth of this statement and recognizing that these are all issues that we have addressed in our steps to becoming stable as discussed above.

Waiting Leads to Change

A third reality is that waiting, instead of rushing and pushing for a quick resolution to my unsettledness, can lead to amazing changes. We sometimes believe that our only choice is to remain in a miserable marriage or else get a divorce. Yet, there is a third choice that often gets overlooked. A study was released in 2002 that was titled "Does Divorce Make People Happy?" It demonstrated some astonishing results.

Using data from the National Survey of Family and Households (a nationally representative survey with a wide-ranging data set that looks at all kinds of family outcomes, including happiness), the research team studied 5,232 married adults who were interviewed in the late 1980s. Of these individuals, 645 reported being unhappily married. Five years later, these same adults—some had divorced or separated and some had stayed married—were interviewed again.

The results of these interviews were astounding. They revealed that two-thirds of the unhappily married spouses who stayed married were actually happier five years later! Among those who initially rated their marriages as "very unhappy" but remained together, nearly 80 percent considered themselves "happily married" and "much happier" five years later.

Surprisingly, the opposite is found to be true for those who divorced. A study conducted by the Institute for American Values confirmed that divorce frequently fails to make people happy because, while it might provide a respite from the pain associated with a bad marriage, it also introduces a host of complex, new emotional and psychological difficulties over which the parties involved have little control. They include child-custody battles, emotionally scarred children, economic hardships, loneliness, future romantic disappointments, and so on. This helps explain why, of *all* the unhappy spouses in the initial survey, only 19 percent of those who got divorced or separated were happy five years later.[12]

These figures stunningly demonstrate one of the benefits of "standing and waiting."

Your Past Doesn't Dictate Your Future

A fourth reality is that failures in the past do not condemn your marriage for the future. Many couples report that there has just been too much pain, too much damage, and too much failure to ever be able to recover. Yet, this feeling and experience of failure can be turned into a marriage rebirth. Communication and levels of understanding can improve, and couples can actually find fulfillment in a relationship that once seemed destined for the trash heap. When couples have committed themselves to the process of reconciliation, I have seen many of them experience a marriage that is better than they have had in 20 years and that they had been convinced was unachievable. Past failure does not preclude hope for the future.

Your Spouse Still Has a Choice

Reality number five is that there are no guarantees. You can only control and are only responsible for yourself. Your happiness is not dependent upon the actions and responses of your spouse. With hard work, many spouses will seemingly come to their senses. But not all do. You may walk through all of the steps that I have discussed. You may follow all of the reconciliation suggestions in the next chapter. You may honestly do all that you know to do, and do it all in a loving manner, only to find that your spouse has walked away. It could happen. But if it does, you will know that you have honestly tried everything possible. You will have honored God, your spouse, and will have grown healthier in the process. Just know that even when we do it all correctly, the results aren't always what we think they should be.

Knowing When to Let Go

A sixth reality is that there is a time for holding on and there is a time for letting go. Knowing when your diligent efforts for reconciliation have not achieved their desired result is important. You may have done all that you could, and your spouse has still continued and successfully acquired his or her divorce. Now you must accept it. Of course, even then, this doesn't mean that reconciliation isn't still possible. I have seen couples remarry after they have divorced and been apart for as long as five years. But for now, you must accept that you are divorced and move forward in being the person that God has called you to be.

One final reality, and I want to stress that it is a reality, *"Rejoice in the Lord always. I will say it again: Rejoice!"* (Phil. 4:4). Paul is not saying to be happy about your circumstances. That would be foolish and an absolute denial of reality. What he is saying is that, in spite of your circumstances, you can rejoice in the Lord. He is faithful, He will sustain, He will never leave us, He loves us, and He has forgiven us with a grace beyond what we can understand. He will redeem our life and, as hard as it may be to see in the moment, He will give us a future. Rejoice in the Lord always!

AFFIRMATION

While I absolutely and honestly believe in all that I have stated about the benefits of the standing and waiting process, I don't want to pretend that it is easy. I have been there. It is one of the most difficult and often painful things that you will ever do. There will be some days that you will declare it impossible, want to give up, and look for a quick emotional fix. There will be other days when it will seem more doable. Your emotions will peak and valley and seem very undependable. During these times, cling to the Word and what you know as opposed to what you feel. Ask God to inhabit both your rational thoughts as well as your irrational feelings. Hang on to what you know to be true.

I want to close this chapter with an encouragement that I received during my own dark time in the valley. It is titled "A Stander's Affirmation" and comes from Rejoice Marriage Ministries.[13]

I AM STANDING FOR THE HEALING OF MY MARRIAGE!...I will not give up, give in, give out, or give over 'til that healing takes place. I made a vow, I said the words, I gave the pledge, I gave a ring, I took a ring, I gave myself, I trusted GOD, and said the words, and meant the words...in sickness and in health, in sorrow and in joy, for better or for worse, for richer or for poorer, in good times and in bad...so I am standing NOW, and will not sit down, let down, slow down, calm down, fall down, look down, or be down 'til the breakdown is torn down!

I refuse to put my eyes on outward circumstances, or listen to prophets of doom, or buy into what is trendy, worldly, popular, convenient, easy, quick, thrifty, or advantageous...nor will I settle for a cheap imitation of God's real thing, nor will I seek to lower God's standard, twist God's will, rewrite God's word, violate God's covenant, or accept what God hates, namely divorce!

In a world of filth, I will stay pure; surrounded by lies, I will speak the truth; where hopelessness abounds, I will hope in God: where revenge is easier, I will bless instead of curse; and where the odds are stacked against me, I will trust in God's faithfulness.

I am a STANDER, and I will not acquiesce, compromise, quarrel or quit. I have made the choice, set my face, entered the race, believed the Word, and trusted God for all the outcome. I will allow neither the reaction of my spouse, nor the urging of my friends, nor the advice of my loved ones, nor economic hardship, nor the prompting of the devil make me let up, slow up, blow up, or give up 'til my marriage is healed.

CHAPTER TWELVE

SAVING YOUR MARRIAGE

"Keep your eyes open before marriage, and half shut afterwards."

—BENJAMIN FRANKLIN[1]

Chuck and Amanda were not much different than many young couples. They had met in high school, hung out with the same group of friends, and enjoyed each other's company. Following high school, marriage seemed like the normal and appropriate thing to do.

While they loved each other and had really liked hanging out together, being married and spending everyday together brought out some differences that they had ignored while dating. Neither one had given their differences much thought. They both assumed that once they were married, the differences would take care of themselves. Actually, if they looked deeper, the expectations were a little more self-centered than that. They each thought that their new partner would just begin to want to spend time doing the same things that they did. But what happened? You already know the answer. Following the wedding ceremony, they both wanted to do their own things.

Chuck was an avid sportsman. Every summer, he liked to play on one (sometimes two!) softball teams. In the wintertime, it was basketball and skiing with friends, and other times of the year he was active on a volleyball team. He had managed his life this way for years and didn't see any reason for it to change. Surely, since he and Amanda were married now, she would want to join him in these activities. But as you have guessed, that was not the case.

Amanda liked to visit with her girlfriends, do some shopping, and watch chick flicks. Chuck had no interest in these things. So, while Amanda might be watching a movie in one room, Chuck would be downstairs playing video games.

Each felt that the other person didn't really love him or her. Otherwise, they would be with them doing what they wanted to do. Neither one was considering how his or her actions were affecting the other person.

Then, as though the stalemate wasn't difficult enough, they had a baby. This new bundle of joy was exciting at first and seemed as though he may be the binding force that would help to draw these two individuals emotionally together. But after a few weeks, the picture took on a familiar look. Amanda would get off work, pick-up their son from day care, prepare dinner, feed and bathe the baby, and get him to bed. Chuck would get off work, come home and change, and go meet his buddies for basketball. Upon returning from the gym, he might hold their son for a few minutes so that Amanda could change clothes. Then while she put the baby to bed, he would watch television.

As you can imagine, it didn't take long for resentments to build up. Add these to the already existing self-centered differences and there was a fireworks display sitting next to a lit blowtorch just waiting for the right connection to cause a seemingly irreparable explosion.

When Chuck and Amanda came into my office this was their plight. They described themselves as "oil and water." They were nothing alike. They didn't have any of the same interests, and as Amanda was quick to say, "They just did life differently." They felt that this marriage was a mistake, and now they wanted to know how to get out. Surely, there was someone else out there that was more like Amanda and someone out there that was more like Chuck that they could both find and with that find happiness and fulfillment. They were tired of being miserable and alone and living in quiet desperation.

Oh yes, they had considered how this would affect their son, but they just didn't see anyway to repair the damage. They could still remember the times when they used to enjoy one another's company, but those times seemed like a distant dream. They admitted that they still cared about each other, but again, they were tired of living alone in a marriage. They saw no other way than to end this marriage with the least pain possible.

It is amazing how many couples come in like this and only see options of misery or divorce. They usually fail to see a third option, reconciliation and restoration. This is the option that I introduced to Chuck and Amanda, and it resulted in a marriage that they long ago had given up hope that they could ever have. But they could—and they did.

RECONCILIATION

I have read many definitions of the word *reconcile*. Webster would say that the word means "to restore to friendship or harmony; to settle or resolve differences."[2] While, another dictionary defines reconcile this way: "to restore to union and friendship after estrangement, and to make agreement of things seemingly opposite or inconsistent."[3]

For the purposes of our discussion I am going to borrow a definition from Jim Talley who states that,

> The primary goal of reconciliation...is to enable those
> of you who are angry, bitter, and hostile to be friendly

again and bring back harmony, whether you are separated, divorced, or remarried.[4]

I think that this is a great place to start. Reconciliation and restoration are not necessarily the same thing, and we will talk more about restoration later. But I want to emphasize that reconciliation is first and foremost a prerequisite to any hope of restoration. Yet, even when a restoration of the marriage is not possible, perhaps due to a remarriage, reconciliation is always possible.

Some people are just looking to get back together. They reason that, "If we are together, then we are reconciled and restored." I can place my cat Patches and my dog Jolee in the same kennel. They will be together, but I assure you they will be anything except reconciled. Reconciliation is so much more than that.

You may currently find yourself in one of these situations: living under the same roof but occupying different rooms in the house and living in a cold silence; separated and living in different locations; in the process of divorce proceedings, just waiting for the final gavel to fall and give it finality; divorced but aching for it not to be; or divorced and remarried, but continuing to deal with your ex-spouse over everything from finances to custody issues. My admonition to you is that some form of reconciliation is possible in all of these situations. If you are hoping to restore a relationship, reconciliation is an absolute necessity. We will look at ways to approach this, some dos and don'ts, things to be prepared for, steps to take, and even sources of strength to complete the task.

Time is a Good Thing

The first, and probably the most difficult, concept to grasp is that time is a good thing. I know, as you sit in your house alone, worrying about your spouse's activities, wanting to somehow fill the void of your own loneliness, time and waiting do not seem like a good thing. Yet, it is a must! This is an opportunity for you to get emotionally, and perhaps even physically, healthier than you have been in a long time. We talked about the benefits of "waiting" in the previous chapter.

It is interesting to watch separated couples do what I would call the "reconciliation dance." This is a dance where one person is in a place desiring to work on the marriage, while the other is not. Yet, given a little time, that person may come around and be ready to give things another look, only to find that the first partner is no longer interested. It seems that the parties usually cycle through a reconciliation phase with some regularity. If that is the case, then time is important.

If you desire reconciliation with your spouse, it is imperative that, whether you are separated or divorced, you not date anyone other than your spouse for two reasons. First, you are probably carrying around emotional baggage with open-heart wounds that do not need to be taken into a new relationship. The other person deserves someone a little more "whole," and that is probably not you at the moment. The second reason is that time allows your former mate to cycle back into a reconciliation mindset. If you have already moved on to another relationship then that reconciliation door is probably no longer open to your mate.

I want to remind you again that one of your first priorities is to become more emotionally stable and healthy. I recall a friend of mine who went through a divorce a few years ago. While he was anxious to not be alone and to find someone new, he also knew that he was not healthy. Yet, he had been living emotionally unhealthy for so many years, he wouldn't have known healthy if it bit him. As he began his journey of healing, he kept periodically asking me, "Do you think I am emotionally healthy?" or "How will I know when I am emotionally healthy?" It takes time and work. Without intentional, deep, soul-searching work, it will take even longer, and health still may elude you. However, with appropriate, self-examination, peeling of layers, and rebuilding, it can happen. But it will still take time. There is no substitute.

How long will it take? I have been asked that more times than I can count, and I wish there was a standard answer, but there is not. It really does have to do with a multitude of factors. My encouragement is to ask yourself some important questions. Are you stable enough to make a time commitment toward reconciliation? I am not talking a week or two here. Can you make a commitment toward this process for say a year or two or longer? Many feel that they just can't be by themselves, which is a sure sign of psychological instability. Are you willing to learn to be single and content? Until you can truly be OK by yourself, you have more deficits than assets to take into any relationship—be that with your spouse or any other person. This is a perfect time to develop good, same-sex friendships. Without them, you will look to opposite-sex relationships to fulfill all of your relationship needs, and that kind of desperation will smother and kill the relationship.

You have to ask yourself whether you can learn to make it on your own financially. This can be important in rebuilding your "stable" self. Probably a more difficult question to ask, if you are the one that initiated the divorce proceedings, is whether you can stop that process and put it all on hold while you pursue reconciliation?

There are many other questions to address regarding how you react to your spouse's friends, your in-laws, whether or not you are in a support group, and so on. I have just raised a few to get you thinking about the importance of, and the commitment that is needed, to really give reconciliation a shot.

It is easy to look at this and think, "This is just too hard. I would much rather just find someone else and start again." As I have mentioned in other places, I would contend that when all is said and done, just starting over really isn't the easier option, but it certainly may look like it right now. We have to remember that reconciliation is a choice. It is a choice against separation and divorce. It is a choice to pursue the type of marital intimacy that

God desires for us. Yet, while it is a choice, Talley points out that it is not optional.

> One of the hardest things to get across to a formerly married single is that reconciliation is not an option for the Christian intent on obeying God. The practical outworking of this is illustrated in Paul's letter to the Philippians, where that marvelous passage about being anxious for nothing is preceded by that admonition we looked at earlier: *I plead with Euodia and I plead with Syntyche to agree with each other in the Lord*" (Phil. 4:2). Imagine coming to church one Sunday morning, and the pastor reads a letter from an evangelist who held a crusade in town a year earlier. Suddenly you start to feel your face getting red as the pastor reads, "I urge Tim and Sherri to live in harmony in the Lord." You have been unwilling to move back to the line of reconciliation, and word somehow reached the evangelist. That is exactly what happened in the church in Philippi. The apostle Paul felt it was vital for Christians to be reconciled to one another.[5]

God pleads with us for reconciliation in our relationships. Paul wrote:

> *All this is from God, who reconciled us to himself through Christ and gave us the ministry of reconciliation: that God was reconciling the world to himself in Christ, not counting men's sins against them. And he has committed to us the message of reconciliation* (2 Corinthians 5:18-19).

The Gospel of Jesus is that reconciliation is possible. God has worked for that throughout our history. He has given Himself to us, time and time again, in the face of mockery, betrayal, and rejection. He continues to pursue us and to pursue reconciliation with us. He models it for us and asks the same of us in our relationships. God did not create marriage for divorce, but for reconciled, intimate, selfless, beautiful relationships.

If you are ready to commit yourself to a process of reconciliation, be aware that you are liable to face some of the same things that God faces with us. Even in His perfect plan of redemption and renewal, He was outright rejected, discarded, laughed at, minimized, and treated as unwanted and unneeded. Know that as you pursue reconciliation with your spouse, in all likelihood you will be responded to in some of these same unkind and discounting ways. But remember, this is not a one-shot attempt. It is a commitment to a process that takes time. The sufficiency of God's grace will see you through this.

STEPS TOWARD RECONCILIATION

While reconciliation is possible, it is not easy nor is it automatic. Just because you may desire it doesn't mean that it will come about. You will have to be intentional—very intentional. I remember a comment made by a young woman following a concert pianist's performance. She said, "I would give anything to be able to play like that." The reality, however, is that she wouldn't really. She likes the idea of being able to play like the professional, but she is neither willing to spend the time learning nor the hours practicing that would be required to enable her to perform at that level. If she would really "give anything," then she would have done so and would be able to play accordingly.

The same is true of reconciliation. It is easy to say that you want reconciliation, but I would ask, "Do you really?" Are you willing to sacrifice of yourself, get past your pride, and really do what is necessary to achieve it? If you are currently separated, going through a divorce, contemplating a divorce, or even divorced but hoping to restore the marriage, then I want to suggest eight steps that you can take in this endeavor toward reconciliation.

Step One—Make a Reconciliation Commitment

As we discussed earlier, you need to make a commitment to a substantial time frame during which your focus will be on reconciliation with your mate. This is not a time to date or consider other relationships. For those of you who are not divorced, remember that if you are not free to marry, then you are not free to date either. If your time commitment is for a year or two years or whatever other length of time you may decide, you are saying that during this period, you are going to view your focus, your energy, and your efforts through this filter of reconciliation. Are your thoughts, words, and actions in line with your goal to be reconciled? I would even suggest that you begin to journal. Write down what it is you are committing yourself to. Make regular entries about what and how you are doing in your efforts. Keep track of your progress including mistakes and successes.

Step Two—Accept God's Authority

We live in a society that prides itself on the fact we are tolerant. We are tolerant of other religions, various nationalities, differing lifestyles, and varying sets of moral standards. Ethics have become relative in a post-modern society. Each person decides for him- or herself what is right. This same philosophy has infected the marriage relationship. Millions of people who label themselves as Christians have gone through the tragedy of divorce. It seems that being a Christian has been very little help in sparing them from the pain that a non-Christian would experience. Why is this? Oftentimes it comes down to an inability to accept God's authority. God has given clear instructions regarding marriage, divorce, and reconciliation. We wouldn't expect nonbelievers to follow those instructions. Yet, we would hope that followers of

Jesus would submit to His desires for our lives. We would expect God's children to heed His instructions.

In order for this to take place, Christians need to remove the word *divorce* from their vocabulary—literally. The use of this word should be stricken from ever being used in a marriage relationship. C. Bruce White, author of *Marriage, Divorce and Reconciliation*, puts it this way:

> We ought to think of divorce as a vulgar word, a profane word! If you never entertain the idea; if you never discuss that particular possibility; if that option is never available; if you just do not use that word, then of course the potential for that developing is not nearly as great.[6]

We should instead replace this word in our vocabulary with the word *reconciliation*.

Step Three—Change Begins With You

In a perfect world, all would be fair. It seems only fair that if I begin to make changes that I need to make, my spouse ought to make changes that she needs to make as well. And she would—in a perfect world. However, as you may have noticed in your years of experience, we live in anything but a perfect world. Therefore, the reality is that change begins with one person, and in this case that one person is going to be you. I counseled individuals who want to understand, clarify, and gain insight first. While these can sometimes be helpful, it is important to understand that insight leads to insight—not change. Change leads to change.

In other words, I have to make a decision to change and then begin to do it, even if I don't fully grasp all of the understanding as to why. Here's an example. Whenever your spouse makes a mistake, you feel that it is your God-given duty to point it out. When you do this, your spouse feels belittled and devalued. You think that pointing out mistakes so that they can be corrected is a good thing, and you don't understand why you should have to change this. Even without fully understanding, you are able to see that your spouse doesn't like it when you do this. It pushes him away, and he doesn't want to be around you. Is this what you want? Probably not. Therefore, you begin (without great insight) to make needed change. When you do, it will eventually lead to a different reaction from him. Again, change leads to change. Don't wait on your spouse to change. You take the lead in doing what you need to do. You don't do it because your spouse is changing too. You do it because it is the best and right thing to do.

Step Four—Get Rid of Bitterness

> Do not let any unwholesome talk come out of your mouths, but only what is helpful for building others up according to their needs, that it may benefit those who listen. And do not grieve the Holy Spirit of God, with whom you were sealed for the day of redemption. Get rid of all bitterness, rage and anger, brawling and slander, along with every form of malice. Be kind and compassionate to one another, forgiving each other, just as Christ God forgave you (Ephesians 4:9-32).

Yes, I understand that you feel that your spouse has severely wronged you, and you just can't seem to get past it. But understand that hanging on to that bitterness will keep you stuck and unable to move forward. Paul's instructions are that we get rid of it, we let go of those old resentments, and we extend forgiveness to our spouse just as God has done to us. If you choose to feed the anger and allow it to live in your heart, the bitterness will remain. It is your choice as to what you will do with it. Michelle Weiner-Davis states:

> As long as you are holding on to resentments of the past, you can't be forgiving. As long as you are not

forgiving, you can't be loving. As long as you aren't loving, you can't do what it takes to make your marriage work.[7]

Step Five—Address Your Own Failures

We are so very good at blaming. If it were an Olympic event, the field of qualified competitors would be wide. John P. Splinter, author of *The Complete Divorce Recovery Handbook*, notes that

> When we encounter personal failure, we tend to resist being completely honest with ourselves about our failure. We are more comfortable casting blame onto others, circumstances, our past, our upbringing, the failures of our parents, our spouse, our financial situation, our education, our body or face, our social circle, even God. We rationalize. We blame. We repress. We fight against accepting personal responsibility, and in doing so we become tied to our failures and the guilt and shame they drag behind them. We also become tied to the probability of making the same mistakes in the future.[8]

During this period of reconciliation, it is imperative that you begin to stop placing blame outside of yourself. This isn't to minimize the wrongs that the other person may have committed. But it is a realization that you can't change or fix them. All you can modify is your own behavior. What have your contributions been to the demise of the relationship? These may be hurtful things that you have done or loving behaviors that you have failed to do. Are you having difficulty finding your failures? Let me ask you this. Are there things that you could have done that would have made the relationships better? Without fail, individuals always answer this question with an affirmative. So, I would encourage you to begin there. As you peel back the layers of your missteps,

I can assure you that you will begin to find more and more work that needs to be done.

Some fear that if they begin to honestly look at their shortcomings, the search will never end because they know that deep down inside there are many. However, my experience has shown that when people begin to authentically examine their stuff, a weight is lifted and true freedom from emotional oppression begins to take place. As that happens, the positive impact on the relationship can be pleasantly surprising. Take the risk. The fear is unfounded and the results are more than worth the risk.

Step Six—Develop Emotional Stability

Do not be anxious about anything, but in everything, by prayer and petition, with thanksgiving, present your requests to God. And the peace of God, which transcends all understanding, will guard your hearts and your minds in Christ Jesus (Philippians 4:6-7).

If we will overlay this instruction on our life, we will have taken the first step toward emotional stability.

I find emotional overdependence to be a frequent problem for both men and women. I see it early on in the teen years. A girl feels that she has to have a boyfriend or else there is something wrong with her. A boy feels that he is somehow lacking if he doesn't have a girl on his arm. I see individuals who are so dependent upon someone else that they are not complete, and certainly not happy, if they don't have that other person. This is not healthy. We were designed to stand as individuals first and to develop as couples second. This unhealthy need to lean on another has caused some to immediately look for someone else when their spouse leaves. They can't seem to stand on their own two feet. They are not complete and have no identity without someone else attached to them. Again, this is not healthy!

If you fit this description, and many will, it is time to take Paul's words to heart and begin to make choices that will allow you to begin to stand on your own, even when it feels awkward and lonely. Let that feeling remind you that you are taking needed healthy steps toward becoming a stable individual.

Step Seven—Develop Action Goals.

I always find it interesting when speaking with a teenager about his or her failing grades. When I ask what they will do to improve those grades next semester, I will typically get a response along the lines of "I will try harder." What that tells me is that he or she can probably expect a failing grade next semester as well. The reason for this is that the student has given me a vague goal with no plans behind it. An action goal would be if he or she said, "Well, I am going to set aside two hours a day to study. I will do my homework at the kitchen table where it is quiet, and I will ask my parents to look it over when I am done." This plan would have a much greater chance of success.

The same concept holds true for marriages. If an individual says to me, "I am going to begin to fix dinner three times a week so that my wife can have a break when she gets home from work," I know that this may really happen. However, if he had simply said that his goal was "to be more loving," I would see this as pretty vague with limited chance for success.

In that vein of thinking, I want to suggest seven action goals that you might begin to pursue. This is by no means an exhaustive list, but rather one to get you primed.

1. Find specific ways in which to show your mate honor and respect.

2. Don't criticize your mate.

3. Make a list of ways that you can express God's love to your mate. Then begin by picking one of the ways and acting upon it.

4. Come up with a list of irritating and annoying things that you do to your mate that you will stop doing. Select one and purposefully avoid doing that behavior.

5. Show kindness. Do this with your words as well as with your actions. Make a list of kind acts that you perform and begin to do them.

6. Build up your mate instead of tearing him or her down. Remember Paul's words from Ephesians,

Do not let any unwholesome talk come out of your mouths, but only what is helpful for building others up according to their needs, that it may benefit those who listen (Ephesians 5:29).

Find specific ways in which to do this.

7. Five to One Positives. Research has demonstrated that it takes five positive behaviors to offset one negative one and its impact upon a marriage. When the ratio falls below this, marriages typically experience trouble. Therefore, work to demonstrate at least five behaviors that are positive in nature for every one that is negative. David and Jan Stoop offer their advice about positive behaviors in their book, *The Complete Marriage Book.*

Positive behaviors include knowing and talking more about our partner's needs and desires, affirmations and praise, affection, date nights, a daily ten-second kiss— all the things we love to do while courting each other.[9]

Step Eight—Constantly Seek God's Help.

A commitment to a process of reconciliation is not an easy one or for the faint of heart. However, not only is it one that God asks you to do, but it is one that He will provide you the strength to see through. One of the fruits of the Spirit is self-control (see Gal. 5:23). All of the steps that I have outlined require this particular fruit. It is nice to know that God doesn't ask us to do something without giving us the tools and the strength to pull it off. He does not leave us powerless. He has given us the Holy Spirit, and by His comforting, strengthening power, we are able to respond to our spouse in ways that we could never do on our own. As a matter of fact, it is probably for this very reason, doing it on your own, that you find yourself in your current situation. Rest assured. God will provide the resources to enable you to experience a far richer marriage. He will provide you what you need during this process of reconciliation.

RECONCILIATION WITH YOUR EX

As I mentioned earlier in this chapter, reconciliation is not just for those trying to get back together. It is also for those who are divorced and even remarried. Remember, reconciliation is about being friendly again and coming back to a place of harmony. If you have children with your ex-spouse, then you will continue to deal with your ex, in some manner, for years to come, perhaps for the rest of your life. Most ex-relationships are ones of acrimony and hostility. How life-draining that can be. Wouldn't it be much better if it weren't that way? I want to encourage you in a couple of important directions that I think can be helpful when it comes to reconciling with your ex-spouse.

Resolve to parent in a manner that is honoring God, your children, your ex-spouse, and yourself. Children are not pawns, trophies, or weapons to be used against your former spouse. Children are a gift and a responsibility from God. Together, you and your ex-spouse must find a way to honestly put your children's needs above your personal hurt. Assume for a minute that your ex-spouse loves your children just as much as you do. Surely, if that is true, the two of you can begin to find a way to parent in a manner that honors all involved.

Learn that peace is better than conflict. God calls us to live at peace with each other. I can't begin to tell you how many people that I see who experience physical and emotional dysfunction because they have chosen a lifestyle of conflict and animosity over one of peace. Review the previous eight steps and see how they might apply to you in order for you to experience reconciliation with your ex-spouse. The effort will be worth it.

RESTORATION

Restoration carries with it the concept of bringing something back to its previous condition or its former status. Yet, I would suggest that it even goes beyond that. Couples frequently talk about restoration with the idea that they want things returned to the way that they were. However, when we more closely examine "the way things were," we often find that they were a mess that had the potential to lead to a chasm in the relationship, which they did. The truth of the matter is, couples rarely want things the way that they were; what they actually want is what they dreamed they would have when they got married. They have probably never had that, but would love to have it.

I wish I could give you a formula to follow so that all could be restored. However, it is an ongoing process, not a formula. I will suggest a few steps below to help you in the process. But please remember that it is *an ongoing process.*

Step One—Begin by following the steps to Reconciliation

Step Two—Rebuild Trust

Yes, trust can be rebuilt, but it must start with a foundation of integrity. It is possible that you will be able to trust your spouse again and be trusted by your spouse, but a pattern of integrity and trustworthiness must come first. If you have not been a person of integrity then you have a challenge ahead of you. It is not easy, but I promise you that change, lasting change, is possible. Trust is essential to restoration.

Step Three—Realize that Marriage Won't Make You Happy

Many people keep searching for the right person to make them happy. They keep trading one partner in for another in their quest to be happy. Their mistake lies in the fact that happiness is a one-person show. You can't rely on someone else to make you happy. You must first learn to be satisfied with your own life, and then seek to develop a significant relationship by offering your God-given strengths to that relationship.

Step Four—Develop Physical, Emotional, and Spiritual Closeness

If a marriage is to be restored to what it was, or to what you both dreamed it would be, it will involve intimacy. Without physical intimacy, it is difficult for spouses to connect emotionally or spiritually. Emotional intimacy develops as intentional and consistent acts of love are built upon a foundation of trust. Spiritual closeness is probably one of the most ignored areas in marriages. It will never happen by itself, but it will be the result of two people intentionally working to develop this area. Structured times of study, authentic sharing of lives, openly bringing your prayer life together before the Lord, and honest communication are all components of spiritual closeness. When a couple truly becomes one, it will be as a result of intimacy in these three areas.

Step Five—Keep Doing All Of It

Dream out loud, talk, pray, play, honor each other, have fun, and then do it all again. These are important pieces to a restored relationship that achieve what was, and more importantly, what can be.

WHAT IF MY SPOUSE WON'T PLAY?

This is a commonly asked question when one person wants to work on the marriage while the other person doesn't. Certainly, it is much easier when both people come to the table ready to give their all and do what it takes to bring their marriage back to a place of honor. When two people do that, their marriage will most likely be salvaged, restored, and brought to heights unseen before. But what if your spouse has taken his toys and gone home? What if he or she refuses to come to the table and work toward restoration? What do you do?

There can be many reasons that this situation exists. It could be that he or she is in the middle of an affair and has no desire to give it up. Most affairs end within six months. If you can wait at the table of reconciliation, there may be an opportunity to get past this. Another possibility is that your spouse doubts the sincerity of your desire and efforts to change. Perhaps he has heard your intentions before, but has not seen any long-term follow through.

For whatever reason, you find yourself at the table alone and your spouse won't participate. What do you do?

I encourage you to *pursue righteousness.* God desires that you be in relationship with Him, that you obey His instructions, and that you live to His standard. This can be a challenge, especially when your spouse may be doing the exact opposite. You have to remind yourself that you do not answer to God for your spouse; you answer for you. Do what is right even when he or she doesn't. If you will do that, God will be there for tomorrow, and the next day, and the next.

Don't Give Up

As you sit at the reconciliation table alone, you will be very tempted to just give up. It would emotionally be much easier, but it will not lead to reconciliation. I promise you that I know what it is like to sit at the table, ready to work, with no one sitting across from you. But I also promise you that, if you will look to your side, you will find the Holy Spirit sitting there with you. You are not alone. Don't give up.

Keep Pushing to Make it Better

You may be separated, or you may still be living at home with your spouse in two very separate worlds. You try daily to do and say and be the right things, but it seems to no avail. Over time, you begin to wear down further and further emotionally until you just accept that it is the way that it is. As a result, you live in quiet desperation and resolve that this is just the way life is going to be. At this point, I want to stand up and scream—"Don't accept it! It is a lie!!!"

God has called us to journey with Him and grow each day in our walk. He calls us to do the same in our marriage. If you don't like the way things are in your marriage, ask for what you want, give the other person what they need, and work to improve it. Don't just accept mediocrity. I was in my office the other day with a couple who has been married 24 years. They had not been on a vacation without the children in almost that long. The husband felt that he was not a priority to his wife, because she never seemed to want to get away with just him. Until the conversation in my office, she didn't know that he felt that way. How sad. This has gone on for years, and they have just accepted the way that it was without understanding. And yet, just a little push to make it better by one or the other could have improved things years ago. Again, don't accept that it has to be this way. It can be better, and you can be the one to initiate work towards that goal.

Set Yourself Up

Finally, I encourage you to *set yourself up.* It is interesting to watch and listen to people as they observe others. I hear comments such as, "They get all the breaks," "They are just so lucky," and "Everything good comes to them." People make these comments as though they are somehow randomly left out of the "good things in life" arena. While I do understand that some people get breaks and others don't, I also know that many times, individuals set themselves up for whatever happens.

For example, I can take two people and enter them in a marathon. One person has been sitting on the couch for weeks consuming nothing but cake and ice cream and watching television non-stop. The other person has been out training each morning, running various distances and different speeds, and building up to 26 miles. The day of the marathon comes. Which of these two people is most likely to win the marathon? I know it seems like a silly question, but hopefully you get my point. The person who has been training will most likely win because he "set himself up" to do so by preparing in an appropriate manner. It will have nothing to do with being luckier or just having things go his way.

In like manner, I want you to set yourself up for success in this relationship. While I cannot guarantee that the results will be exactly what you are looking for, I can promise you that you are greatly increasing the odds by adopting this mindset.

If you have followed the steps of reconciliation and restoration, if you will pray without ceasing, if you will fix your hope on Jesus, and will continue to do these things on a daily basis, you will be prepared and set-up for good things to happen.

> *And we know that in all things God works for the good of those who love Him, who have been called according to His purpose* (Romans 8:28).

Notice that this Scripture doesn't just say that God will make good things happen for you. He says that to those who love Him and have been called according to His purpose. If that statement fits you, then it will be manifested in your actions of obedience, trust, and perseverance, as you rely upon God's strength.

COUNSELING

One item that I have not mentioned up to now is counseling. This component should actually be included in the steps for reconciliation, the steps for restoration, and the steps for when your spouse won't join you at the table. I believe that martial or individual therapy is an essential part of the reconciliation and restoration process. Trained Christian therapists can help unpeel your layers of self-deception, offer godly counsel and direction, teach you healthy marital skills, and so much more. They are equipped to walk with you and speak truth into your life.

One warning: there are gazillions of therapists out there, and I can tell you, from being in the field, that some of them are pretty scary and do more damage than good. Others are priceless and can play a significant role in saving your marriage. You need to find the latter. There are a number of ways to pursue this. You might talk with friends who have had successful therapeutic encounters. Talk with your minister about his or her recommendations. You can even contact some Christian organizations such as Focus on the Family and get a list of Christian counselors in your area.

Make sure that you are comfortable with the therapist and his or her values. Ask them questions until you feel certain that you are on the same page when it comes to your values about marriage and family. Remember, you are about to allow them to speak into your life in significant ways. You are about to give them the ability to influence your future. Be certain that this is the person that you want to trust to do that.

I know that people sometimes are afraid of the stigma of seeing a therapist. To that I say, get over it! If the transmission is about to fall out of your car, you won't hesitate to get the car to your mechanic before it is too late. I submit that your marriage is more important than your transmission. Get your marriage into the shop before it is too late. Get over your pride, get over yourself, and do what needs to be done to save what God has joined.

A COUPLE

I know that even with all that I have given you in this chapter, you still may feel that your situation is hopeless and irreparable. While I don't know about your particular situation, I want to share with you one that I do know about. This particular couple faced not one but several complicating problems that might be similar to something you are facing.

Dakota and Martha had been married just a few years when it began. Martha was a Christian while Dakota was not. From the commencement of the marriage, Martha knew that this might pose a problem, but she always felt that Dakota would come around with time. At first, he just ignored her prayers and her church involvement. However, with time this grew to resentment. He didn't like it that their Sunday mornings were interrupted by Martha always going to church. At first, he just told her how he felt, but with time his tone turned angry and developed into regular verbal abuse. This became such a struggle for Martha that she eventually pulled back from the church until she had separated herself completely.

Dakota liked to go out drinking on the weekends and wanted Martha to go as well. She tried to do this for a while, but she found the whole bar scene pretty distasteful and eventually stopped going all together. As you can imagine, this led to more resentment and more verbal abuse from Dakota.

By the time they had been married five years, Dakota was drinking every day, and it was beginning to affect his job performance. Martha attempted to talk with Dakota about her concerns, but this just sent him into a rage escalating both his drinking and his verbal abuse. One night, actually early morning, Martha received a call from one of Dakota's friends at the bar asking her to come and get him, as he was passed out. Dutifully she went, with help she got him to the car, and then somehow managed to help him into the house, where he passed out again on the couch.

As she was taking off his clothes, she came across a woman's phone number. With the help of a friend, she began to do some investigating and the results just about crumbled the remaining bits of her world. She discovered that Dakota had been having an affair for four months with this woman and that she wasn't the first. She also learned that he had been using heroin with her on a regular basis.

Martha was devastated. Her husband had become an unfaithful, drug abusing, alcoholic. He degraded her constantly, expressed contempt and disdain for her, and on top of all of this, had recently lost his job because he couldn't seem to stay sober long enough to go to work. She was at the end of her rope.

Well-meaning friends encouraged her to get out of there as quickly as possible and divorce the bum. They told her that she didn't have a marriage anymore. She initially agreed, but something inside kept gnawing at her—she had married Dakota for better for worse, for richer or poorer, and in sickness and in health for the rest of their lives. She knew that right now he was worse, poor, and sick. It would have been easy to leave—very easy. But she just knew that it wasn't that simple.

Martha contacted the minister at her old church and poured her broken heart out to him. He listened intently, saying very little. When she had just about emptied his Kleenex box, she said "I don't think that I have any tears left. I want to be faithful to

God and my husband, but I just don't know where to begin. I am spent."

This wise minister began to lay out for her God's desire and design for restoration in her marriage. Without going into all of the logistics of Martha's daily routines and struggles, I will tell you that she set out on a course to save her marriage when only she was willing to come to the table. She reconnected with a body of believers. She joined an Al-Anon group, and she began to set boundaries in place with regard to Dakota.

He didn't come around quickly. Actually, the drinking and verbal abuse became even worse for a while. But Martha continued loving her husband through godly actions, tough love approaches, and an unwavering faith that her husband could change with the power of God. The day finally came when Dakota hit rock bottom. He had spent the night at another woman's house and had become violent. The police were called, and Dakota found himself in jail with no one to call except his wife. Martha was there. This was a beginning.

Dakota could not understand why Martha was still around. Her behavior baffled him. As he watched her deal with him, he became convinced that either she had a dozen screws loose or there was something to this "God thing." He asked her if she could set up a time for him to talk with her minister.

That meeting was the beginning of a changed life. Over a period of time, Dakota gave his life to Jesus, checked himself into an alcohol treatment center, and began individual and marital therapy. Dakota's heart was changed, but it took more time and the love of his wife for the bad habits and mistreatment of her to completely be healed.

As a result, this couple not only salvaged their marriage, they restored it to a level beyond their original dreams. And they spent their 15th anniversary speaking at and leading a marriage retreat. Because one person remained faithful, and another was able to see enough to eventually come to the table, God was able to do an amazing restoration. This is great story because there are so many difficult components in it. But it is just one story. There are thousands more out there. Stories of seemingly broken, irreparable marriages about to be added to the divorce junk heap were pulled from the landfill in time for God to bring healing. I don't care what ugliness you have going on. I don't care how different your personalities may seem. I don't care if the two of you represent the term "oil and water." Every marriage is salvageable—if two people are willing to submit and do the work necessary to achieve true peace and harmony. God is here to tell you that reconciliation and restoration are within your grasp. Come to Him and be surprised.

SECTION FOUR

ACKNOWLEDGING AND PRACTICING GOD'S DESIGN

CHAPTER THIRTEEN

JUST WHAT IS GOD'S WILL?

"Be careful not to start or end a prayer by blindly saying, 'if it be Your will.' Rather, you should seek to know God's will in the situation and then base your prayer upon it."

—GLORIA HUMES[1]

"God's Will" is a very common phrase in Christian circles. Whether we are discussing where we will live, our occupational choice, or the person we are dating, we often do so under the umbrella of what we think God's will is. We talk, we seek counsel, we pray, and we think—all in an effort to discern this seemingly mysterious, and somewhat elusive, piece of information. If we could just determine this, all would be well—or so we think.

Certainly there are subjects where God's will seems less than crystal clear or perhaps comes with many options. Thus, we include a variety of pieces in an effort to best understand what He would want. However, on this particular subject matter—marriage and divorce—we can sit back and relax. We don't have to go through any mental gyrations in order to know God's will. He has made it relatively simple and pretty clear for us. So, let's examine this together.

WHAT DOES GOD DESIRE?

You may remember that Samuel said, *"To obey is better than sacrifice"* (1 Sam. 15:22). Jesus reemphasizes this when He says, *"If anyone loves Me, he will obey My teaching"* (John 14:23). We could look at a number of other Scriptures that teach that God desires we obey Him. Certainly, we try to rationalize how our disobedience will make sense in our particular situation, because it is for a good cause, and somehow the ends will justify the means. But I don't think that we will find that God necessarily takes this same view.

Remember when Ananias and Sapphira decided to donate a sizeable gift to the early church. They sold a piece of property and apparently wanted to donate some of the proceeds and keep some of them as well. While they were certainly free to do this, what they weren't free to do (at least not without some problems) was to lie to the church about it. Rather than just say "Hey we sold some land and want to donate part of the money," they chose to say they were donating all of the profit to the church. What happened when they came into the church and attempted to pull off this scheme? God took their lives. (See Acts 5:1-11). Whoa! But they were giving money to the church; they were still doing a good thing. Why was lying about it such a big deal when they were still doing a good thing? God didn't want deception and didn't need their money. What He wants is honesty and obedience.

Or what about Uzzah? *Who?* Uzzah: the man who seemed to have the best of intentions to protect God's stuff. In First Chronicles 13, we read about what happened when King David decided to have the ark of the Covenant moved. The Israelites were assembled and the priests had their assigned duties about how the ark was to be transported. By God's decree, only certain people were allowed to touch the ark.

They moved the ark of God from Abinadab's house on a new cart, with Uzzah and Ahio guiding it. David and all the Israelites were celebrating with all their might before God, with songs and with harps, lyres, tambourines, cymbals and trumpets. When they came to the threshing floor of Kidon, Uzzah reached out his hand to steady the ark, because the oxen stumbled. The Lord's anger burned against Uzzah, and he struck him down because he had put his hand on the ark. So He died before God (see 1 Chron. 13: 7-10).

It is easy for us to look at this passage and find ourselves feeling a bit indignant. If you read on in the story, you would find that King David even became angry. Again, we rationalize that Uzzah was doing a good thing. Didn't God understand that? What was He thinking? But you have to remember the overriding principle. It is not that God doesn't appreciate a person's sacrificial efforts in life, but above and beyond that, He desires obedience more than sacrifice. His desire was that Uzzah obey what he knew to be right, not to take it upon himself to re-decide whether or not God really meant what He said. Do you think that God, the Creator of all that is, was capable of taking care of the unstable cart? Sure He was. But we often act as though God is incapable and ineffective, and that if we don't step in and act, even if it is different from what God has said, then somehow God's Kingdom will crumble. Is our God that small, or is it just that our egos and sense of self are that overinflated?

Matthew 5:48 states that we are to be "perfect." Perhaps a better translation might be "complete" or "mature" just as God is. Our desire should be to be mature and complete in our obedience to God. Our desire should be to be more and more like God.

Jim Talley also comments on obedience:

> Jesus committed Himself to me when He died on the cross for me. Out of that commitment flows my

commitment to His will for my life, and His will clearly is that I be married to [my wife]. That then becomes the basis of my commitment to [her].[2]

My commitment to obedience is manifested in my relationships with others.

In his book, *Reconcilable Differences,* Talley discusses the cycle of divorce.

After years of working in the area of divorce recovery and reconciliation, I am convinced the most effective remedy is spiritual renewal on the part of one or the other or both. Someone has to say, "I will obey God. I will do what He tells me to do in His Word."[3]

What does God desire? He desires that I obey Him and do whatever He tells me in His Word to do!

GOD HONORS OBEDIENCE

I want to briefly look at three individuals and how they chose to obey God even in the face of seemingly impossible circumstances. They could have easily said, "Wait a minute! My very life is on the line here, and God's plan appears to have flaws and weaknesses. I had better do this my way instead." But they didn't. Let's see what happened.

Joseph

Joseph, the favored son of Jacob, had more than his share of challenging times. You may remember the story of how his father Jacob gave Joseph a beautiful coat of many colors or one that was richly ornamented. His brothers were quite jealous, contemplated killing him, and ultimately sold him into slavery in Egypt. Once in Egypt, a man named Potiphar, the captain of the guard, purchased him.

Potiphar realized that Joseph was different, that the Lord was with him, and that he could be trusted. As a result, Joseph was placed in charges of Potiphar's entire household, which in turn led to success and blessings for Potiphar.

All was going well, until Potiphar left town and his wife began to proposition Joseph. Being the man of principle and integrity that Joseph was, he consistently refused her seductive invitations and eventually was forced to flee the premises. Good for Joseph! He didn't falter but was obedient and God blessed him. One would hope so, but that is not exactly what happened—at least not immediately. Potiphar's wife lied about what happened and Joseph was thrown into the King's prison. *Wait—are you saying that Joseph took a stand, obeyed God's will, and wound up in prison for it?* That's right. Yet, Joseph never wavered. He didn't obey because of what it would get him or because it would make him happy. He obeyed because it was the right thing to do and because *it would please God.*

Joseph was soon given a leadership position in the prison, was called up to interpret a dream for the king, and ultimately became the king's number two man. But as cool as Joseph's vindication is, it is not the reason that Joseph obeyed. He was content to obey whether or not he ever saw daylight out of prison. He was aware that the story was not about him, but about God. This is a difficult lesson for us to learn, but it is essential.

Gideon

Gideon was a man chosen by God to lead Israel during a period of time as described in the Book of Judges. Gideon was given the task of leading Israel into battle against the Midianites. Gideon was a bit nervous and had been seeking signs of assurance from the Lord to make sure that God was really going to take care of him. Gideon was feeling pretty good because he had gathered the army of Israel together and it consisted of about 32,000 men. This gave Gideon confidence that they might experience some success.

The Lord said to Gideon, "You have too many men. I cannot deliver Midian into their hands, or Israel would boast against me, 'My own strength has saved me.' Now announce to the army, 'Anyone who trembles with fear may turn back and leave Mount Gilead.'" So twenty-two thousand men left, while ten thousand remained. (Judges 7:2-3).

I feel sure that Gideon was in a state of shock while he worked on a new game plan of how he would pull off this battle with only 10,000 men. But just as he began to strategize with his war advisors,

...the Lord said to Gideon, "There are still too many men. Take them down to the water, and I will sift them for you there. If I say, 'This one shall go with you,' he shall go; but if I say, 'This one shall not go with you.' He shall not go" (Judges 7:4).

The Lord told Gideon that He would sift through them for Gideon. I can imagine that Gideon was thinking "Sift through them? Are you kidding me? I need all of them that I can keep!"

Yet, Gideon did as the Lord commanded, went through the process down by the water, and left with a mere 300 men. He only had 300 men to attack an entire army! This was not looking good. But God had a plan. All that Gideon had to do was obey and follow it, whether he understood it or not, whether it made sense or not, whether it seemed foolish or reasonable; Gideon just needed to be obedient. If he would be willing to do that, the outcome might be surprising. While you can read the incredible account in Judges 7, just be assured that Gideon did obey. He allowed God to come up with the plan for the group of 300, and the result was an amazing rout of the Midianites.

Daniel

Daniel was part of a group of royalty and nobility that King Nebuchadnezzar brought in for training after he took over Jerusalem. The king considered Daniel and three of his friends to be the best and brightest when it came to wisdom and understanding. Daniel was called upon more than once to interpret dreams for the king and was later placed in a position of prestige and power by the king.

Nebuchadnezzar's son Belshazzar succeeded him as king, followed by King Darius. King Darius was also more than impressed with Daniel's wisdom and integrity. Darius planned to elevate him to a position over the other administrators, which led to a conspiracy by those who were jealous of Daniel. This wicked group of men appealed to the king's vanity and persuaded him to issue an edict that for 30 days all of the people were only allowed to pray to the king. Anyone who violated this order would be thrown into the lion's den. When Daniel heard about this he was disturbed.

When you think about it, it would have been quite easy for Daniel to rationalize a behavior that would have kept him out of trouble, at least with Darius. He certainly could have reasoned that God had placed him in this powerful position of influence. It was important that he remain there in order to spread God's influence among the leadership and the people. God needed him there. Besides, he knew that the king didn't have God's power and couldn't answer prayer. So, what harm could be done by just going through the motions? He could humor the king and therefore keep his position, not to mention, his life. Sounds like a feasible plan. But this isn't what Daniel chose to do. The Cambridge scholar, F.M. Cornford is quoted as saying, "The only reason for doing the right thing is that it is the right thing to do; all other reasons are reasons for doing something else."[4]

Daniel 6 tells us that when Daniel heard about the edict he a) panicked—no; b) ran to his friends and complained—no; c) fled the country—no; but d) went right home and prayed to God. *Hmm—isn't that the very thing that the king said not to do?* Yep! But Daniel was intent on obeying God. Would it be a good thing for Daniel's influence in the kingdom to continue? Perhaps. But it is an even better thing to obey the Creator of the Universe. He can then deal with Darius and Daniel's position of power if He chooses to. If you have read the story, then you know that the king was quite distressed when he heard about Daniel praying to God. He wasn't distressed because of what Daniel did; rather he was upset because he knew he had to adhere to his own decree and throw Daniel to the lions. Try as he did to find an escape clause, King Darius could not, and he placed Daniel in the den.

I find it interesting that we don't see Daniel crying, upset, pleading for his life, worried about his loss of influence, or any other number of things that we might find ourselves resorting to. We find just the opposite. Daniel was at peace and accepted his fate. All the while, the king was stressed, couldn't sleep, and worried all night about Daniel's welfare. So, what happened? The next morning the king found Daniel alive and well because God had sent an angel to protect him.

Now we can't always assume that obedience will prevent us from being eaten by the lions in our life. But we can know that our obedience to what God desires thoroughly honors and pleases Him. Do you really think that if Daniel had quit praying to God, and given lip service to the king, that God would have continued to use him in a powerful way in the King Darius' kingdom? I sincerely believe that we would have seen just the opposite. I think that Daniel's influence would have faded from the scene more quickly than a bad cell phone signal. I am reminded of Jesus' statement in Matthew 10:39, *"Whoever finds his life will lose it, and whoever loses his life for My sake will find it."* Had Daniel hung on to his life of power and made that his priority, he would have certainly lost it all. However, because he was willing to give up all that he had in order to please God, life was granted to him. The fullness of life that is afforded because of obedience far outweighs any seeming temporary gains achieved by our rationalized disobedience.

BACK TO THE QUESTION

I asked the question earlier, "What does God desire?" We looked at the simple fact that God desires obedience, and we examined some of the ramifications of that. You may be thinking, *"I need to know more specifically His will in this area of marriage and divorce. What does He want me to do in this situation?"* I am so glad you asked. But before I tell you, I want to set the stage with an important premise that was briefly mentioned earlier in this book. It is important that you make and carry out your decisions from a point of conviction and not convenience. This is such a critical concept that I want to say it again and perhaps a little louder. *make and act upon your decisions based on conviction and not convenience!*

In other words, study to see exactly what God says and allow that alone to determine what you do. Too many times, I see individuals enter the discussion with preconceived ideas and desires. They know what they want to do before the discussion even begins. So, they work diligently to create an intellectual scaffolding to support their preconceived desires. This is what I call a decision that comes from convenience. People do mental and intellectual gymnastics to create an argument, to build a defense, for what they want, regardless of the facts. This is being intellectually dishonest with yourself and with God. Set your course of action based upon conviction that comes from understanding God's Word.

With that being said, we are reminded again of Jesus' words in Matthew 19.

> For this reason a man will leave his father and mother and be united to his wife, and the two will become one flesh?' So they are no longer two, but one. Therefore what God has joined together, let man not separate.

God's plan is clear, but it makes people uncomfortable. Why? God's plan is what *God* wants. When things are difficult or hard, God's plan is not what we want. In our limited and twisted wisdom, we want things that are easy, things that make us happy, things that please us, and so on. It is sad to say, but true. We are frequently more interested in what will please us than we are with what will please God. As Humes says, "Therefore, God has orchestrated everything that we endure for His divine purpose for our lives."[5] Why can't we accept that? Why do our behaviors indicate that we don't truly believe that God knows what He is doing? We think that He doesn't get it or is asleep, because we take matters into our own hands. We act as though He hasn't orchestrated anything. Rather than see Him as the orchestra director, we view Him more as an out-of-work tuba player. As Ron Durham, author of *Happily Ever After*, writes:

> There are explanations; there are excuses, but I don't think we ever stand before God and explain the circumstances of our divorce and God says, "Well, in your case..."[6]

God knows what He designed, how we are meant to work, what is best for us, and overall He knows what He is doing! What a concept! God's will is not that we divorce, but that we love, forgive, reconcile, and redeem our marriages in order to honor Him. We also receive an amazing by-product of achieving satisfaction ourselves. Gary Chapman says, "The key principle we may glean from the Lord's dealing with [the prophet] Hosea is that God's will for divorced or separated couples is always reconciliation."[7]

Chapman discusses God's clear will in this matter when he writes, "Your prayer must not be: 'Lord, if it is Your will, bring him/her back.' We already know it is God's will for marriages to be restored, though God respects humanfreedom."[8] Richards continues this thought:

> No, the Lord's will is clear: marriage unions are not to be broken or put aside by men—even for "spiritual" reasons. Jesus expects us to find grace within the relationship, not by denying its validity.[9]

At this point, you may find yourself saying "But—what about this, or you haven't been in my shoes, or how can God want..." Remember our discussion in Chapter 6 regarding our very logical sounding rationalizations. I cannot discuss and cover every conceivable conflict and dysfunction that may appear in your marriage. What I can say is what God states clearly: You are to leave your parents, be completely committed to your spouse, build a united and intimate marriage that lasts for the rest of your life, and honor God's will, your commitment to your spouse, and the very vows that you offered. This is God's will. God's will is not confused or conflicted, but quite clear!

THIS BLIP CALLED LIFE

There are two basic views of life. Either we see life as an end in itself or as a means to an end. If it is an end in itself, then this is all there is. My 80 or 90 years on this planet is it. I have one shot, and I had better enjoy it all I can while it lasts, because when my time is up, we're done. There is nothing else. This is it. This view will certainly impact decisions that we make about marriage and divorce. With this mind-set, divorce becomes a very rational option. "If I am miserable or unhappy, I must get out because life is too short to live this way. I am not going to live like this. I am going to jettison this negative baggage and move on in pursuit of a fulfilling life."

However, if my perspective is that God is here and in complete control, then life is a blip on the radar screen. By that I mean that this life is but a dot on a continuum of eternity. I realize that the end, the goal, is spending all of time in the presence of God. That relationship is my goal and where my efforts are directed. How does my marriage fit into this? There are many ways, but I will just mention a few. Marriage provides me a partner with whom to travel and serve. Marriage allows God to work through another human to mold, shape, and grow me in His image. If you are married, then you know, as much as you may hate it, your spouse knows you and your faults unlike anyone else, except God. I have heard couples sometimes say, "We bring out the worst in each other," to which I respond—"Great!" I truly believe that God can use our mate to bring out our garbage, which in turn allows us to see it, own it, address it, and get rid of it. God can use our mates to help us grow into becoming more like Him. Marriage honors God, and it honors people.

I have heard people complain about various aspects of their jobs. They might say, "I am supposed to be planning and leading sales meetings, but yesterday they wanted me to make photocopies for the boss. I felt so demeaned." My first question might be, "Would you stay at this job if you knew you had to make copies from now on?" The individual's response would probably be "No." But if I asked, "How about if you only had to make copies for three days. Could you do that?" The answer might be "I guess so." But if I continued, "How about if you only made copies for three days, but you realized that what you were copying during those three days were materials that would make your planning meetings go better, would ultimately increase sales by 50 percent, and would lead to a promotion in the company?" The employee's response is likely to be a resounding "Yes!" In the scheme of things, those three days is but a blip.

Again, this life is a blip on the eternity continuum. I can choose to live for the blip or for what comes next. (If the sales leader lives for the blip, he might have a terrific three days of doing what he wants, but then be out of a job after that.) However, if I look closely, I might find that how I choose to deal with this blip will impact my relationships in eternity as well as the quality of this blip.

Please don't misunderstand me and think that this life is irrelevant, or that I am minimizing the difficulties of it. Believe me; I know better than that. It is significant and can even seem all-consuming. I would like to be happy and enjoy this blip called life. All I am saying is that if my goal is God's purposes for all of eternity, my relationship with Him will be intimate, and my blip will be meaningful, very possibly satisfying, and even happy at times. However, if my focus is the blip and my happiness now, I will likely be very disappointed, unfulfilled, and anything but happy.

Yet, when I am in the middle of a seemingly oppressive relationship, an unsatisfying marriage, a downright miserable and depressive life, even the blip can seem like more than I want to handle. How am I to begin to look beyond the blip to see God's bigger picture? I am reminded of Paul's words regarding God's power,

> *"My grace is sufficient for you, for my power is made perfect in weakness." Therefore I will boast all the more gladly about my weakness, so that Christ's power may rest on me. That is why, for Christ's sake, I delight in weaknesses, in insults, in hardships, in persecutions, in difficulties. For when I am weak, then I am strong* (2 Corinthians 12:9-10).

Does it sound like Paul is focused on the blip? Not at all. As a matter of fact, he doesn't say, "Boy, this blip is hard, but somehow I will struggle through, because it is the right thing to do. I will somehow survive." No, he says, "I delight." *Whoa! Time out! Delight?* That is what he says. "I delight in weaknesses, insults, hardships, persecutions, and in difficulties." Does that sound like your marriage? Have there been hardships, be they financial or otherwise? Sure there have. Do you get insulted? You may be thinking—*"All the time!"* How about difficulties? You get my point. Paul is saying that if I have an eternity perspective instead of a blip perspective, then all of these things are mere opportunities to grow and become more complete like God. We cry out to God, *"Yeah, but it is really hard!"* God's grace is sufficient. It is all we need. In our weakness, God's power is made complete.

If we are going to have an eternity perspective, then our language needs to reflect that. Craig Hill, author of *Marriage: Covenant or Contract,* adds:

> I believe, as Christians, we must answer questions and live consistently with our choices. If we choose to live for self and personal happiness, we are free to do so, but let's not continue to say that Jesus Christ is Lord and misrepresent His name and image to others. If we choose to value our subjective experience above the written Word of God, then let's just say so and not claim that the Bible has authority in our lives. If we believe that marriage is a contract rather than a covenant, then let's act accordingly and not perform the ceremony as though it were a covenant before God using covenant language such as "until death do us part" and other such phrases which are really not consistent with a contract belief.[10]

I WANT TO LOVE GOD

You may come to this point and think, *"I really do want to love God, obey Him, and do His will. Tell me where to begin."* Chapman states,

> The only true way to express our love for God is by expressing our love for each other. When we fail to love each other, we have failed in our love for God. Therefore, we must confess the failures of the marriage to God.[11]

And as we discussed in the previous chapter, begin to love our spouse.

Have you ever thought about what would happen if we all did what this chapter advocates? If we followed God's expressed will regarding marriage instead of diligently looking for loopholes? If we said, I will not try to construct an argument for what I want, but I will act upon God's conviction in my life. If I took the first step and said, I am going to obey God and do His will pure and simple. What would happen?

Olan Hicks suggests the following ramifications.

> We have established in scripture that God approves the practice of marriage. It is His appointed way for the entire human race, including those who have sinned against it in the past. We have established also that God forbids the practice of marriage sundering [splitting apart]. In the viewpoint we have set forth here, it is right to be in a marriage and wrong to sin against a marriage. This is precisely in line with the fundamental facts of scripture. If it were to be accepted by all, the end result would be a total annihilation of divorce, for all who have done it would repent and resolve never to do so again, and all who plan to divorce would change

their minds and determine not to do it. It might not be possible to prevent in some cases because the other party in the marriage may be unwilling. But if all parties accepted the viewpoint set forth here, divorce would be eradicated. We would have no divorces because they would have been erased in forgiveness. No future divorces would be coming up, because the minds so intending would have been changed.[12]

This would be an amazing consequence of actively doing God's will!

CHAPTER FOURTEEN

OUR REFLECTION

"It is not in the calm of life, or the repose of a pacific station, that great characters are formed... The habits of a vigorous mind are formed contending with difficulties. All history will convince you of this, and that wisdom and penetration are the fruit of experience, not the lessons of retirement and leisure. Great necessities call out great virtues."

—ABIGAIL ADAMS,
letter to her son John Quincy Adams[1]

"You cannot make yourself feel something you do not feel, but you can make yourself do right in spite of your feelings,"

—PEARL BUCK[2]

The words to an old song begin, "In the light of the silvery moon." The moon has created fascination in people's minds for generations. It is associated with everything from romance to werewolves to rising tides to lunar landings. We gaze at it through our telescopes observing the various craters and even find faces.

As children, we used to think that it was made out of cheese. On most nights, we see at least a portion of the bright moon in the sky, but not because of anything that the moon does other than exist. We see the moon only because it reflects the light of the sun. We gain a little perspective on just how bright the sun is when we realize that the moon reflects only 5 to 18 percent of the sun's light.[3] And yet that percentage results in light that is sometimes bright enough to hike or drive by. As long as there are no obstacles, we are able to clearly see the sun's light reflected from the moon. However, when it is blocked, such as during an eclipse, we are able to see little if anything.

Another amazing reflector is water. I marvel at some of the most beautiful photographs taken of mountain lakes. You have no doubt seen pictures where the mountain is reflected in the water of the lake with such clarity that it looks like two identical pictures in reverse position. I have seen some that were so clear that you could turn the picture upside down and almost be fooled as to which half was the mountain and which half was the lake reflection. However, if I were standing on the shore of that lake admiring the scene when a cloud came by, causing the lighting to change, it might alter the reflection. Or perhaps if someone tossed a large rock into the lake, creating the ripples caused by such a disruption, we would find the reflection of the mountain to be significantly blurred and changed. Only when the water is still and untouched is the reflection accurate.

Bathroom mirrors are probably some of the most common reflectors that we encounter on a regular and daily basis. We use them when combing our hair, brushing our teeth, shaving, putting on make-up, and adjusting our clothes. We do so because they are an extremely accurate reflector of what stands before them. Of course there are exceptions to this. If you have ever been to the Haunted Mansion at Disneyland®, you may recall as you near the end of the ride that you look into a mirror. In that reflection, you see yourself, but you also see a ghost in the car with you. Needless to say, that is not an exact reflection because the ghost is not really in the car with you. Perhaps you have been to the circus or arcade where there have been mirrors that intentionally distort the image causing you to look incredibly thin or fat. But for the most part, mirrors can help us to see an exact reflection. Certainly, if the mirror is dirty, fogged up, or cracked we may not see a realistic image.

By now you are probably saying to yourself, *"OK. This is interesting, but what in the world does all of this discussion about the moon or water or mirrors have to do with my marriage? I don't understand why we are talking about reflection."* Bear with me as I set this discussion aside for a few minutes. Think of this as one of those movies that begins with a story line that you think you are following when it suddenly switches to what seems like a completely different train of thought. Eventually, the plots connect and begin to make sense. In the same manner, I promise that I will come back to this discussion of reflection, I will connect the dots, and the relevance will become very clear.

BY THE GRACE OF GOD

How do you view God? I know that may seem like a strange question, but it is an important one. Some view God as an all-powerful entity that is constantly waiting for us to mess up. As a result, they see themselves as vacillating between being saved one minute and lost the next. God seems to be looking for a way to kick them out of heaven. As Craig Hill says,

> This creates a tremendous fear of abandonment even in relationship with God and results in an intense performance orientation and perfectionism in life. "I had better do everything just right and never sin, or Jesus will leave me and find someone else who does things right.[4]

However, this view is quite different from what Scripture portrays.

Jesus stated very clearly in John 3:16 that, *"God so loved the world that He gave his one and only son, that whoever believes in Him shall not perish but have eternal life."* The next two verses go on to affirm that God is intently interested in loving and saving people. His agenda is not to condemn and kick people out. If that were the case, then He didn't need to send His son. Based upon the law that God had given humankind, and humanity's blatant disregard for it, He was more than justified to kick us all out. But again, that is not His agenda. He has chosen to reach out to us with Jesus to bridge the sin gap so that we might enter a secure relationship with Him for all of eternity.

Listen to just a few of the passages that affirm the security of the relationship that we have with our Creator and Savior. John wrote, *"Yet to all who received Him, to those who believed in His name, He gave the right to become children of God—children born not of natural descent nor of human decision or a husband's will, but born of God"* (John 1:12-13). By God's choice, we have been made His children, and being a child is a secure relationship. Think for a moment about your own children. They are cute and adorable when they are a year old, but can be quite a bit more challenging when they are 15. Yet, they are still our children. We give them instructions and guidelines to follow. They obey sometimes but frequently rebel and disobey. What did you do the first time that they disobeyed? You may have punished them in some manner, and you were no doubt disappointed. Were they still your children? *"Well,"* you say, *"that's a dumb question. Of course they were."* OK. How about the second time or 15th or one 100th time that they disobeyed? At what point did you go to the courthouse and disown them and make it official that they were no longer your child? I know—it still seems like a ridiculous question. But I hope that you are seeing the reason for the question.

My children have done some pretty crazy, disobedient, even illegal things. I have been furious, devastated, shocked, grieved, and beside myself. But no matter what my emotions were, my children never ceased to be my children. It was never even a consideration. Oh sure there have been times of distance. Due to their own choices and guilt, they have even chosen at times to limit their communication with me. There were times of pain and growth as well as times of joy and exhilaration. But through it all—they were always my children. They have my name and my genes. They are my children! It is no different with God. As a matter of fact, from whom did we learn to parent? Who is our model, our example? God! We are His children and are even more secure with Him than our own children are with us.

Listen to what Paul writes in his second letter to the church at Corinth.

> *Now it is God who makes both us and you stand firm in Christ. He anointed us, set His seal of ownership on us, and put His Spirit in our hearts as a deposit, guaranteeing what is to come* (2 Corinthians 1:21-22).

We are owned by God, and we bear His seal of ownership, and that seal marks His guarantee of what is to come. Notice Paul doesn't say, "You are in Christ for awhile, and God really hopes that good things will come your way." No, he says we are sealed, and His Spirit is our guarantee of the future. You can't get much more solid than that.

As God's child, I am more than aware of what a flawed and disgraceful mess I can be. I can't even imagine how the God of the universe could even listen to my prayers, let alone call me "friend." For this reason, I find the encouraging words in Philippians meet me right where I live. Paul writes that he is confident of this, "*that He who began a good work in you will carry it on to completion until the day of Christ Jesus*" (Phil. 1:6). He didn't write that God would discard me unless I get it together and straighten up and fly right. No, Paul says that God began a good work in me and refused to stop with just beginning the work. As one songwriter phrased it, "He'll be faithful to complete it."[5] Even when I am unfaithful and undeserving, He will be faithful and will carry it, not partway, not halfway, but will carry it to completion. What a refreshing drink of promise to a parched sinner such as myself. He will not abandon me! One final powerful passage that I want us to look at is Romans 8:31-39. The apostle Paul wrote the following:

> *What, then, shall we say in response to this? If God is for us, who can be against us? He who did not spare His own son, but gave Him up for us all—how will He not also, along with Him, graciously give us all things? Who will bring any charge against those whom God has chosen? It is God who justifies. Who is he that condemns? Christ Jesus, who died—more than that, who was raised to life—is at the right hand of God and is also interceding for us. Who shall separate us from the love of Christ? Shall trouble or hardship or persecution or famine or nakedness or danger or sword? As it is written: "For your sake we face death all day long: we are considered as sheep to be slaughtered." No, in all these things we are more than conquerors through Him who loved us. **For I am convinced that neither death nor life, neither angels nor demons, neither the present nor the future, nor any powers, neither height nor depth, nor anything else in all creation, will be able to separate us from the love of God that is in Christ Jesus our Lord."***

I want to pay special attention to the last couple of verses that are in bold print. Notice the power of what is written. We are secure in Christ. There is nothing in the spirit world, nothing in time, no powers or extremes, not **anything** in all of creation that can separate us from the love of God. Can you think of anything else in life that offers this kind of absolute security? Anything else that I attempt to come up with pales in its solidity and security. I cannot come up with a position, a job, a relationship, a manufacturer's warranty, not anything that matches up with the absolute permanent unbreakable security that God offers and guarantees me if I am His child. How is this kind of relationship with my Creator even possible? It is possible by the amazing and unmatchable grace of God. By His grace, and His grace only, this offer of security is made. I wholeheartedly accept!

You may once again be wondering where this chapter is going. We have talked about the power of reflection as well as the grace of God. I certainly hope that you are moved by the discussion of God's grace and His offer to you. But you are probably still wondering how these discussions made their way into a book about marriage and divorce. Hang with me, and I promise in this next section to put the pieces together.

EPHESIANS 5

This powerful passage has been read, reread, used, and abused. Therefore, I believe it is important that here we take another look at it with a bit of a different twist.

As Paul wrote this letter to the church at Ephesus, he led up to this section with a discussion about how to live as the Body of Christ. Early in Chapter 5, he wrote such things as: we are to live as children of light; we are to be careful that we live in a manner that uses and demonstrates wisdom; and we are *"to submit to one another out of reverence for Christ"* (Eph. 5:21). The stage was set and warmed for what Paul was about to discuss next: the roles of husbands and wives.

Wives, submit to your husbands as to the Lord. For the husband is the head of the wife as Christ is the head of the church, His body, of which He is the Savior. Now the church submits to Christ, so also wives should submit to their husbands (5:22-24).

I often find that the men are cheering at this verse and saying, "Way to go, Paul; that's telling them the way it ought to be." Conversely, women frequently find that the hair on the back of their neck is standing on end, and they are ready to attack something or somebody. Why do Paul's words elicit such polarized feelings? Because the passage has been abused in ways that were never intended.

Some think that Paul must have been writing to a 1950s cultural mindset. However, he wrote nearly 2000 years ago, simply expressing truths about God's design for the family. He said that in God's design, there are structural and hierarchical roles that function best. And in that context, he says that wives are to submit to their husbands as though they are submitting to the Lord. He likens the husband's relationship to the wife as Christ's is to the Church. This is not a mere outward expression, but is an inward attitude.

The problem is that men have used this passage to demand that a wife bow to his every word and obey whatever he says. No wonder women get upset with Paul over this passage. However, it needs to be clearly understood that this kind of relationship is not what Paul is talking about. He does acknowledge that in God's design the husband is head of the house and the wife is to acknowledge that role. The problem is that simply bossing others around doesn't make a man the head of anything. He merely demonstrates his expertise at being a jerk. Demanding that everyone cower to his authority does not mean that he is leading as Christ leads the Church.

Many men love to read this passage and stop at verse 24. That is the problem. When you look at what comes next, you begin to realize why men don't want to read any farther and why the wife was actually given the easier role. You begin to understand the kind of leadership that Paul wants a wife to submit to. Let's look at the next few verses.

> *Husbands, love your wives, just as Christ loved the church and gave Himself up for her to make her holy, cleansing her by the washing with water through the word, and to present her to Himself as a radiant church, without stain or wrinkle or any other blemish, but holy and blameless. In this same way, husbands ought to love their wives as their own bodies. He who loves his wife loves himself. After all, no one ever hated his own body, but he feeds and cares for it, just as Christ does the church—for we are members of His body. "For this reason a man will leave his father and mother and be united to his wife, and the two will become one flesh"* (Ephesians 5:25-31).

Wow! This is powerful. A man is not to play boss, making demands, and insisting that everything is his way. He is to love his wife as Christ loves the church and gave His life for her. Paul states that as a husband, men are to lay down their lives for their wives. Oh, I know that a lot of husbands would say, *"Well, of course I would die for her. I mean if somebody broke into the house, I would protect her and give my life."* While that is important and honorable, Paul is talking way beyond that. He is saying that men should even give up their lives, give up their desires, and give up the things that they want for the purpose of loving a woman.

"Wait, you mean I might have to give up what I want? Can't I just die for her in the event of a robbery instead?" Physically dying is one thing, but a man giving up his life for his wife is entirely

different and can be much harder. Reread that passage, men, and see how we are to present our wives—as Christ will the Church—radiant, without stain, wrinkle, or any other blemish. He is not talking about Botox® injections to prevent wrinkles. This is what He's talking about: *God has given me this woman to love, and it is my job to present her back to God, radiant and better than when I received her.* Now how can we do that? Certainly it won't happen by being the boss who demands his own way. It is going to happen when we learn to love our wives as our own bodies. Guys, you have been given a difficult charge that will require all of who you are. That is what being a husband is all about.

I could talk more about what a wife's submission should look like as well as a husband's all-encompassing love. However, since that is not my purpose here, I will leave that for another time or for someone else. Just know that if men and women would truly grasp the equal but different roles that God has given them, they would find it easier to fulfill them if their mate were also coming to the table honoring God's design.

While I want you to grasp the significance of this passage in terms of our roles with each other, there is a larger point that I want to make. This is where the dots will begin to connect. Let's look at the remainder of Chapter 5.

After stating that the two will become one flesh, Paul wrote:

> *This is a profound mystery—but I am talking about Christ and the church. However, each one of you also must love his wife as he loves himself, and the wife must respect her husband* (Ephesians 5:32-33).

First, I want you to notice that Paul has taught that men are to love their wives, and women are to respect their husbands. This is a reminder that we are not talking about some subjective feelings that come and go. We don't always have control over what we feel. But we do have control over what we do. Paul wouldn't ask us to do something that we have no control over. He has stated that we are to love and we are to respect, and because these are choices of behavior, we absolutely are capable to doing them.

Secondly, Paul has drawn parallels throughout this passage and has sealed the comparison when he says that he is talking about Christ and the Church. He is presenting a clear picture that our marriages are a reflection. Just as the moon reflects light from the sun, just as the water reflects the mountains, or the mirror reflects an image, our marriages are a reflection of Christ's relationship to the Church. Allow that to sink in for a moment. Our marriages are no more stand-alone than the moon is when it comes to reflection. Our marriages are to be an accurate reflection of what we see in Christ. Christ loves the Church and gave His all for her. Husbands are to reflect that sacrificial relationship. The Church is to submit to and respect Christ's headship, just as the wife is to do with regard to her husband.

In other words, people should be able to look at our marriages and see a reflection. They should be able to stand back, observe us, and gain an understanding of God's relationship to His people. Our marriages are a testimony of how God relates to His people, or at least they were meant to be. But how are we doing? We read earlier in this chapter that absolutely nothing can separate us from the love of Christ. Christ loves us, gave Himself for us, and doesn't give up on us. The Church and her Lord Jesus are inseparable. Do our marriages bear witness to that fact?

Unfortunately, with a divorce rate in the Church that equals or exceeds that of the world, it is clear that we are getting in the way and pursuing our own agendas rather than being a reflection of what God desires. Rather than look at our marriages and see an example of God's unceasing love for His people, nonbelievers are more likely to walk away with a belief that God just throws His people away when He tires of them and finds other people. When they become difficult to deal with, He gets rid of them. When they no longer please Him, they are gone. That is what 50 percent of our Christian marriages demonstrate. That is not a reflection; it is an obstruction; it is an eclipse. Listen to what Craig Hill says about this:

> I believe that the primary issue here is the defamation of the image and name of God in the sight of others. As the Body of Christ, we bear the image of God on the earth to others around us. Unbelievers look at the Body of Christ to see who God is and what He is like. When we, as the body of Christ, embrace the values of society around us rather than Jesus' values, we defame the character of Christ in the sight of those around us and become a stumbling block and hindrance to their salvation.[6]

Ron Durham, author of *Happily Ever After*, continues this thought:

> Now add to this truth the biblical idea that in marriage, man and woman become "one." The implication is that the union of two people in marriage reflects the unity or oneness of God. Unfortunately, the breakup of a marriage is a reflection on God also—a false reflection. The divorce of two married people makes the false claim that God is not one after all, because people are made "in His image."[7]

J. Carl Laney adds:

> Just as a union is formed in marriage when two people commit their lives to each other, so a union is formed when the believer is joined to Christ as he trusts Him for salvation. Will Christ ever break the relationship between himself and His church? Absolutely not! (See Hebrews 13:5.) Will Christ ever be "divorced"

or separated from the believer? Never! (See Romans 8:35-39; John 10:28.)

Since the marriage union is a picture of the permanent relationship between Christ and His church, the marriage union itself must be permanent. If marriage were a dissoluble relationship, it would be an inaccurate representation of the indissoluble relationship between Christ and His church.[8]

Today's wedding ceremonies often include vows that the couple has created. Yet, even then many of the traditional phrases are still retained because of the significance they have communicated throughout generations. The most often repeated vows include some form of the following:

Do you promise to love, honor, and cherish this person
in sickness and in health, for richer for poorer, for
better and for worse, as long as you both shall live?

It is a short question that is packed with commitments that carry huge ramifications. Let's examine some of the key words. We begin by promising. Definitions of all types could be explored ad nauseam, but when all is said and done, most of us have a pretty clear idea of what *promise* means. Whether we are promising to keep a secret, make loan payments, show up to an event, or love our spouse, we know what is expected. The question then becomes—is your word good? If it isn't, several things can happen. Your friends will cease to confide in you, your credit score will stink and no one will loan you money, and people will no longer count on you if your word does not mean something. Our marriage vows are possibly the most important human promise that we will ever make. Will you keep your promise?

You have promised to love, honor, and cherish your spouse. Again, these are not sentimental, gooey feelings. They are decisions about how you will choose and commit to behave. As you stand before the altar, the minister, or the justice of the peace, you look at your beautiful or handsome spouse, and you easily say the words of a promise that, at the moment, seem easy to keep. Yet, most vows wisely include conditions that will challenge the best of promises.

You will notice that we commit to loving "in sickness and in health." "Here I am at the altar," you say. "He seems pretty healthy to me. Sickness isn't an issue. This will be an easy statement to follow through on." What about when an unexpected disease is discovered? When aging deteriorates his body, how will you react?

We promise to love and cherish for "richer or poorer." *"Obviously we have enough money to get married. We have jobs and can afford nice things. Poorer shouldn't be a problem so I can sign up for that."* Yet, how will you respond when your spouse is laid off from work due to a downturn in the economy or as a result of outsourcing? What if he or she cannot find another job?

And then, of course, there is "for better or worse." *"Goodness, here we are getting married. We love each other; she is gorgeous; and I have finally found the one who will always be there for me. How could there ever be worse?"*

Here is where the rubber meets the road. When we are employed, in good health, and life seems good, we can easily pronounce these words of lifelong commitment. It is not difficult. But the very reason that we say, "in sickness and in health, for richer or poorer, for better or worse" is because, rest assured, there will be sickness, poorer, and worse. You can bank on it as much as the sun coming up in the morning. It is when we are in the middle of those times that we find out what our promise of love, cherish, and honor are made of. During these difficult, challenging, and sometimes horrendous times, a person's depth of character is revealed. When things are going the way that we believe that they ought, life is good and smiling is easy.

However, when they are not, is our promise still good? Did I truly mean that I would love, cherish, and honor even when it is absolutely awful and has become my worst nightmare? I suppose the same question could be asked of God. He has promised to love us as His children and He has promised that nothing can separate us from that. But what about when we are rebellious, disobedient, mean-spirited, arrogant, proud, duplicitous, and deeply hurting the other children that God loves? Does He say, "Well, yes, I promised to love you, but that was before you became all of these things that are unlovable. Now I have changed My mind and it is a different story"? Thank God that He doesn't do that. His love for us is secure and it brightly shines from His presence. In turn, that is what we are to reflect, if we will.

One great unchanging truth is this—things change. How will I deal with them when they do? I have seen marriages end because a wife put on 40 extra pounds, because he or she had an affair, a husband didn't make enough money to satisfy his wife's taste, a wife unexpectedly came down with a debilitating, terminal illness, a husband lost his job, or because a child was born with special needs. All of these situations and more fit under the umbrella of "in sickness and in health, for richer or poorer, for better for worse."

I have also been privileged to see marriages survive the same list of maladies. Committed spouses deal with and weather difficult changes. Frequently they do more than that. Many have grown stronger, healed, and soared as they allowed God to redeem and restore what had become ugly and repulsive. God is not in the business of discarding and throwing us away. Rather, He specializes in healing, making new, and restoring. He has called us to be in the same business. In Second Corinthians 5:18 we read, *"All this is from God, who reconciled us to Himself through Christ and gave us the ministry of reconciliation."* In the spirit of First Corinthians 13, I may be the greatest public speaker, the best CEO, or an outstanding conflict mediator at work, but if I an unwilling to build bridges of reconciliation with my spouse, I am nothing! The rest doesn't matter if I have not been faithful to love my spouse and my Lord.

SUMMARY OF THE DOTS

Understanding that we are a reflection is critical to our understanding of marriage and its purposes. We are called to be defogged and uncluttered mirrors. We are called to accurately reflect God to the world around us. God's relationship with us is based upon a permanent, relentless, never-ending love. He fully knows us and then, by choice, unconditionally loves us fully. He has placed love in our lives to reflect to those around us. We are truly a reflection to other couples, to each other, to our children, to other Christians, as well as to nonbelievers. This reflection, whether we want it to or not, tells a story: a story of God's love and relationship with His people. Does your story tell of a God who offers security and will never leave, or does your story tell of a God whose love is completely conditional and who will change His mind, break His promise, go back on His word, and leave when He is not satisfied?

If your marriage tells of a God who is conditional, then you are telling your story. However, if your marriage paints a picture of a God who never leaves, then you are reflecting God and His story. To this end, we were called. What do you want the world to know about God? What they will believe is not the words that you speak, but the kept or broken promises that you live.

CHAPTER FIFTEEN

SOME COMMON SENSE THOUGHTS

"I look to the future because that's where I'm going to spend the rest of my life."

GEORGE BURNS,
at age 87; he lived to be 100.[1]

"But you don't understand my situation!"

"We should not judge but should just live and let live."

"We will just have to pray that God will show us His will."

We have discussed these statements and others like them in previous chapters, so I won't repeat that material here. Our purpose here is simply to focus on one of two common sense approaches to this whole issue of divorce.

APPROACH #1—ROUND UP WHAT I NEED AND BUILD THE SCAFFOLDING

In this approach, we embark on what we called making a "decision of convenience." I know the difficult position that I am put in by looking to God's Word for answers. The difficulty is that the answers aren't the answers I was hoping to find. Therefore,

I find myself on a quest for loopholes. I have been there before, and I remember thinking, "Surely there is a loophole to get me out of my situation." So, I would look harder, read more, pray more—all aimed at finding the answer that I wanted. If I just look deeper into Scripture, maybe I will find some hidden passage that I somehow missed before that will excuse the vows that I made. If I pray more, perhaps God will grant me the feelings that I am looking for that I can then interpret as His will. If I seek enough advice from different people, certainly I will eventually find someone with clout, such as a therapist or clergy person, who will say what I want to hear. Then I will be off the hook.

Paul described this approach in Second Timothy 4:3 when he wrote,

> *For the time will come when men will not put up with sound doctrine. Instead, to suit their own desires, they will gather around them a great number of teachers to say what their itching ears want to hear.*

As a parent, we have all probably had those Christmases where we bought our children something that required a great deal of assembly; perhaps a bicycle or dollhouse. Imagine if you will that it is late on Christmas Eve, and the children are finally in bed. You drag out the box that has the unassembled bicycle in it. You open it and discover that "some assembly required" means "complete assembly required." Every nut, bolt, sprocket, and spring must be fitted together. There are several bags of different sized screws, washers, cotter pins, and so on. There are no letter or number labels on any of the components, and worse, the box is missing the instructions. The stores are closed on Christmas Eve, and no manufacturer hotlines are open or available. What will you do? *"Well,"* you think, *"I guess I will just have to look at the picture and do my best."* You look at the outside of the box only to find that the brand name and the word "Bicycle" are printed on it. No picture! The task just became geometrically more complicated.

But, being the dedicated parent that you are, you dive in and do your best. You are determined that tomorrow morning, there will be a bicycle next to that tree! In fact, tomorrow morning there is one there. You did your best. However, your best leaves something to be desired. The back wheel doesn't spin quite right; the front wheel rubs on the frame; the brakes squeak; and the chain keeps slipping off. Many of us have been in similar situations to this, and it is not fun. It is not fun because we worked very hard to accomplish our task, and the end result was quite disappointing. We would have fared better if we had paid the extra little bit of money and allowed the store to assemble the bike for us. Then it would have worked properly and all parties involved would have been much more satisfied.

This experience is not unlike what we encounter when we take off on our loophole search. God has not given us an alternative set of instructions that are different than those revealed to us through His Word. There is no alternate picture to view. But we go ahead and try to build our clever, theological scaffolding that is based upon our sin-based selfish desires. When we do so, we, and all those involved including God, are not truly satisfied. There may be a momentary feeling of reprieve, but this is far from fulfilled, God-pleasing satisfaction and holiness. The myths of our own ability to create something from disobedience that will honor God and people far exceed actuality. But the myth is a powerful attractor, and people frequently buy into the lie.

People in pain make many statements that sound valid. And because people are in pain, we certainly want to be understanding and helpful. But we need to do so without compromising the truth of who God is.

I hear statements such as:

- "You deserve better."

- "I didn't seek God's will before I married the person."

- "I didn't know what I was getting into."

- "This isn't what I thought I was signing up for."

- "He/she is abusive—physically, verbally, or psychologically."

- "I didn't listen to my parents or friends."

- "I need to be happy and fulfilled."

- "My spouse abuses alcohol or drugs."

- "My spouse uses pornography."

- "God surely doesn't want me to live my life..."

- "I've wasted enough years, and I am not wasting any more."

- "I can't stand this anymore."

- "I can't do this anymore."

- "I shouldn't have to..."

All of these statements evoke feelings of understanding and sympathy. We don't want to be rigid, legalistic, and inflexible. We want to be people of grace. Yet, we have to be people of grace and love who are grounded in the truth. In Chapter 6, we looked at this in depth when we discussed rationalizations.

I have heard people proclaim that they were married to this or that person before they became a Christian. They didn't know any better, but now they do and therefore should be able to nullify the marriage and find someone else. In First Corinthians 7, Paul reaffirmed that God wants us to reconcile with our mates. We don't divorce them just because we became believers.

Instead, we reconcile with them because we are now believers. When I hear comments like, "I can't stand this" or "I can't do this anymore," I can't help but wonder if their statements are true—wouldn't that mean that God is a liar. Paul wrote in Philippians 4:13, "*I can do everything though Him who gives me strength.*" Paul assures us that there will not be more put on our plates than we can endure (see 1 Cor. 10:13). God knows our limitations, and He will give us the strength, the wisdom, the stamina, and the endurance required to live in obedience to Him. He tells husbands to love their wives and wives to respect their husbands. Again, He doesn't tell us to do something that we can't. It is within our power to choose and to do, because He has given us the wherewithal to do so.

APPROACH #2—A TRANSFORMED MIND

Paul wrote a powerful passage in Romans 12:1-2:

> *Therefore, I urge you, brothers, in view of God's mercy, to offer your bodies as living sacrifices, holy and pleasing to God—this is your spiritual act of worship. Do not conform any longer to the pattern of this world, but be transformed by the renewing of your mind. Then you will be able to test and approve what God's will is—His good, pleasing, and perfect will.*

In this approach, we no longer have to concoct our own shaky scaffolding; we no longer have to assemble our instruction-less bike. We can purchase it from the store completely assembled. But in order to do that, we have to be transformed by the Almighty, the Creator of the Universe. We must stop watching the world and adopting its methods of addressing difficult marriages. The world's view has led to pain, devastation, and the tearing apart of people's souls. Why oh why would we choose to be conformed to that approach? But we continue to do so at breakneck speed.

This is why Paul says that we must be transformed by the renewing of our minds. When we do this, we will discover a very different perspective. Gary Chapman comments:

> Many have expected a spouse to provide that which only God can give. Peace of mind, inner security, a confidence in the outcome of life, and a sense of joy about living do not come from marriage, but from an intimate relationship with God.[2]

God wants to be the absolute source of life for us. Truly, if He is our source, at the core, the very essence of who we are—nothing can shake us. All of the seemingly commonsense comments fall right out the window. By virtue of His strength and faithfulness, I no longer need to look for loopholes. He is my source and life—not my husband or wife. When I encounter seemingly insurmountable problems with my spouse, He is my source and strength for patience and love. When I hurt, He is my comfort. When I am exasperated, He is my peace. When I am unfairly accused, He is my truth. When I feel that I just can't do it anymore, He gives and is all I need to not just endure, but to be victorious over my situation.

When I am transformed by the life-changing power of God, I will be a part of the people that Paul describes in Colossians 3.

> *Since, then, you have been raised with Christ, set your hearts on things above, where Christ is seated at the right hand of God. Set your minds on things above, not on earthly things. For you died, and your life is now hidden with Christ in God. Therefore, as God's*

chosen people, holy and dearly loved, clothe yourselves with compassion, kindness, humility, gentleness and patience. Bear with each other and forgive whatever grievances you may have against one another. Forgive as the Lord forgave you. And over all these virtues put on love, which binds them all together in perfect unity (Colossians 3:1-3;12-14).

Common sense would say, "This religious stuff sounds good, but it doesn't address my pain." We must be reminded; this isn't just "religious stuff." These aren't just nice words to put on a plaque in my office that don't permeate my life. *These words are God's truth!* Do you believe that? If you do, if you really do, then it is time to allow God to transform you by allowing Him to renew your mind. He promises that He will do this if you will let Him. There is nothing more powerful than this truth. He can change your life and your marriage. God understands divorce, and He wants us to understand it and all of its devastating ramifications as well. He wants us to understand His heart in this matter. When we do, we will be prepared to love our mate as God intends and to build a marriage that reflects His love for us and absolutely glorifies Him in our lives!

APPENDIX A

As mentioned in Chapter Five, in order to gain a more accurate picture of what is taking place in the Church today, I gathered data from churches across the United States. All of these churches offered some type of a divorce recovery program and ranged in size from a few hundred to thousands. The questionnaire was sent across all denominational lines. Of the 100 churches to receive the request for information, 39 responded from 24 different states. The Divorce Questionnaire asked the following:

Regarding Divorce Recovery Programs

1. Specific goals and objectives of your divorce recovery program.

2. Do you divide participants in your divorce recovery program into categories—such as: length of time since divorce, children at home, etc.?

3. How do you address issues of people that are separated but still married?

4. Do you address issues of people dating other people in the workshop or at least during the duration of the workshop?

5. How long have you been conducting your workshops?

6. How many individuals typically attend your workshops?

7. Do you accommodate nonbelievers in your workshops? How?

Regarding Single's Ministry

8. Please describe your single's ministry. Example— size, age, breakdown of different groups, types of monthly activities, etc.

9. Does your church have any programs that address divorce prevention or marriage restoration?

10. How do you address moral issues in your single's ministry?

11. What is your church's position concerning the issues of remarriage?

12. Does your church utilize church discipline as described in Matthew 18:15ff?

Responses to half of the questions (1,3,8,9,11, and 12) were addressed in Chapter Five. Data is provided here in relation to the other six questions.

Question 2 asked if the participants are divided into categories. The majority (79 percent) indicated that they do not divide the people into any kind of homogeneous groups. Approximately 7 percent said that they do divide into groups, as their numbers are large enough to support this, while the remaining 14 percent reported that they only divide their groups into male and female.

With regard to the issue of dating while in the divorce recovery workshop (Question 4), a full 93 percent of the churches discuss, emphasize, and discourage participants from dating during the workshop. The focus is on using this time to begin to get healthy within one's self.

The average length of time that workshops have been conducted in churches (Question 5) is just a little over 10 years, with the shortest time being 1 year and the longest 24 years.

Question 6 asked for the average number of participants in the divorce recovery workshops. The average size of a workshop is 19 individuals, ranging from the smallest of 3 to the largest of 60. One church who has been conducting workshops for many years indicated that they have had over 1500 participants come through their program.

One Hundred percent of the churches reported that nonbelievers are more than welcome in their workshops. Some go to great lengths of advertising in the community through newspaper and websites. One church stated that by the end of their divorce recovery program, most nonbelievers have come to a faith in Christ. Crisis has a way of bringing people to a point of facing life and its meaning. What an opportunity to touch lives with the Gospel of a loving and healing God.

Answers to question 10 ran the gamut. Some churches rely on different speakers in large venues to address moral issues. Others hope that materials in the divorce recovery workshops will be sufficient. The majority of churches reported that they attempt to address moral issues in a biblical manner, holding people accountable, confronting when needed, and some even utilize church discipline. I appreciated the response of one church that answered the question this way: "Loving in a biblical manner. We attempt to restore individuals and godly relationships, at the same time walking a fine line of compassion and firmness."

APPENDIX B

Resources For Churches and Individuals

This is not intended to be any kind of exhaustive resource list. One only needs to get on the Internet today to discover hundreds of Web-based resources. I recommend just a few Web resources below that I believe make some exceptional contributions. Again, these are only a few of the outstanding resources available.

For additional printed materials, I would recommend any of the publications that I have referenced. They can be found in the notes section.

Websites:

www.marriage.family.org

www.marriagebuilders.com

www.CaMarriage.com

www.divorcebusting.com

www.divorceremarriage.com

www.garychapman.org

www.fivelovelanguages.com

www.smalleyonline.com

www.marriagesavers.org

Mentoring Engaged and Newlywed Couples video kit
Drs. Les and Leslie Parrott, Center for
Relationship Development
Seattle Pacific University
3307 Third Ave. West
Seattle, WA 98119

ENDNOTES

Chapter One

1. Anonymous (commonly attributed to Abraham Lincoln or Shearson Lehman), "Commitment Quotes," Quoteland, http://www.quoteland.com/topic/Commitment-Quotes/285/ (accessed June 20, 2011).

2. All names in this book have been changed to protect the privacy and identity of individuals.

3. C. Bruce White, *Marriage, Divorce, and Reconciliation* (Columbus, GA: Brentwood Christian Communications, 1984), 60.

Chapter Two

1. John Maxwell, *Developing The Leaders Around You* (San Diego, CA: Injoy Inc, 1995), 56.

2. Barry Ham, "The Effects of Divorce on the Academic Achievement of High School Seniors," *Journal of Divorce & Remarriage*, no. 38 (2003): 3-4.

3. Ibid.

4. U.S. Bureau of the Census, *Marital Status: 2000, Census 2000 Brief,* (Issued October 2003): 1-3.

5. Ibid.

6. Ibid.

7. Ibid.

8. Ibid.

9. *Merriam Webster Dictionary,* s.v. "Anatomy," Merriam Webster's Online Dictionary, http://www.merriam-webster.com/dictionary/anatomy, (accessed June 21, 2011).

Chapter Three

1. Carl Sagan, "Quotations by Author: Carl Sagan: Emotions: *Blues for a Red Planet,*" Quoteland, http://www.quoteland .com/author/Carol0Sagan0Quotes/20/ (accessed June 22, 2011).

2. John Eldridge, e-mail message to author, Oct. 30, 2003.

Chapter Four

1. Aristotle, "Quotations by Author: Aristotle: Selfishness," Quoteland, http://www.quoteland.com/author/Aristotle -Quotes/155/?pg=5, (accessed June 26, 2011).

2. Michael McManus, *Marriage Savers* (Grand Rapids, MI: Zondervan Publishing House, 1993), 123

3. Ibid., 123.

4. http://en.wikipedia.org/wiki/No-fault_divorce.

5. Michael McManus, *Marriage Savers* (Grand Rapids, MI: Zondervan Publishing House, 1993).

6. Norman H. Wright, *The Premarital Counseling Handbook* (Chicago, IL: Moody Press, 1992), 48.

Chapter Five

1. C.S. Lewis, *Mere Christianity* (New York: MacMillan Publishing Co., 1952), 96.

2. David Instone-Brewer, *Divorce and Remarriage in the Bible: The Social and Literary Context* (Grand Rapids, MI: William B. Eerdmans Publishing Company, 2002) 304.

3. Ibid., 3.

4. Olan Hicks, *What the Bible Says About Marriage, Divorce, & Remarriage* (Search, AR: Gospel Enterprises, 1987), 9.

5. David Instone-Brewer, *Divorce and Remarriage in the Bible: The Social and Literary Context* (Grand Rapids, MI: William B. Eerdmans Publishing Company, 2002), 121.

6. Ibid., 73.

7. Ibid., 73.

7. Ibid., 72.

8. Ibid., 85.

9. Ibid., 91.

10. Ibid., 92.

11. Ibid., 123.

12. Ibid., 201.

13. Ibid., 204.

14. Ibid., 280.

15. Ibid., 282.

16. Ibid., 299.

17. Ibid., 85.

18. Gloria Humes, *Divorced Marriage Over!...But God!* (Baltimore, MD: Publish America, 2002), 41.

19. Olan Hicks, *What the Bible Says About Marriage, Divorce, & Remarriage* (Search, AR: Gospel Enterprises, 1987), 40.

20. This source is unlisted to protect the privacy of this particular church.

21. These workshops were sponsored by Woodmen Valley Chapel and First Presbyterian Church in Colorado Springs, Colorado.

Chapter Six

1. Mark Twain, http://www.twainquotes.com/Lies.html

Chapter Seven

1. Gary Smalley, *Love is a Decision* (Dallas, TX: Word Publishing, 1989), 16.

2. J. Carl Laney, *The Divorce Myth* (Minneapolis, MN: Bethany House Publishers, 1981), 26.

3. David and Jan Stoop, *The Complete Marriage Book* (Grand Rapids, MI: Fleming H. Revell, 2002), 25.

4. J. Carl Laney, *The Divorce Myth* (Minneapolis, MN: Bethany House Publishers, 1981), 56.

5. David and Jan Stoop, *The Complete Marriage Book* (Grand Rapids, MI: Fleming H. Revell, 2002), 37.

6. J. Carl Laney, *The Divorce Myth* (Minneapolis, MN: Bethany House Publishers, 1981), 59-60.

7. Olan Hicks, *What the Bible Says About Marriage, Divorce, & Remarriage* (Search, AR: Gospel Enterprises, 1987), 102.

8. John P. Splinter, *The Complete Divorce Recovery Handbook* (Grand Rapids, MI: Zondervan Publishing House, 1992), 39.

9. J. Carl Laney, *The Divorce Myth* (Minneapolis, MN: Bethany House Publishers, 1981), 85.

10. Michelle Weiner-Davis, *The Divorce Remedy* (New York: Simon & Schuster, 2002), 22.

11. Gary Richmond, *The Divorce Decision* (Waco, TX: Word Books, 1988), 66-67.

12. Michelle Weiner-Davis, *Divorce Busting* (New York: Simon & Schuster, 1992), 13-14.

13. Ibid., 35.

14. Ibid., 38.

15. John P. Splinter, *The Complete Divorce Recovery Handbook* (Grand Rapids, MI: Zondervan Publishing House, 1992), 143.

16. Ibid., 188.

17. David and Jan Stoop, *The Complete Marriage Book* (Grand Rapids, MI: Fleming H. Revell, 2002), 50-51.

18. Ibid., 55-56.

Chapter Eight

1. *Readers Digest* (Pleasantville, NY: January 2008).

2. Bruce C. White, Marriage, *Divorce, and Reconciliation* (Columbus, OH: Brentwood Christian Communications, 1984), 32.

3. Ibid., 61.

4. Ron Durham, *Happily Ever After* (Wheaton, IL: Victor Books, 1993), 28.

5. Ibid., 29-30.

6. Ibid., 9.

7. Michael McManus, *Marriage Savers* (Grand Rapids, MI: Zondervan Publishing House, 1993), 30.

8. Gary Chapman, *Hope For The Separated* (Chicago, IL: Moody Press, 1996), 88-89.

9. Ibid., 89-90.

10. Gary Richmond, *The Divorce Decision* (Waco, TX: Word Books, 1988), 94.

11. Michelle Weiner-Davis, *The Divorce Remedy* (New York: Simon & Schuster, 2002), 21-22.

12. Ibid.

13. Gary Richmond, *The Divorce Decision* (Waco, TX: Word Books, 1988), 128.

14. Ron Durham, *Happily Ever After* (Wheaton, IL: Victor Books,1993), 35.

15. Ibid., 34.

16. John P. Splinter, *The Complete Divorce Recovery Handbook* (Grand Rapids, MI: Zondervan Publishing House, 1992), 122.

17. Ibid., 27.

18. Ibid., 33.

19. Ibid., 40.

20. Ibid., 40.

21. Ron Durham, *Happily Ever After* (Wheaton, IL: Victor Books, 1993), 32.

22. Barry D. Ham, *Journal of Divorce & Remarriage* (Tucson, AZ: The Haworth Clinical Practice Press, 2004), 168-176.

23. William Hettich Jeynes, *Assessing Socio-economic Theory's Explanation for the Effects of Divorce and Remarriage on Academic Achievement* (doctoral dissertation, University of Chicago, March 1997), 227.

24. John P. Splinter, *The Complete Divorce Recovery Handbook* (Grand Rapids, MI: Zondervan Publishing House, 1992), 126.

25. Ibid., 126.

26. Ibid., 126.

27. Michelle Weiner-Davis, *The Divorce Remedy* (New York: Simon & Schuster, 2002), 21.

28. Ibid., 21.

29. Gary Richmond, *The Divorce Decision* (Waco, TX: Word Books, 1988), 13.

30. Ibid., 61.

31. Ibid., 146.

Chapter Nine

1. Oprah Winfrey, "Oprah Winfrey Quotes: Potential," Quoteland, http://www.quoteland.com/author/Oprah-Winfrey-Quotes/2031|/ (accessed June 26, 2011).

2. Gary Richmond, *The Divorce Decision,* (Waco, TX: Word Books, 1988), 147.

Chapter Ten

1. Daniel Taplitz and Kathy Gori, *Chaos Theory,* Drew's Script-O-Rama, http://www.script-o-rama.com/movie_scripts/a2/chaos-theory-script-transcript.html, (accessed June 26, 2011).

2. Brennan Manning, *Abba's Child* (Colorado Springs, CO: NavPress, 2002), 129-130.

3. Gary Chapman, *The Five Love Languages* (Chicago, IL: Northfield Publishing, 1992), 28-29.

4. Jim Talley, *Reconcilable Differences* (Nashville, TN: Thomas Nelson, 1991), 70.

5. Gary Chapman, *Hope For The Separated* (Chicago, IL: Moody Press, 1996), pg. 62.

6. Michelle Weiner-Davis, *The Divorce Remedy* (New York: Simon & Schuster, 2002), 54.

7. Ed Wheat, *How To Save Your Marriage Alone* (Grand Rapids, MI: Zondervan Corporation, 1983), 20.

8. Gary Smalley, *Love is a Decision* (Dallas, TX: Word Publishing, 1989), 26.

9. Ibid., 210.

10. Ibid., 99.

11. John P. Splinter, *The Complete Divorce Recovery Handbook* (Grand Rapids, MI: Zondervan Publishing House,1992), 116.

12. Gary Chapman, *Hope For The Separated* (Chicago, IL: Moody Press, 1996), 73.

13. Michelle Weiner-Davis, *Divorce Busting* (New York: Simon & Schuster, 1992), 132.

14. Gary Chapman, *Hope For The Separated* (Chicago, IL: Moody Press, 1996), 82-83.

15. Gary Smalley, *Love is a Decision* (Dallas, TX: Word Publishing, 1989), 183.

16. Ibid., 107-108.

17. Ibid., 27.

18. Ibid., 31.

Chapter Eleven

1. Leo Tolstoy (n.d.), quoted on FamousQuotes.com; http://www.1-famous-quotes.com/quote/251119 (accessed July 14, 2011).

2. *Andy Griffith Show,* "Man in a Hurry," Season 3, Episode 79, Written by Everett Greenbaun and Jim Fritzell, Directed by Bob Sweeney, Original Air Date January 14, 1963. (Charlotte, NC: United American Video).

3. C.S. Lewis, *Prince Caspian: The Return to Narnia* (New York: Collier Books, 1970), 124.

4. Ibid., 136-137.

5. Jim Talley, *Reconcilable Differences* (Nashville, TN: Thomas Nelson,1991), 141.

6. Gary Chapman, *Hope For The Separated* (Chicago, IL: Moody Press, 1996), 69.

7. Jim Talley, *Reconcilable Differences* (Nashville, TN: Thomas Nelson,1991), 106.

8. Gary Chapman, *Hope For The Separated* (Chicago, IL: Moody Press, 1996), 42.

9. Jim Talley, *Reconcilable Differences* (Nashville, TN: Thomas Nelson,1991), 79.

10. Ibid., 140.

11. Gary Chapman, *Hope For The Separated* (Chicago, IL: Moody Press, 1996), 33.

12. Family News from Focus on the Family, September 2002.

13. www.rejoiceministries.org.

Chapter Twelve

1. William J. Federer, *America's God and Country: Encyclopedia of Quotations* (St. Louis, MO: Amerisearch, 2000), 243.

2. *Merriam Webster's Dictionary,* s.v. "Reconcile," Merriam Webster's Online Dictionary, http://www.merriam -webster.com/dictionary/reconcile (accessed June 27, 2011).

3. The New Grolier Webster International Dictionary of the English Language, "Reconcile", (New York: Grolier Inc., 1970).

4. Jim Talley, *Reconcilable Differences* (Nashville, TN: Thomas Nelson, 1991), 11.

5. Ibid., 142.

6. C. Bruce White, *Marriage, Divorce, and Reconciliation* (Columbus, GA: Brentwood Christian Communications, 1984), 85.

7. Michelle Weiner-Davis, *Divorce Busting* (New York: Simon & Schuster, 1992), 232-233.

8. John P. Splinter, *The Complete Divorce Recovery Handbook* (Grand Rapids, MI: Zondervan Publishing House, 1992), 100.

9. David and Jan Stoop, *The Complete Marriage Book,* (Grand Rapids, MI: Fleming H. Revell, 2002), 279.

Chapter Thirteen

1. Gloria Humes, *Divorced Marriage Over!...But God!* (Baltimore, MD: Publish America, 2002), 37.

2. Jim Talley, *Reconcilable Differences* (Nashville, TN: Thomas Nelson, 1991), 16.

3. Ibid., 138.

4. Brennan Manning, *Abba's Child* (Colorado Springs, CO: NavPress, 2002), 1994.

5. Gloria Humes, *Divorced Marriage Over!...But God!* (Baltimore, MD: Publish America, 2002), 21.

6. Ron Durham, *Happily Ever After* (Wheaton, IL: Victor Books, 1993), 99.

7. J. Carl Laney, *The Divorce Myth* (Minneapolis, MN: Bethany House Publishers, 1981), 134.

8. Gary Chapman, *Hope For The Separated* (Chicago, IL: Moody Press, 1996), 60-61.

9. Larry Richards, *Remarriage: A Healing Gift From God* (Waco, TX: Word Books, 1981), 120.

10. Craig Hill, *Marriage: Covenant or Contract* (Littleton, CO: Family Foundations Publishing, 1992), 63.

11. Gary Chapman, *Hope For The Separated* (Chicago, IL: Moody Press, 1996), 48.

12. Olan Hicks, *What the Bible Says About Marriage, Divorce, & Remarriage* (Search, AR: Gospel Enterprises, 1987), 241.

Chapter Fourteen

1. Abigail Adams, "Quotations by Author: Abigail Adams: Difficulty," Quoteland, http://www.quoteland.com/author/Abigail-Adams-Quotes/2396 (accessed June 27, 2011).

2. Pearl Buck, "Quotations by Author: Pearl Buck: Feelings," Quoteland, http://www.quoteland.com/author/Pearl-Buck-Quotes/1635, (accessed June 27, 2011).

3. http://www.jimloy.com/astro/moon0.htm

4. Craig Hill, *Marriage Covenant or Contract* (Littleton, CO: Family Foundations Publishing, 1992), 7.

5. Jon Mohr, "He Who Began a Good Work in You" (Jonathan Mark Music & Birdwing Music, 1989).

6. Craig Hill, *Marriage Covenant or Contract* (Littleton, CO: Family Foundations Publishing, 1992), 33.

7. Ron Durham, *Happily Ever After* (Wheaton, IL: Victor Books, 1993), 57.

8. J Carl Laney, *The Divorce Myth* (Minneapolis, MN: Bethany House Publishers, 1981), 122-123.

Chapter Fifteen

1. George Burns, "Quotations by Author: George Burns: The Future," Quoteland, http://www.quoteland.com/author/George-Burns-Quotes/391/, (accessed June 27, 2011).

2. Gary Chapman, *Hope For The Separated* (Chicago, IL: Moody Press, 1996), 45.

ABOUT DR. BARRY D. HAM

Dr. Barry Ham is an educator in a variety of forms: as a college professor, an adolescent counselor, and as a Marriage and Family Therapist in practice in Colorado Springs.

He received his BA and BS degrees in ministry and music from Dallas Christian College. His first graduate degree was a Masters in Psychology from Abilene Christian University, followed by a Masters in Marriage and Family Counseling from California State University, Fresno. Finally, he received his Ph.D. in Clinical Psychology from Southern California University.

He was born in Tulsa, Oklahoma, and was raised there and in Houston, Texas. He currently lives in the Colorado Springs area with his two goldendoodles: Jolee and Bailey. He has two grown children who also live in the area.

Dr. Ham is available to speak at your church or gathering and is also available for weekend seminars

For booking and additional information, he can be contacted at:

Dr. Barry D. Ham

c/o Integrative Family/Individual Therapy

P.O. Box 63241

Colorado Springs, CO. 80962

drbdham@msn.com

www.ifithearpy.com

IN THE RIGHT HANDS, THIS BOOK WILL CHANGE LIVES!

Most of the people who need this message will not be looking for this book. To change their lives, you need to put a copy of this book in their hands.

> *But others (seeds) fell into good ground, and brought forth fruit, some a hundred-fold, some sixty-fold, some thirty-fold* (Matthew 13:8).

Our ministry is constantly seeking methods to find the good ground, the people who need this anointed message to change their lives. Will you help us reach these people?

> *Remember this—a farmer who plants only a few seeds will get a small crop. But the one who plants generously will get a generous crop* (2 Corinthians 9:6).

EXTEND THIS MINISTRY BY SOWING
3 BOOKS, 5 BOOKS, 10 BOOKS, OR MORE TODAY,
AND BECOME A LIFE CHANGER!

Thank you,

Don Nori Sr., Founder
Destiny Image
Since 1982

DESTINY IMAGE PUBLISHERS, INC.

"Promoting Inspired Lives."

VISIT OUR NEW SITE HOME AT
WWW.DESTINYIMAGE.COM

FREE SUBSCRIPTION TO DI NEWSLETTER

Receive free unpublished articles by top DI authors, exclusive
discounts, and free downloads from our best and newest books.
Visit www.destinyimage.com to subscribe.

Write to: Destiny Image
             P.O. Box 310
             Shippensburg, PA 17257-0310

Call: 1-800-722-6774

Email: orders@destinyimage.com

For a complete list of our titles or to place an order
online, visit www.destinyimage.com.